By the same author

THE BATTLE FOR NORTH AFRICA
HITLER AS MILITARY COMMANDER
THE BATTLE FOR THE ARDENNES
THE BATTLE FOR BERLIN
EL ALAMEIN
A HISTORY OF THE S.A.S. REGIMENT

co-author
THE THIRD WORLD WAR

THE ITALIAN CAMPAIGN

JOHN STRAWSON

Carroll & Graf Publishers, Inc.
New York

Copyright © 1988 by John Strawson

First published in Great Britain by Martin Secker &
Warburg Ltd 1987

First Carroll & Graf edition 1988

Carroll & Graf Publishers, Inc.
260 Fifth Avenue
New York, NY 10001

Library of Congress Cataloging-in-Publication Data

Strawson, John.
  The Italian campaign / John Strawson.—1st Carroll
  & Graf ed.
     p.   cm.
  Includes index.
  ISBN 0-88184-368-7 : $18.95
  1. World War, 1939-1945—Campaigns—Italy.
  I. Title.
D763,I8S76   1988
940.54'21—dc19   87-19871
                                               CIP

Manufactured in the United States of America

CONTENTS

ACKNOWLEDGEMENTS

I would like to thank Barley Alison of Martin Secker & Warburg, together with her colleagues, for the encouragement they gave me in writing this book. At the outset I was somewhat doubtful about it, as so many excellent books, either about the Italian campaign in general or particular parts of it, have already appeared. Indeed, while putting the finishing touches to it, another detailed account of the battles was published, this one by those two eminent historians, Dominick Graham and Shelford Bidwell. Their scholarship, narrative power and judgements would be hard to better, but I was obliged to console myself with the reflection that my own treatment of the campaign, as one who took part in it, is so different that it might have some appeal to the general reader.

In Martin Gilbert's latest volume of his biography of Winston Churchill, *The Road to Victory*, there are some very interesting observations as to the Prime Minister's strategy with regard to Italy. In particular it is clear that Churchill was consistently in favour of a cross-Channel operation, but at the same time appreciated to the full how operations in a secondary theatre – the Mediterranean and Italy – could contribute to success in Normandy and N.W. Europe. Hence his passionate advocacy that every advantage should be wrung from the Italian campaign. And he was always conscious of the fact that so large a contingent of the Allied armies fighting there was British. As the American contribution to Allied strength grew and their consequent influence on strategy increased, therefore, Churchill's obsession with bringing off a British coup in what was primarily a British theatre of operations may be understood. His hopes, however, were not fulfilled. Italy remained essentially a secondary affair.

I am most grateful to Tom Hartman for his assistance in editing the text and putting together both the maps and photographs to illustrate the text. I would like to thank my old friend, Colonel Humphrey Weld MC for drawing my attention to an article which appeared in the *Cronaca di Rimini* of 20 September 1975. Finally I wish to thank my wife for all the help and support she has given me during the production of this book.

The author wishes to thank the following for permission to quote from the books mentioned: F. Majdalany, *Cassino*, the author's estate; Viscount Montgomery, *Memoirs*, A P Watt Ltd on behalf of Viscount Montgomery of Alamein; Sir Winston Churchill, *The Second World War*, Cassell (1948–54); Eric Newby, *Love and War in the Appenines*, Collins; Raleigh Trevelyan, *Fortress: The Diary of Anzio and After*, the author; and the following article: 'On This Day' from *The Times*, 19 May, 1944.

LIST OF ILLUSTRATIONS

The author and publishers are grateful to the following for permission to reproduce copyright photographs: Imperial War Museum, Nos 1, 2, 3, 11, 14, 18, 19; The Robert Hunt Library, Nos 5, 6, 7, 8, 9, 10, 12, 13, 15, 16, 17, 20, 21, 22.

MAPS

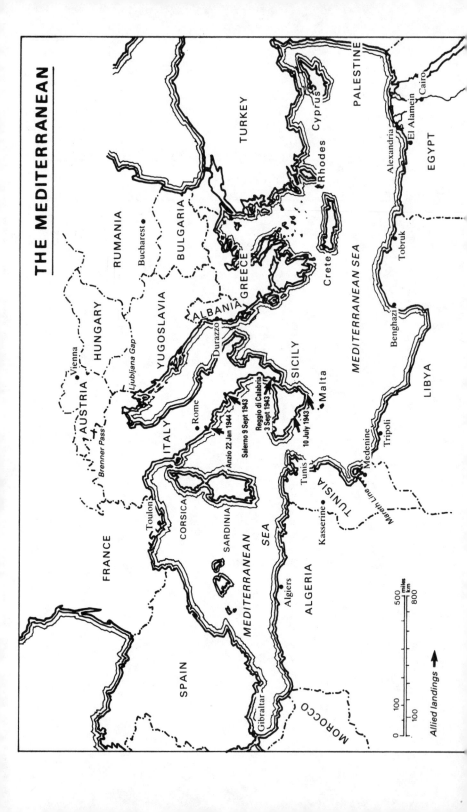

THE MEDITERRANEAN

FRANCE

SPAIN

Gibraltar

MOROCCO

ALGERIA

Algiers

Toulon

CORSICA

SARDINIA

MEDITERRANEAN SEA

Rome •

ITALY

Anzio 22 Jan 1944

Salerno 9 Sept 1943

Reggio di Calabria 3 Sept 1943

SICILY

10 July 1943

Malta •

Tunis

TUNISIA

Kasserine •

Mareth Line

Medenine •

Tripoli •

LIBYA

Benghazi •

MEDITERRANEAN SEA

Tobruk •

AUSTRIA

Vienna •

Brenner Pass

HUNGARY

Ljubljana Gap

YUGOSLAVIA

Durazzo

ALBANIA

GREECE

Crete

RUMANIA

Bucharest •

BULGARIA

TURKEY

Rhodes •

Cyprus

PALESTINE

Alexandria •

EGYPT

El Alamein •

Cairo •

500 miles
800 km

0   100   100

Allied landings →

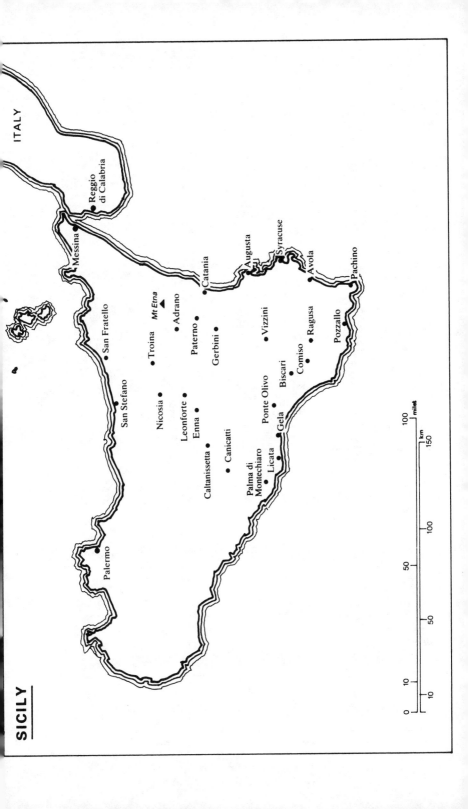

SICILY

ITALY

Messina
Reggio di Calabria
San Fratello
Mt Etna
Troina
Adrano
Paterno
Catania
San Stefano
Nicosia
Leonforte
Enna
Gerbini
Augusta
Syracuse
Vizzini
Avola
Caltanissetta
Canicatti
Ponte Olivo
Biscari
Comiso
Ragusa
Pozzallo
Pachino
Palma di Montechiaro
Licata
Gela
Palermo

0 10 50 100
0 10 50 100 km
150
miles

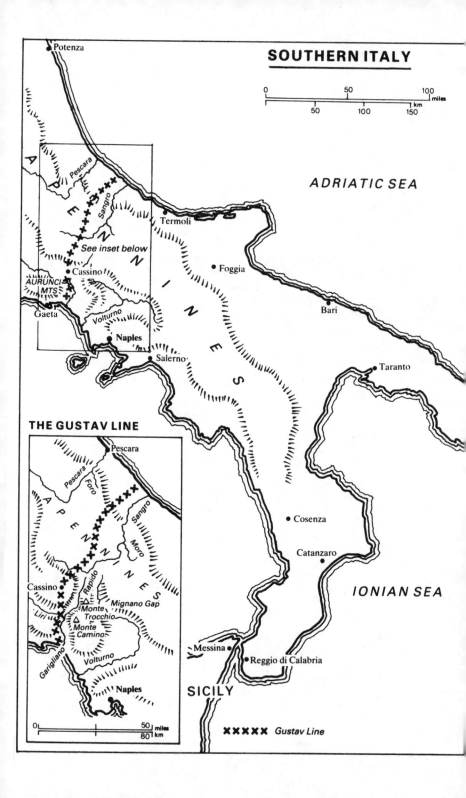

SOUTHERN ITALY

• Potenza

0   50   100
miles
50   100   150
km

ADRIATIC SEA

Pescara

Sangro

• Termoli

See inset below

• Foggia

A P E N N I N E S

• Cassino

AURUNCI MTS

• Bari

Gaeta

Volturno

Naples

• Salerno

• Taranto

THE GUSTAV LINE

Pescara

Pescara

Foro

Sangro

A P E N N I N E S

Moro

Cassino

Rapido

△ Monte Trocchio

Mignano Gap

Liri

△ Monte Camino

Gargliano

Volturno

Naples

• Cosenza

• Catanzaro

IONIAN SEA

Messina •

• Reggio di Calabria

SICILY

0   50
miles
80
km

✕✕✕✕✕ *Gustav Line*

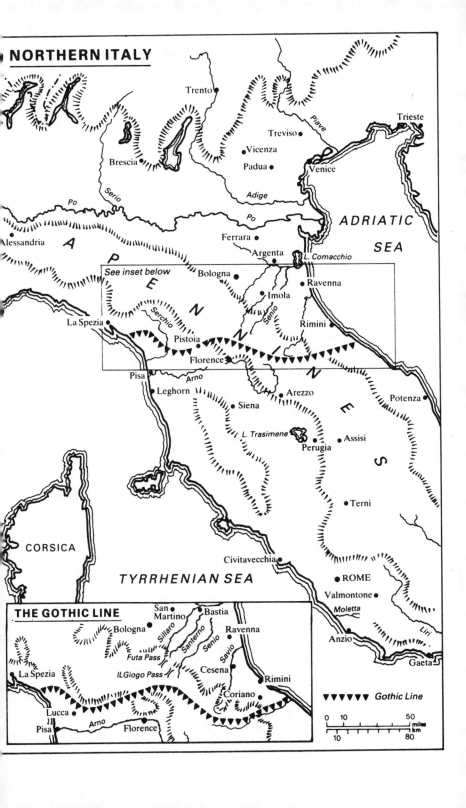

NORTHERN ITALY

Trento

Trieste

Piave

Treviso

Vicenza

Padua

Venice

Brescia

Serio

Po

Adige

Po

ADRIATIC

Alessandria

A

Ferrara

Argenta

L. Comacchio

SEA

See inset below

Bologna

Ravenna

P

E

Imola

N

Senio

Serchio

N

Rimini

La Spezia

Pistoia

I

Pisa

Florence

N

Arno

Leghorn

Arezzo

E

Potenza

Siena

L. Trasimene

S

Assisi

Perugia

Terni

CORSICA

Civitavecchia

ROME

TYRRHENIAN SEA

Valmontone

Moletta

Anzio

Liri

Gaeta

THE GOTHIC LINE

San
Martino

Bastia

Bologna

Sillaro

Santerno

Ravenna

Futa Pass

Senio

Savio

IL Giogo Pass

Cesena

La Spezia

Coriano

Rimini

Lucca

Arno

Pisa

Florence

▼▼▼▼▼ Gothic Line

0   10   50
                miles
     km
10   80

PROLOGUE

We can recognize July 1943 as the month the tide finally turned
against Hitler.

David Irving

This book is not a detailed account of the battles for Italy. Such an
account has been so well done by General Sir William Jackson that it
requires neither repetition nor revision.* What is more the latest
Official History volumes, which complete the story of the war in the
Mediterranean and Middle East, are majestic in their range and
authority. What I have tried to do here, as one who took part in the
Italian campaign, is to record some reflections on it, seen in part with
the benefit of *Ultra* and the 30-year rule, but first and foremost to put
the campaign into perspective. In doing so it is important for the reader
to remember that by the time Allied troops set foot on Italian soil – in
September, 1943 – the tide *had* turned against Hitler; indeed the mere
fact that the Allies with an armada of three hundred ships and absolute
domination of the skies had been able to land in Sicily two months
earlier with virtually no interference from Axis forces was part of that
tide's turning. With the game beginning to go wrong everywhere, in the
East, in the South, in the Atlantic, in the dreadful, endless bombing of
Germany, *and* – for even though the Atlantic Wall was being built, the
expected invasion from the West could not be long delayed – the
ever-to-be-feared and shunned bogey of war on two fronts, east and
west, was not a thing of fancy any more; with such a chapter of
accidents to read, what was Hitler to do? Short of some miracle, such as

*More recently another book, *The Tug of War*, by Dominick Graham and Shelford
Bidwell, has given us an enthralling and detailed account of all that happened.

the acquisition of atomic weapons before the Allies, the outcome of the war seemed no longer to be in doubt. The United States grew stronger month by month, the Red Army appeared to have inexhaustible reserves, the British were still powerful – it looked as if Germany's military position was hopeless. Is it not remarkable, in political, military and human terms, that, in spite of all this, it still took so long to finish the thing off? It is the part the Italian campaign played in this finishing-off process which is the theme of my reflections. Was it necessary? Was it significant? Was it inevitable? What, ultimately, will be the verdict of history?

By the autumn of 1943, despite being, as he himself had put it, 'the hardest man in centuries', Hitler was beginning to acknowledge the true state of affairs. As Speer has told us, however, he somehow succeeded in turning his despondency and disappointment into a kind of forced optimism. 'Even in desperate situations,' wrote Speer, 'he displayed confidence in ultimate victory. From this period I can scarcely recall any remarks on this disastrous course of affairs, although I was expecting them. Had he gone on for so long persuading himself that he now firmly believed in victory? At any rate, the more inexorably events moved towards catastrophe, the more inflexible he became, the more rigidly convinced that everything he decided on was right.' There was, of course, one area of weapon development from which Hitler could draw comfort and hope – the so-called 'secret weapons'. While the great Kursk offensive, Operation *Zitadelle*, was under way at the beginning of July, 1943, the Commander-in-Chief, Navy, Admiral Dönitz, had shown him the blue-prints of the new all-electric submarine, which would have so great an underwater speed that it would defeat all the tactics and defensive systems which the Allies possessed. Moreover the new U-boats would have an anti-radar detection device. Dönitz explained that the first of these new boats would be ready for action by November, 1944, but that he had already made plans with Speer [Minister of Armaments and Munitions] for more rapid production. It was agreed between them that this important new submarine should have priority over all other armaments. Nor was this all. At the same time Speer had introduced to Hitler those responsible for developing the A-4 rocket, subsequently known as the V-2. Although Hitler had originally been cool about the project because he felt that only mass production would enable their use to be effective, and they were very demanding in expensive material, he had heard from Himmler only a month earlier about a successful launch and landing – complete accuracy at a range of 100 miles – and the Army was backing the whole idea with great enthusiasm. Hitler was assured by the experts that the rockets would be operational against England by the end of 1943.

It is when we understand the reliance which Hitler began to place on these secret weapons, which would be operational in 1944, that we also see why it was that he was determined to hang on to certain territory, to keep his enemies at bay, giving him the time and the space to develop these weapons to their full potential. Thus the need to defend Italy once it was under threat becomes clear. It was always to be a holding operation, and the big question, which so exercised Hitler, Kesselring and Rommel on the German side, Churchill, Eisenhower and Alexander on the Allied side, and Badoglio and his advisers in between, was – how far south would the Germans hold? The answer from the German point of view, although not directly expressed as such, would always be – as far south as possible consistent with what the Allies and Italians were likely to do. And it is in this respect that two considerations assume great importance. One is best summarized by Montgomery's entry in his diary on 5 September, 1943, when he himself landed in Italy:

> Before we embark on major operations on the mainland of Europe, we must have a master plan and know how we propose to develop those operations. I have not been told of any master plan and I must therefore assume there was none.

The second consideration concerns the Allied attitude to the Italians themselves, and also the German view of what influence if any the Italians might have on the whole affair. Fundamentally the difference between the Allies and the Germans was the difference between talk and action. Hitler's position was quite clear. He was not prepared to allow the military situation in Italy to get out of hand simply because Mussolini had been dismissed. Indeed on the very day that this happened, he made it quite plain to his staff that they must plan everything on the assumption that the Italians would not remain loyal, no matter what their protestations. 'Of course they won't remain loyal. . . . We'll play the same game while preparing everything to take over the whole area with one stroke, and capture all that riffraff.' Even the

Vatican would not cause Hitler any embarrassment. It could be taken over too, including the 'entire rabble' of a diplomatic corps. He would get 'that bunch of swine' out. Apologies could be made later. Hitler's coalition of political and military power made such decisive action easy for him. In believing that the Allies would behave with comparable speed, boldness and decisiveness to exploit Italy's defection, however, he greatly overestimated their capacity for such essentials in waging war. The Allies were so obsessed with the precise terms of surrender and the arrangements to be made on the ground when their armies arrived that six weeks were to elapse between Mussolini's fall and the announcement of an armistice by the Badoglio Government. Six weeks had been more than enough for the German Army to establish a firm grip on most of the peninsula. And any fears Hitler had had that the Allies would make maximum use of their air and sea power to seize Rome and force the Germans to establish their defence of Italy as far north as the Pisa-Rimini line astride the Apennines from the very beginning were soon put to rest. Montgomery's 8th Army landed on the toe of Italy, Clark's 5th Army at Salerno, well south of Naples. By this time the Germans had sixteen divisions in Italy, the Italian Army had been disarmed and immobilized, and it soon became clear to the Germans that they would be able to defend a Winter Line only just north of Naples. Rommel's advice that the inadequacy of the Italians made it necessary for the defence of the country to be based in the north had no appeal to a Führer anxious to hang on to as much ground as possible, whereas Kesselring's argument that the sheer nature of the Italian countryside would make it possible to defend successfully much further south without any reliance on the Italians found an instant response from Hitler. As far as 1943 was concerned all the Allied armies would achieve in Italy would be to get a good taste of rain, mud, cold, mountains, German skill and courage in defence, and the total impossibility of trying to exploit their superiority in air forces and armoured troops in such conditions. If mobile operations on the grand scale could not be conducted in Italy, elsewhere they could be, notably on the Eastern front, and there – at the time of the Allied invasion of Sicily – Hitler had indulged in one more huge offensive to try and wipe out the Kursk salient.

It will help us to comprehend the scale of the Italian defensive campaign by the German Army if we note that in July, 1943, of its 280 divisions, nearly 190 were deployed on the Eastern front. For

Operation *Zitadelle* Hitler had assembled the cream of the Wehrmacht. General Hoth's 4th Panzer Army contained no less than nine veteran panzer divisions – *SS Totenkopf, SS Leibstandarte, SS Das Reich, Gross Deutschland*, 3rd, 6th, 7th, 11th, and 19th Panzer. Model's 9th Army had five Corps, three Panzer and two Infantry. The idea Hitler had – even though he had admitted to Guderian that the mere thought of the offensive made his stomach turn over – was not just to smash the Russians in their Kursk salient, but drive them back to the Don, even to the Volga, and then at last do what he had for so long been aiming at and sweep up from the south-east to take Moscow from the rear. The attack failed and caused the Germans serious losses, but the fact that the battles were waged at all at a time when the Allies had just set foot in Sicily enables us to put into context the impact on the Eastern front of what was happening in the south. It lends strength to the contention of Norman Stone, to which we will refer again, that the Allied invasion of Italy did not cause Hitler seriously to alter his military activities in other theatres. Indeed, Norman Stone goes so far as to maintain that 'experience of the Allied invasion of Italy caused the German generals to recover their will to win'. Perhaps this may not surprise us when we consider the comparative actions of the Germans and the Allies at the beginning of September, 1943. Norman Stone has admirably summed it up:

> Divisions were sent south, to hold a very strong position in the mountains. Two divisions near Rome throttled the Italian revolt. Hitler sent his daredevil SS chieftain, Otto Skorzeny, to kidnap Mussolini, by glider, from his mountain retreat, and the hotel guards were startled out of their wits for a sufficient length of time for Mussolini to escape. Hitler installed him as a puppet ruler of a Fascist republic in northern and central Italy. The German Tenth Army, under von Vietinghoff, threw a cordon across the mountains of southern Italy. By contrast, the Allies were very slow indeed. Montgomery made an enormous bombardment of the extreme southern tip of the Italian peninsula, and then landed from Sicily. He found no resistance at all – the sledgehammer had not been used against even a nut. Then it took three weeks for the Allies to reach Naples, helped by another amphibious affair at Salerno. With winter, they stuck, with six German divisions holding fifteen double-strength Anglo-American ones. So it remained until the late spring of 1944.

While allowing for some hyperbole here, we can see what Professor Stone means about a renewal of German confidence. Although there was to be Allied confidence too, more amphibious operations, excessive use of air power and some grand strategic aspirations, the pattern for the Italian campaign had been set – a pattern of slow, ponderous, frustrating, costly advances and attacks which yielded no decisive results, and were redeemed only by the courage and perseverance of the ordinary soldiers.

The Italian campaign may be conveniently divided into four phases: the initial invasion by 8th Army at Reggio and 5th Army at Salerno in September, 1943, followed by an advance to the winter line; the struggle to capture Rome during the winter and spring of 1944, involving the two great battles at Cassino and Anzio; the advance from Rome to close up to the Gothic Line and the battle to break through there which bogged down in the autumn of 1944; the final battles in the spring of 1945 in which the German armies were defeated south of the Po, resulting in their surrender at the beginning of May. Great expectations during the first phase, when the Allies enjoyed more than a 50 per cent superiority in divisions over the enemy, were quickly disappointed as a result of bad weather and the removal of that numerical advantage by taking divisions away for *Overlord*; it is important to put these events into the context of the war as a whole at that time. While the Allies were keeping some eleven German divisions busy, the Russians, having defeated the German attack at Kursk, advanced and simply went on advancing. They captured Orel and Kharkov in August, Poltava and Smolensk in September, Kiev in November and Zhitomir on the last day of 1943. Hitler's policy of standing fast and not yielding any ground had the inevitable consequence of his losing hundreds of thousands of soldiers, including many from the satellite armies, and losing too areas of great strategic importance to him, like the Crimea and the Donetz basin. The great difference between these two theatres of war, of course, was that of space. In the East setbacks could be tolerated, space was plentiful, there was room for what Hitler called 'strategical operations', it was possible to cushion the blow, to hold on and on. In Italy space was at a premium, but at the same time the countryside was such that it favoured the defence time and time again.

It favoured Kesselring's defence of the Gustav Line so much that it was not until May, 1944, that Alexander succeeded in breaking it, with by this time a 40 per cent superiority of Divisions. We may bear in mind that in these battles for Rome between January and May, 1944 – at a time when the Normandy invasion was about to be launched and the

Russians were shortly to sweep forward to threaten East Prussia in their gigantic summer offensive – the bitter and bloody struggle for Cassino was waged at a cost of 185,000 men killed or wounded. Death may be a necessary end. Whether it was necessary to meet it on the slopes of Monte Cassino is questionable, when relatively few German divisions were engaged there, and it was unlikely in the extreme that Hitler would denude the Italian front and leave the Allies an option of motoring forward into the Balkans and central Europe. The capture of Rome, however great a political prize it might be, had little strategic significance. Soon after its capture, by July and August, 1944, it was plain that the European war had become a battle for Germany itself – the Russians had broken through in Poland and Eisenhower had, on 1st September, taken over command of the land battle from Montgomery, and was about to advance against Germany on a broad front. In Italy the Allies were embarking on the third phase – an attempt to break through the Gothic Line, having just imposed conditions on themselves, by withdrawing six divisions for the strategically irrelevant operations in southern France, which would render them incapable of doing so. Another series of costly and bloody battles took place in mountainous country, which, just like Cassino, wholly favoured the defenders. And during a second and, like the last one, miserably frustrating winter, Hitler with a final gambling throw in the Ardennes both chucked away his last reserves, enabling Eisenhower's armies to resume their advance in the west, *and*, having weakened the Eastern front in order to indulge in this fruitless gamble, simply opened the door to the Russians who stormed their way forward to the Oder, some forty miles from Berlin itself. By April, 1945, when Alexander's armies in the fourth phase of their campaign at last broke into the plains of Lombardy and defeated von Vietinghoff's Army Group C, the Red Army was in Berlin, Eisenhower was advancing across his entire front, halting only to prevent accidental clashes with the Russians, and the Supreme Commander of the Wehrmacht, after a final shouting match in which he condemned everyone as treacherous, married his mistress and then arranged for her and his own death. In this way the game was brought to an end.

Although the Italian campaign was essentially a subsidiary part of the game, a side-show, if you like, it fielded some memorable players. Among them, of course, was the principal advocate and architect of the Allied Mediterranean strategy, Mr Winston Churchill. Sir Isaiah

Berlin has described Churchill as 'a gigantic historical figure . . . superhumanly bold, strong and imaginative, one of the two greatest men of action his nation has produced' and he considered Churchill's account of the Second World War and his part in it to be that of an actor on history's stage, who 'speaks his memorable lines with a large, unhurried, and stately utterance in a blaze of light, as is appropriate to a man who knows that his work and his person will remain the object of scrutiny and judgment to many generations'. After the Allied victory in North Africa Churchill set forth his case for an attack on Italy, bearing in mind that a large number of Allied divisions – American, French and most of all British or British-controlled – would be to hand, even after what had to be removed to the United Kingdom for the build-up there was taken account of. These so-called 'Background Notes' of 31 May, 1943, had this to say:

> His Majesty's Government feel most strongly that this great force, which comprises their finest and most experienced divisions and the main part of their army, should not in any circumstances remain idle. Such an attitude could not be justified to the British nation or to our Russian allies. We hold it our duty to engage the enemy as continuously and intensely as possible, and to draw off as many hostile divisions as possible from the front of our Russian allies. In this way, among others, the most favourable conditions will be established for the launching of our cross-Channel expedition in 1944. Compelling or inducing Italy to quit the war is the only objective in the Mediterranean worthy of the famous campaign already begun and adequate to the Allied forces available and already in the Mediterranean basin. For this purpose the taking of Sicily is an indispensable preliminary, and the invasion of the mainland of Italy and the capture of Rome are the evident steps. In this way the greatest service can be rendered to the Allied cause and the general progress of the war, both here and in the Channel theatre.

Churchill went on to speculate as to the likely enemy reaction. He consoled himself with the thought that whatever they did would be to the Allies' advantage. If Sicily and southern Italy were strongly reinforced by the Germans, then the aim of diverting powerful forces from the Russian front would have been realized. If they did not do so, it should be easy to capture Rome quickly. What Churchill did not foresee at this time was a moderate reinforcement by the Germans which would be sufficient to conduct a successful defence in particularly suitable country, and at the same time not cause too serious a draining of resources from the Eastern front. He went on to argue that if Allied action obliged Italy to quit the war, the Germans would have to provide troops to defend the Riviera, to man a new front on the Po or Brenner, *and* to replace the Italian divisions which were at present deployed to defend the Balkans. While conceding that any attempt to foresee what the German action in the Mediterranean might be was highly speculative, Churchill continued to suggest that great strategic prizes were to be won by the course of action which he was proposing. The German position had greatly deteriorated; the Allied situation had greatly improved; events on the Russian front would go on absorbing much of the enemy's strength. He concluded his paper like this:

> It must therefore be considered unlikely (a) that the Germans will attempt to fight a major battle in Sicily, or (b) that they will send strong forces into the leg of Italy. They would be wiser to fight only delaying actions, stimulating the Italians in these regions and retiring to the line of the Po, reserving their strength to hold the Riviera and the Balkans. If the battle goes against them in Russia and if our action upon or in Italy is also successful the Germans may be forced by events to withdraw to the Alps and the Danube, as well as to make further withdrawal on the Russian front and possibly to evacuate Norway. *All these results may be achieved within the present year** by bold and vigorous use of the forces at our disposal. No other action of the first magnitude is open to us this year in Europe.

Here in a nutshell is the British justification for the Italian campaign. The reality was somewhat different, for Hitler did not choose the 'wiser' course of fighting delaying actions. Nor did the Germans withdraw to the Alps or Danube. And Hitler hung on to Norway. Yet Churchill was surely right to urge action in the theatre where so many Allied forces were. To have done nothing, to have allowed these British and British-controlled divisions to remain idle, would have been inexcusable. So the idea of a further containing operation, making North Africa 'a springboard, not a sofa' in order to oblige the Germans to dissipate the Wehrmacht, to capitalize on their obligations to a weak ally, to go on grinding down the Axis strength – all this was a proper strategic concept. But Churchill, of course, was hoping and went on

---

* My italics.

hoping for something more. He longed for a kind of military *coup de maître* in the Mediterranean area simply because of his passionate desire that armies principally British should bring off some great strategic decision. Time after time he returned to this theme – in sponsoring the Anzio attack; in supporting Alexander's efforts to conquer Cassino; in trying to get *Anvil* [Dragoon], the landing in southern France, cancelled so that Alexander could push through the Gothic Line; even in reading too much into the final offensive in Italy. It never happened. Yet in insisting that success in North Africa had to be exploited in one way or another, even though such exploitation did not yield the spectacular results he had hoped for, Churchill was surely right. It must always be remembered that Churchill's commitment to *Overlord*, the invasion of N.W. Europe, was absolute and unwavering. He may have *hoped* for spectacular results in Italy, but he came to see that the real value of this essentially secondary theatre was that it contained enemy divisions which might have been more decisively employed elsewhere.

The attitude of the second principal player in the game, the Führer himself, was more ambivalent. When, after the fall of France, he was urged by Admiral Raeder, Commander-in-Chief of the German Navy, to forestall the inevitable British attacks on Italy by destroying the British position in the Mediterranean – 'the pivot of their world empire' – a process which would be achieved by seizing Gibraltar in conjunction with Spain and Vichy France, then capturing the Suez Canal and advancing towards Turkey through Palestine and Syria, Hitler turned him down. He had his eye all too firmly on Russia, arguing that with Russia out of the way, Britain's position would be hopeless. Even America would then be too concerned about Japan's power to come to Britain's aid. Raeder did not give up easily and kept on returning to his theme, particularly when Rommel brought blitzkrieg to the desert and twice threatened the British position in Egypt. By that time, of course, Mussolini's disastrous adventures in Greece had forced Hitler to come to his aid there, as well as des-patching Rommel's panzer forces to rescue the Italians in Cyrenaica, but even though the Führer gave half promises to Raeder that *after* Russia's defeat he would return to the idea of a grand encircling movement of the British Middle East base by striking through Egypt and the Caucasus, for him the Mediterranean area remained first and always a side-show. *Decision* lay in destroying the Soviet Union. He was certainly correct in judging that decision was to be found on the Eastern front. What he had not foreseen was that this decision would be not for, but against, him. Throughout it all the Italian campaign remained a mere holding operation. And how well the Germans did hold on there!

The third great player on the Mediterranean stage, President Roosevelt, put himself there only because it was the only area in which he found it possible to send American forces into action against the Germans in 1942, having promised Stalin that some sort of Second Front would be established before the end of that year. The decision to launch Operation *Torch*, the Anglo-American landings in French North Africa, had profound consequences in that it committed the United States to take part in what many of their leaders regarded as an indirect, Mediterranean strategy, totally at odds with what they saw as the proper course of action – to strike at the centre of Germany as soon and as directly as possible. It was necessary for Roosevelt to overrule his own Chiefs of Staff in order to get the North African invasion executed. General Marshall, whose strategic ideas were on the whole sound and who had great influence over the President in military affairs, called the decision a momentous change in Grand Strategy. Eisenhower called it 'the blackest day in history'. Yet as most responsible historians now agree, given Roosevelt's undertaking to engage the German armed forces somewhere on land during 1942, there was no feasible alternative.

Nonetheless, even a recent biographer of Roosevelt, Ted Morgan, revives the controversy when he claims that the President could have mounted a successful Second Front in Europe within less than a year of entering the war, that is by the autumn of 1942. Morgan claims that it was only the devious arguments of Churchill which persuaded Roosevelt to move away from the jointly agreed strategy of building up forces in the United Kingdom with a view to a cross-Channel operation not later than 1943. But, of course, Morgan is talking nonsense. Even Marshall himself admitted later that with only two or three American divisions available for an early attempt at invading western France – the rest would have had to be British – together with the German capability for reinforcement and build-up, the result would have been suicidal. And indeed the Dieppe raid of August, 1942, was suicidal. In any event once the Anglo-American landings had taken place, both countries, like it or not, were committed to some sort of Mediterranean strategy. It was in the emphasis and purpose of this Mediterranean commitment that differences between the two Allies were to be found. For the Americans on the whole it constituted a necessary, but sometimes frustrating, distraction. For the British it continued to offer great military and political prizes. These different views were epitomized by the attitudes of two more great actors on the Mediterranean stage, General Marshall and General Sir Alan Brooke, whom we must examine shortly and who served their principals, Roosevelt and Churchill, with such devotion both to duty and their own convictions. But the fundamental difference between the principals themselves should not be overlooked, and it is here that Sir Isaiah Berlin once more summarizes so eloquently for us what it is we need to understand:

The differences between the President and the Prime Minister were at least in one respect something more than the obvious differences of national character, education and even temperament. For all his sense of history, his large, untroubled, easy-going style of life, his unshakable feeling of personal security, his natural assumption of being at home in the great world far beyond the confines of his own country, Mr Roosevelt was a typical child of the twentieth century and of the New World; while Mr Churchill for all his love of the present hour, his unquenchable appetite for new knowledge, his sense of the technological possibilities of our time, and the restless roaming of his fancy in considering how they might be most imaginatively applied . . . despite all this, Mr Churchill remains a European of the nineteenth century.

It is when we consider these splendid phrases, this acute analysis of character and inclination, that we may perhaps perceive why it was that Roosevelt, without hesitation or a backward glance, followed the advice of his military advisers and recoiled from the prospect of involvement in the cockpit of Europe's struggle for power in the previous century, preferring instead the direct, uncomplicated approach to the centre of Hitler's Reich; while Churchill, with his long and close experience of both the Great Game and the desperate slaughtering on the Western Front in a previous war, was anxious to exploit the potential offered to wear down the German war effort and come to the aid of his Russian ally by extracting every ounce of benefit obtainable from the success already achieved on the enemy's vulnerable southern flank.

At the same time it is important to recognize, as Churchill and

Roosevelt both did, together with their military advisers, how much the whole notion of a Mediterranean strategy owed to sheer opportunism. The British were in the Mediterranean 'because they were there'; the Americans had arrived there largely because of Roosevelt's determination to do something in 1942; it had been accepted by both countries that it would be impossible to move all these forces back to the United Kingdom in time to mount a cross-Channel operation in 1943; they had to do something unless they were to remain idle for the remainder of that year while the Russians alone bore the brunt of the Wehrmacht; it was in this way that the so-called Mediterranean Strategy acquired some sort of respectability. Operations therefore had to be pursued, after the successful conclusion of the North African campaign, in order to go on distracting German forces from the Russian front and if possible to bring about the collapse of Italy. What was decided on, therefore, was the invasion of Sicily. What was not foreseen was that this step would lead inevitably to the continuation of the campaign on the mainland of Italy, and that this latter commitment, while still no doubt having an effect on operations elsewhere, would turn out to be so demanding and, at the same time, so inconclusive. It was in this area that the views of Marshall and Alanbrooke varied so markedly.

Alanbrooke's first impressions of Marshall were, as indeed they should have been, favourable. They first met when Marshall came to London in April, 1942, in order to persuade the British as to the soundness of the American plan – to build up maximum military strength in the United Kingdom during 1942 so that either an 'Emergency' offensive could be mounted across the Channel *in 1942*, or in any event that a proper invasion would take place in 1943. In his wish to strike at the bulk of the German armed forces as soon as possible, Marshall had the whole-hearted support of Eisenhower. Brooke thought otherwise. He regarded Marshall's plan as 'Castles in the Air', but this did not prevent his liking for the American Chief of Staff, whom he thought of as a 'great man, a great gentleman, and great organizer, but definitely not a strategist'. Brooke was quite clear at this stage of the war what the proper Allied policy should be: 'We were desperately short of shipping and could stage no large-scale operations without additional shipping. This shipping could only be obtained by opening the Mediterranean and saving a million tons of shipping through the elimination of the Cape Route. To clear the Mediterranean, North Africa must first be cleared. We might certainly start preparing plans for the European offensive, but such plans must not be allowed to interfere with the successive stages of operations essential to the ultimate execution of this plan.'

It is this last point which might be said to highlight the different approach of the two men. Alanbrooke, while acknowledging the need to prepare for the invasion of North-West Europe, insisted on pursuing operations elsewhere in order to ensure the success of this invasion. He was always anxious to exploit opportunity in theatres where the German Army was already being engaged, pinned down and distracted from either the Russian front or the potential 'Second Front'. Marshall, on the other hand, saw the cross-Channel assault as the supreme purpose for the great armies he had created and armed; he saw the blow there as the be-all and end-all of his strategy, and was loath to contemplate, still less sanction, what he thought of as their dissipation in secondary pursuits. For him other operations in other theatres would simply weaken and delay the build-up for what became known as *Overlord*. Both men were, of course, right, and our judgment as to which one was more right than the other springs essentially from the answer we give to a question which has exercised historians since the war's end – what was the earliest date that a successful invasion of Normandy could be mounted? The answer which enjoys most support is, despite all that John Grigg and others have written, 1944, and if this is the correct answer, then all that Brooke sought to do in 1943 in the Mediterranean area, both for its own sake and for the contribution it made to the Eastern and later the Western fronts, stands without serious challenge as having been necessary and right.

It was at the Casablanca Conference in January, 1943, that Brooke succeeded in convincing the Americans that victory in North Africa would have to be exploited by invading Sicily, and as David Fraser has pointed out in his masterly biography of Alanbrooke, once the decision to invade Sicily had been made, the only operations on land against the Germans during 1943 which were possible would be in the Mediterranean area. Alanbrooke's whole strategy at this time was to keep the pressure on Italy, as General Fraser writes:

the German Army should be driven to replace the Italian throughout the Mediterranean theatre and possibly be induced to spend effort on defending Italy itself. To leave Italy unmolested – and combatant – after the victories of Tunisia would have relaxed a point of pressure on Germany. To

Alanbrooke this would have been indefensible. To him the pressure had to be exerted and constantly maintained until North-West Europe was invaded.

It is in considering this last point that further controversy between Brooke and Marshall went to the heart of the strategic argument. Brooke, like Churchill, was from time to time seduced by the – almost certainly illusory – prospects of some triumph in Italy and the Balkans which would transform the whole course and duration of the war. We find him complaining in his diary in the autumn of 1943, after Italy had been invaded, about the slowness of the build-up there. He even goes so far as to suggest that the Americans had thrown away great opportunities in the Mediterranean by their insistence on 'the very problematical cross-Channel operations' and makes a bitter, ironical comment on Marshall's strategy. Yet in fact, as was to be shown, the battles in Italy *did* contribute to success in Normandy and *did* distract German forces from the Eastern front. What more could have been asked of these battles? When Brooke goes so far as to suggest in his diary that he has failed in the Mediterranean, and that if only he had been able to swing the Americans to his way of thinking, the Balkans would have been ablaze and the war finished in 1943, we must conclude that he was allowing disappointment and frustration to get the better of his reasoned judgment. That the Allies had perhaps expected too much from the elimination of Italy was understandable. That they should still not comprehend both the manner in which Hitler conducted his war and the staunchness with which the Wehrmacht would carry out his commands was less so. It was Kesselring's staunchness in doing so – and indeed in convincing Hitler that it would be possible to hang on to so much of Italy for so long – that was to cause Alexander and his fellow generals to reconcile themselves to a long, hard, slogging battle of attrition.

One of the most astonishing misjudgments made by Eisenhower, when he was considering who should command the armies to undertake the Normandy invasion, was made clear when he asked for Alexander, rather than Montgomery. It can only be comprehended when we consider Eisenhower's own style of command and inability to understand a battlefield. What is even more surprising, given that Brooke had observed the way in which the Alexander/Montgomery team had been so effective in North Africa – Alexander providing the political and logistic support, Montgomery running the battle itself – is that Brooke too was initially undecided. It would have been wrong to have teamed Eisenhower and Alexander for the supreme Allied operation of the war. Each had a great capacity for getting on well with others and running a good team. Neither had the tactical grasp and relentless perseverance of Montgomery. It was fortunate, therefore, that the intervention of the Secretary of State for War, Grigg, in recommending to Churchill the War Cabinet's preference for Montgomery was conclusive. Alexander would remain in command of 15th Army Group.

With this command he three times launched an Army Group attack – in May, 1944, in August, 1944, and in April, 1945. Only the last fully achieved its object. For the first two attacks he was up against a very skilled and determined opponent, Kesselring, who by April, 1945, had been removed by Hitler to rescue an unrescuable situation on the Western front. We shall see later how these events developed. Of all the military players in the game, there is little doubt that Alexander was the most gentlemanly. Indeed this was a reason for the limit on his success. Liddell Hart called him a born leader, but qualified his praise by saying that had he not been so nice, 'so deeply a gentleman', he might have been a greater commander. This 'niceness' sometimes robbed him of the ruthless determination which at times commanders in war had to draw upon. At Anzio, for example, he urged the man on the spot to advance more rapidly and more deeply. He should have ordered, required, demanded it. Nigel Nicolson suggested that although Alexander did win his battles, he could have done so more economically had he been mentally tougher. His preference for smooth relations in top Allied counsels tended to result in confusion and even waste further down the chain of command. As Montgomery was often to say, Alexander did not appear to be certain as to exactly what it was he wanted to do. It was no surprise therefore that those lower down did not know either.

If Alexander was too much the gentleman, the same could not be said of Kesselring. The mere fact that he was a Luftwaffe general, and not, as Hitler would have put it, 'a gentleman of the General Staff with a handle to his name', would have been enough in itself to appeal to the Führer. But he was much more than this. A shrewd strategist – it was he who saw all along that success in North Africa could not be achieved without the elimination of Malta – a Nazi idealist and a military optimist, he was just the man to command in the south. As capable of having shouting rows with Rommel as he was of firmly disagreeing with Hitler himself when he thought the situation warranted it, he was above all a *stayer*. Defeat and retreat did not dismay him, rather the reverse. Douglas Orgill summed it up admirably when he wrote: 'Kesselring's outstanding qualities were the strong will-power with which he managed to rally his staff and armies at successive desperate moments, and the swiftness of reaction and adaptability with which he greeted any unexpected threat'. His optimism, of course, went well with the campaign he was required to conduct. In Italy it was possible to hold on, withdraw, hold on again, and go on repeating the process irrespective of what was happening elsewhere on other fronts, where such ideal defensive country did not exist. The curious side of Kesselring's character was that while he could be realistic enough about strategic and tactical matters, he maintained a romantic, idealistic view of his Italian allies, refusing to believe in their likely defection until it happened. But this did not stop his ruthlessly suppressing them when the time came. To some extent the whole long-drawn-out Italian campaign might be said to be a result of his conviction, shortly after the Allies invaded the mainland, that he could fight a successful defensive battle south of Rome, at a time when Rommel and others were advocating withdrawal to the Pisa-Rimini line there and then, in the autumn of 1943. Such a coalition of sanguineness and determination was just what Hitler wanted in his senior commanders at that stage of the war. No wonder Kesselring got the command. His fulfilment of promises to hold on and successfully defend line after line was such that it was only in the south that Hitler did not constantly chop and change his top commanders during the last years of the war.

Both Kesselring and Alexander were on the whole well served by their subordinate commanders. On the German side, von Vietinghoff, von Mackensen and von Senger und Etterlin respectively commanded 10th Army, 14th Army and XIV Panzer Corps. All were brave, able and experienced commanders, and von Vietinghoff eventually succeeded Kesselring. For the Allies, Montgomery had of course been selected to command *Overlord* before the end of 1943, and was succeeded by Oliver Leese, who concealed a good deal of thorough ability behind a somewhat casual, easy-going manner. He commanded 8th Army until the autumn of 1944 when General McCreery, who combined great love of and skill with horses, a fine intellect and an almost eccentric originality, took over. Perhaps the most controversial figure on the Allied side was General Mark Clark, commanding 5th Army. Clark believed in a personal public relations campaign and was quite successful at it, not as successful as Montgomery, of course, but then no one was. A fellow American general had this to say of Clark: 'A cold, distinguished, conceited, selfish, clever, intellectual, resourceful officer who secures excellent results quickly'. What General Devers missed out was how suspicious Clark was. He always seemed to fear that the British would rob him of credit due to himself. And it is in his subsequent assessment of his British colleagues revealed in his private papers – he has nothing good to say about Montgomery, Leese, McCreery or even Alexander, all of whom supported him so well – that Clark shows himself to be less than a great man. Like Churchill and Alexander he saw the Italian campaign as something of greater significance than it was, always hoping for decisive results, but even this view, wrong as it was, would have been formed only because it would reflect greater glory and importance on himself. Yet despite his faults, despite even his failure to carry out Alexander's orders after breaking out of the Anzio beachhead, orders which if obeyed could have resulted in far greater damage to the German 10th Army, it must be said that Clark commanded 5th Army competently and firmly.

So far we have been touching only on the court cards in the game, the kings, knights and castles. What about the pawns, the ordinary soldiers that these great men commanded, cared for and condemned? There are perhaps still few better ways to catch the atmosphere of battle, the conditions under which men lived and fought and died, than glancing at war's literature. Siegfried Sassoon's *Counter-Attack*, written to describe the sheer awfulness of the trenches in the Great War, might have been produced to depict some of the circumstances which prevailed at Cassino or the Gothic Line:

> The place was rotten with dead; green clumsy legs
> High-booted, sprawled and grovelled along the saps;
> And trunks, face downward, in the sucking mud,
> Wallowed like trodden sandbags, loosely filled;
> And naked sodden buttocks, mats of hair,
> Bulged, clotted heads slept in the plastering slime.

The battalion in which Fred Majdalany served was already accustomed to such sights. They got a further ration of it all at Cassino, when they took over part of the line from the Gurkhas:

> I wondered if it made any sense at all to a Gurkha, to find himself brought all the way to Italy to help Englishmen to kill Germans. This musing was cut short abruptly, for at that moment we cleared the crest of the spur, and there, staring us in the face, was the Monastery. Two rough, evil-looking prongs of masonry sprouting from an untidy chaos of rubble – all that remained of the southernmost tip of the building – like jagged fangs. This first close-up view was unexpected and slightly startling, and we edged over to the right so as to get out of sight of it. As we worked our way up the terraced, shell-torn slope towards the ruin of a building that looked like the headquarters we were seeking, the smell of death – the old familiar smell became increasingly powerful. . . .
>
> When you smell that smell, then you know you've arrived. You are once again in the world of the Infantry. It is universal and haunting. It is the same, whether it is caused by dead Englishmen, dead Americans, or dead mules. This place was worse than any we had ever known before because there were hardly any parts of these hills where you could go unobserved. So many of the dead had to lie where they fell. Dead English, dead Scots, dead Americans, dead Indians. A grim record of races and regiments that had fought up here, the distinctive uniforms and badges alone identifying the mouldering bodies within them – like a stark inventory of crucifixion. . . .
>
> As soon as it was dark that night our companies filed up from the Bowl, and one by one took over from the Gurkha companies. While this was going on, shells were poured into the Monastery, partly to distract the Germans, partly to drown any noise made by our men as they groped their way into those rocky positions, some of which were within fifty yards of the enemy. One by one the company commanders reported themselves in. The two colonels stood together in the ruined building that was headquarters.
>
> Two hours before dawn the last of our men was in position: the last of the Gurkhas set off at high speed down the mountain track so as to get clear of the valley before daylight. The Adjutant picked up the telephone and said three words to Brigade: 'Take-over completed'. It was ours – the Monastery, the mountains, the smells. A cemetery for the living.

Here we have a picture of the sheer mechanics of soldiering, the drills of hand-over and take-over, which were so necessary and which became so familiar to all those involved in an infantry war. War in Italy was essentially one for the infantry and, of course, the artillery. In his book about the campaign General Jackson stresses the importance of artillery in *saving* lives. German casualties in all the battles in Italy were more than half a million. The Allies lost some three hundred thousand, despite the fact that they were always attacking and the Germans conducting a defensive battle in country which might have been made for it. The explanation lay in the Allied skill in deploying and concentrating their artillery fire. The Allies' great superiority in tanks availed them little, not only because of the unsuitability of the country for mobile operations, but also because too often the tanks were not used in close support of, or closely supported by, infantry.

The battle for Cassino lasted four months, and when it eventually fell in the latter part of May, 1944, Raleigh Trevelyan, fighting as a platoon commander in the Anzio beachhead, noted the fact in his diary and noted too that his battalion was called together to be told by some staff officer that they were to 'have the honour of being the first to break out'. Worse was to come when he learned that the Company he belonged to was to lead the attack across the Moletta, and that his own platoon would be the front one. In preparation for it, he would have to go on a reconnaissance patrol two nights before the actual attack:

> We passed in single file along an unmarked 'secret' track through our minefield and into the Moletta via a depression where no doubt cattle used to go to drink. The banks farther down were steep, about fifteen to twenty feet high on the average. We waded along the river for at least a hundred yards in this no-man's-land. I thought we were going unnecessarily far; anyone could lob grenades down on us, and before long we would be running into the outposts of the Jerries. . . .
>
> When we returned to the depression, there was an argument between Jim and the sapper corporal about the correct way home. This argument seemed stupid to me. I was quite sure of the route we had come by and offered to lead the way. . . . I had hardly taken twenty steps when everything went up in a dazzling green flame, and I was numbed by a fierce stab on the nape of my neck. My ears were hammering, and I had the impression that Jim was lifted bodily over me and thrown into a bush. . . . I turned and saw a man lying very still, and beyond him there was another, making soft quick moans. The sapper corporal and I lifted the first. It was the sapper officer. His face was mostly blown away. He was dead, there was no doubt. I lifted the other, who was no longer uttering any sound. This was Lance-Corporal Atkinson. The whole of the lower half of his body was gone. I had his head in my hands, and he gave a little gurgle from right inside, and I knew he had died too.

This was a mere, almost routine, reconnaissance patrol. Trevelyan, who by this time had had some experience of battle, admitted he had been shaken by it. When it came to the crossing of the Moletta itself, he had a very unpleasant time of it, lost more of his friends and was himself wounded. His account of the closing phases of the Anzio battle shows what a grim, bitter business it was. The whole idea of Anzio had been to make the battle for Cassino easier. In the event both battles were desperate, costly and prolonged. They were in this respect representative of the Italian campaign as a whole.

Yet not all the writings about the campaign depicted the misery and waste of it. We all remember Private Angelo, who, in Eric Linklater's delightful book, ruminated so long and painfully about his apparent deficiency in *il dono di coraggio*. Reflecting on this long afterwards, I would recall to what an extraordinary extent the gift of courage was possessed by an Italian cavalry officer, Filippo Senni, who was attached to my Regiment for the Gothic Line and subsequent battles until the war's end. He would fearlessly tour the front line in an open jeep, while most of us enjoyed the protection of our Sherman tanks. The Italian Army may not have greatly distinguished itself in the round. Some of its individuals were among the bravest of the brave. One of their number, although in a different setting, was of course Don Camillo, and Giovanni Guareschi in presenting to us the little world of that master of fisticuffs allows himself a reference to the war, the partisans and the British Army. In his more or less perpetual struggle with Peppone, the Communist mayor and former partisan leader, Don Camillo is appalled to find that 'A People's Palace' is to be built by the Communists, while there is no money for his own cherished recreation centre for the children. But Don Camillo is able to resort to blackmail when he discovers the source of Peppone's 'treasure'. Peppone explains that, by pretending that one of his wounded partisans was dead and had to be buried, they had succeeded in extracting looted treasure from under the soldiers' noses. 'It was all of it stuff looted by the Germans – silver, cameras, instruments, gold, etcetera. If we hadn't taken it, the British would have had it.' When Don Camillo accuses Peppone – 'that coffin to which the British presented arms was full of what you found in the cellars of the Villa Dotti, where the German Command had hidden it', the mayor blusters, but the sight of a tommy-gun under Don Camillo's right arm convinces Peppone that a share-out of the treasure so that *both* 'The People's Palace' and the children's recreation ground can be built might solve the problem. For all those of us who fought in Italy and learned to love the country and the people, Guareschi's portrait of his little world commands a special place in our affections, these people who 'are attractive and hospitable and generous and have a highly developed sense of humour'. But perhaps the greatest tribute to the Italians, who took so many risks in helping escaped British prisoners and were endlessly to be wondered at and admired for their courtesy and resourcefulness, comes from Eric Newby in his *Love and War in the Apennines*. His particular fear was that those who had sheltered and helped him after his escape from a P.O.W. camp would suffer revenge from German hands:

> The enemy had already arrived at the house. Normally, from the outside like a tomb at night, it was now illuminated by a couple of portable spotlights which also showed up a little knot of men standing in the rain who were wearing the same sort of caps with long peaks that Oberleutnant Frick had done. Nero [the dog] was silent. Fearful for the safety of Luigi and Agata . . . I walked into the woods where my rucksack was hidden. After what seemed a long time I saw the men pick up the lights and go off in the direction of the Colle del Santo. The next hour or two seemed an eternity. I was in anguish at what might have happened to Luigi and Agata. So far as I knew they were the only people in the area who had been sheltering an escaped prisoner and therefore the only ones who were actually liable to be shot for doing so. . . .
>
> I must have dozed off because the next thing I remember was being shaken awake, shivering. It was Luigi. 'Drink this,' he said. 'It's *grappa*.' I took a couple of huge swigs and felt better. . . .
>
> 'What happened to Nero?' I said. 'I didn't hear him bark'.
>
> 'When the *Tedeschi* came I was in the yard. They shone their lights on my face and for a while I couldn't see anything. Nero was barking . . . and went for them, just as he does for everyone. There was one very big *Tedesco* who was in command, a sort of sergente-maggiore I would think, and he went towards Nero . . . he shouted at him in his own language, and Nero ran away into his kennel and he hasn't moved from it since. I wish I knew what he said to him.'

Time after time and in different places the Italians risked their lives for Newby. Yet one of the most extraordinary encounters he had was with a German officer who found him sleeping, guessed that he was an escaped British prisoner, but being a professor of entomology, and at that very moment looking for butterflies, simply talked to Newby and promised not to reveal their meeting. He told Newby how unpleasant it was to feel that one was hated for being German, because of what the

Germans were doing, and that because of this Germany would lose the war:

> 'It's going to take you a long time to lose it at this rate,' I said. 'Everything seems to be going very slowly.'
>
> 'It may seem so to you,' he said. 'But it won't be here in Italy that we shall be beaten. We shall hold you here. . . . What is going on in Russia is more than flesh and blood can stand. We are on the retreat from Smolensk; we are retreating to the Dnieper. According to people who have just come from there we are losing more men every day than we have lost here in the Italian peninsula in an entire month. What are you doing?' he asked.
>
> I told him that I was on my way south towards the front. . . .
>
> 'If you take the advice of an enemy,' he said, 'you will try to pass the winter here, in these mountains. By the time you get to the battle front it will be very, very cold and very, very difficult to pass through it. Until a few days ago we all thought we would be retiring beyond the Po; but now the winter line is going to be far south of Rome. It has already been given a name. They call it the *Winterstellung*.'

Newby was recaptured later, but returned to Italy after the war to meet again and marry the schoolmaster's daughter, Wanda, who had taught him Italian and risked her life time and again to help him. It is a moving story, and although only an appendix to the fierce, destructive battles that took place in Italy, serves to remind us of the country and people who endured them. We are reminded also of the curious circumstance that while within a short time of the war being brought to Italian soil our former enemies became our allies, Mussolini's folly had resulted in a tragedy which had never previously been performed – Italy and England at war. As we shall see later, there were a great many grand ideas about what the Italian campaign was for and what it was going to achieve. For those of us who took part in it at the sharp end and at a low level in the military hierarchy, Italy was simply somewhere to fight the Germans and help win the war. Perhaps it was just as well that we took this view. For this in the end was what the campaign amounted to. And it is the *measure* of this help by which the campaign's importance and value must be judged.

1

PERSPECTIVES

Hitler was able to meet the Allied invasion of Italy almost without serious disruption of the war elsewhere.

Norman Stone

The second time I met Mr Churchill was in Italy in August, 1944.* The Prime Minister had managed to squeeze in among his many other duties a visit to his old Regiment, the 4th Hussars, then bivouacked not far from Ancona and about to move north to take part in the Gothic Line battles. I, as a troop leader in the Regiment, was one of those on parade to welcome the most illustrious Colonel that the Regiment has ever had. We were paraded with our tanks on a huge grass airfield and shortly after Mr Churchill's aircraft had landed, and he together with General Alexander had been greeted by our Commanding Officer, a bizarre occurrence interrupted, although only momentarily, the planned programme. Despite efforts to guide him to the saluting base by another route, the great man, dressed as Colonel 4th Hussars, stepped out purposefully in a direct line from the aircraft towards the position where the Regiment was paraded, only to be confronted soon afterwards by an anti-tank ditch, part of the airfield's defences. None daunted, he plunged down into it to the obvious distaste of General Alexander, as always elegantly attired in bush-shirt

---

* The first time had been in Egypt when Mr Churchill was at the Cairo Conference in 1943. As on this occasion he was inspecting his Regiment, the 4th Hussars, and found everything to his satisfaction except that we were not yet wearing the ribbon of the Africa Star, authorized months before. A few words were spoken and that evening a team of Egyptian seamstresses arrived at our camp to sew the ribbon onto our battledress tunics.

and shorts. Nevertheless Alexander, our Commanding Officer and various aides-de-camp followed. It was just as well for when the Prime Minister attempted to climb *out* of the anti-tank ditch, he found it beyond his powers and only combined heaving at his not inconsiderable posterior by the Commander-in-Chief and other lesser military mortals succeeded in extricating him. The inspection and parade then proceeded and was brought to a close by Mr Churchill's indicating that all ranks should close round him while he stood on a jeep to address us. Then came one of those fine extempore declarations about the state of the game, concluding in his expression of pride that his old Regiment would shortly be giving the Hun another knock. Finally he had tea with us in a tent when all the officers were presented to him. His optimism as to the outcome of the Gothic Line battles, however, was not to be borne out by events. On the contrary there was to be a repetition of much that had gone before. It had long been Churchill's hope that his Mediterranean strategy would yield decisive results. Had it done so at the time he came to see us in August, 1944? Indeed, would it ever do so?

The answer seems to be a matter of opinion. A. J. P. Taylor, in his superb *English History 1914–1945*, makes the point that late in 1943 Churchill had asked his closest advisers the all-important question as to whether or not Germany was likely to be defeated in 1944. Surprisingly enough the British seemed to think that victory in 1944 might be possible. It may be doubted whether Montgomery, at that time engaged in the Sangro battle, would have returned so optimistic a view. On 23 November, 1943, he noted:

> Heavy rain all day. The Sangro valley is completely waterlogged, and for the moment offensive operations are at a standstill.

A few days later he was writing to the Vice Chief of the Imperial General Staff:

> In spite of continuous rain and acres of mud I managed to get a good bridgehead over the Sangro; the trouble was to get any tanks and supporting weapons over, as the river was in flood and low level bridges merely disappeared . . . I don't think we can get any spectacular results so long as it goes on raining; the whole country becomes a sea of mud and nothing on wheels or tracks can move off the roads.

What was becoming clear to Montgomery and Churchill and everyone else was that the Allies were failing in their bid to reach Rome. Both men blamed this failure on the Americans' insistence that resources should be removed for other purposes. The real reason was that the Allies' lack of planning, boldness and concentration of force had easily been countered by the Germans and the weather. This failure, however, did not deter Churchill from trying once more to reinforce efforts in Italy at the inevitable expense of the main effort in France. As A. J. P. Taylor puts it, the British gamble on victory in 1944 'might have been expected to make Churchill eager for the Second Front. On the contrary, his persistence for the Mediterranean was undimmed'. During the Cairo conference in November, 1943, he put it more diplomatically to his fellow leaders, Roosevelt and Chiang Kai-shek, in admitting that while *Overlord* must remain top of the bill, it should not be so tyrannical as to rule out all other activities in the Mediterranean. But in the immediately following meeting in Teheran between Churchill, Roosevelt and Stalin, it was firmly established that *Overlord* must predominate. If there were to be any secondary operations, they would be in southern France, not anywhere further east. All Churchill's arguments were in vain. Yet still he did not give up, and back in Cairo again, having obtained Roosevelt's agreement that there would be no question of imminent amphibious operations in the Indian Ocean, he seized his chance. Faced with stalemate short of Rome and determined to get things moving, his intentions were revealed by a telegram to his Chiefs of Staff, sent after he had persuaded Eisenhower and Alexander to his way of thinking:

> We cannot leave the Rome situation to stagnate and fester for three months without crippling preparations of *Anvil* [attack on the south of France] and thus hampering *Overlord*. We cannot go to other tasks and leave this unfinished job behind.

The job was to remain unfinished for another six months, and when it finally was finished and Rome was taken on 4 June, 1944, it was totally eclipsed by the landing in Normandy two days later. With this, A. J. P. Taylor recorded, 'British strategy in the Mediterranean lost all significance'. Why did it take so long to reach Rome? One reason was Cassino, the other Anzio. In order to try and break the standstill and get the Allied armies in Italy moving again, Churchill proposed that some of the landing craft and other shipping should be kept in the Mediterranean a bit longer before returning to England, even though this might mean a June D-Day for *Overlord* rather than May – the date promised to Stalin. In this he was supported by General Sir Alan Brooke who recorded in his diary on 14 December: 'We are stuck in our offensive here, and shall make no real progress unless we make greater use of our amphibious power'. The idea was that a landing south of Rome in the area of Anzio would shake loose the front and assist the Allied armies to break through the German defences in the mountainous Cassino country, and advance at last to Rome. As we shall see in more detail later, it did not work out that way. In spite of the landings at Anzio taking the Germans by surprise – as usual they were surprised not by the Allies' boldness, but their lack of it – the sheer sluggish inactivity of the American general in command, Lucas, allowed the Germans rapidly to seal off the bridgehead and subject it to the most severe and dangerous counter-attacks. 'Anzio,' observes Professor Taylor, 'was like Gallipoli all over again: inspired by the same man and with the same result.' It was not to be Anzio which shook loose the Germans at Cassino; it was the final battle of Cassino which came to the rescue of the Allied troops at Anzio.

No wonder Norman Stone wrote that the Allied conduct of war in Italy gave the German generals fresh hope and allowed them to recover their will to go on resisting. Anzio was also like Salerno all over again. And just as Salerno and its ponderous aftermath, together with the speed and totality of the German grip on Italy, persuaded Hitler to listen to Kesselring and conduct a delaying campaign in southern Italy, so the indecisiveness of Anzio, even though Rome was eventually taken in June, allowed the Germans to orchestrate *another* successful withdrawal to *another* winter line and to impose on the Allied armies a delay of *another* year before finally the elastic band snapped in May, 1945. Yet we have General Warlimont, a staff officer at Hitler's headquarters, writing that 'Hitler's Mediterranean strategy threw a far greater strain upon the German war potential than the military situation justified'. After the war was over, of course, German generals became very good at making Hitler the repository of all the strategic errors and all the tactical blunders of the German Army. Yet given the situation as it was in the latter part of 1943, with all ideas of further German offensives in the east merely chimerical, with fears of an Allied invasion of the west daily growing, and with an obsession about the need to hang on to the Balkans come what may, what was Hitler to do? He could not simply abandon the Italian mainland and allow the Allies to play ducks and drakes there as they pleased. Some stand had to be made. It all depended on – how much? Michael Howard called his decision 'to commit the maximum available resources to the defence of the Mediterranean' a mistake, a step which was simply playing the Allies' game for them. This judgement hardly squares with Norman Stone's contention that Hitler was able to meet the Allied invasion of Italy almost without serious disruption of the war elsewhere.

There are other serious discrepancies of view. Chester Wilmot claimed that the Italian front turned out to be a far greater drain on Germany than on the Allies. 'In October, 1943,' he wrote, 'Eisenhower's eleven divisions were holding down a German force double that size in Italy alone. By his decision to fight south of Naples, Hitler was compelled to keep ten divisions idle in Northern Italy.' This arithmetic hardly tallies with the facts. In his definitive history of the battle for Italy, General Sir William Jackson shows that in October, 1943, the Allied order of battle of 5th U.S. Army, 7th U.S. Army and the British 8th Army was made up of nineteen divisions. In the same month the Germans had *exactly the same number* of divisions, nineteen, eight under Kesselring, eleven under Rommel.

All this talk of holding down so many German divisions needs to be seen in perspective. We should bear in mind that in December, 1944, less than six months before the war's end, Hitler had succeeded in collecting no fewer than *twenty-six* divisions, of which seven were Panzer divisions, to indulge in the final, and as it turned out, futile gamble of the Ardennes counter-offensive, while still holding firm on the eastern, western and southern fronts. Think of that! We should also bear in mind John Grigg's* contention that it is fallacious to suppose that 'the pinning-down of German troops in southern Europe depended upon the Allies maintaining a major fighting front there'. He points out that there were more German divisions in the Balkans at the end of 1943 than there were in Italy, yet in the Balkans there was no fighting, only the threat of invasion or of local resistance activity. There is much to be said for this. When, however, he goes on to argue that in the autumn of 1943 *thirty* Allied divisions, each one being of greater strength than their German equivalents, were tied down in Italy, he weakens his case by straying a long way from the facts. Nevertheless, his point that had Allied troops not been committed to fight in southern Europe the massive deployment of Allied resources there would have

---

* *1943: The Victory That Never Was.*

been unnecessary is incontrovertible. It is true too that one of the purposes of clearing the Mediterranean – avoiding the need for shipping to go round the Cape and thus generally enable the Allies to husband their shipping – was partially offset by the demands made on this shipping by the Italian campaign itself. It is when Grigg maintains that 'the Germans were entitled to feel that the Italian campaign, though very costly to them, was far costlier in strategic terms to the Allies' that he touches on the nub of the matter. It prompts the question – what else could the Allies have done? His own answers to the question are designed to support the whole theme of his book – that victory in 1943 would have been possible had the Allies determined on a cross-Channel assault then instead of a year later. It was not the view of Allied intelligence staffs, the logisticians, the Combined Chiefs of Staff or those commanders likely to be responsible for executing such a venture. Indeed the power of the Wehrmacht was still formidable in 1944, let alone a year sooner. And the battle of the Atlantic itself was only finally won in 1943.

But leaving that aside, would it have been possible, as Grigg suggests, to deal with Italy either by capturing most of it in the early months of 1943 or not attempting to capture it at all? The first of these notions supposes that the Allies could have mounted an invasion of Sicily, while still engaged in reducing the Tunisian bridgehead and then persuading some unnamed successor to Mussolini to allow the Allies to occupy most of Italy; the second idea makes the bizarre assumption that circumstances under which the Allies did *not* invade Italy would have brought about as great a distraction to the Germans as those in which they did – by encouraging Italian partisans to fight the Germans. We may perhaps recall here Hitler's contempt for the Italian Army.

It was, of course, possible that the Allies, hard-pressed though they were to finish off the Tunisian campaign in time, could have mounted simultaneously an amphibious operation against Sicily, an operation of immense complexity, demanding huge resources of air and sea power, most of the experienced divisions that the British and Americans could muster, and the undivided attention of their most renowned and successful commanders; it was possible that had this been done, the Germans, with all the powerful reinforcements which they poured into Tunisia towards the end of the game there, would have decided against diverting some of them to the much more dangerous and politically vulnerable target of Sicily; it was perhaps possible that the Italians, suddenly displaying martial qualities reminiscent of Theodoric's reflection on the Romans,* would rise against their German oppressors with such ferocity that the veterans of the Wehrmacht would fling down their arms and run off bawling for quarter; it was no doubt possible that Hitler, who had long foreseen and prepared for defection on the part of the Italians, would lose his nerve, not act with lightning decision and ruthlessness, forfeit gratuitously a major strategic advantage, and simply allow his former allies to withdraw from the war and settle down to *la dolce vita*, drinking wine, singing opera and making love; it was even possible that while the British and Americans transferred all their military strength from the Mediterranean area, leaving a few garrisons in North Africa and some ships and aircraft to patrol without interference the formerly disputed seas and air, and concentrated this power in the United Kingdom ready for the crucial invasion of France, the Germans would leave countless divisions in the Balkans and Italy idle, uncommitted and content, while fierce battles raged on the eastern front and the construction of the Atlantic Wall began to be taken seriously by Rommel and others. All these things were possible. But they were so hugely improbable that they could form but a poor foundation for determining the future conduct of war at a moment in that titanic conflict when a major strategic error by the Allies might have had incalculably disastrous consequences.

The fact is that the Italian campaign must always be seen as an essential subsidiary to the really decisive military activities which were taking place or were about to take place elsewhere. In the first place there was the urgent need to draw forces away from the Eastern front and bring significant help to the Soviet Union; later there was the equally important requirement to ensure that the invasion of France should take place at a time when everything had been done to weaken the German capability there. Alexander was of the opinion that the campaign in Italy fulfilled its strategic mission. As he was Supreme Allied Commander there, his judgement is hardly surprising. Yet he concedes that it was not a matter of capturing ground vital to either side, nor did the Allied armies engage the main German forces. It was the effect on the war as a whole which mattered. It is the *extent* of this

---

* *Romanus miser imitatur Gothum; et utilis Gothus imitatur Romanum;* or as Gibbon put it: 'Distress might sometimes provoke the indigent Roman to assume the ferocious manners which were insensibly relinquished by the rich and luxurious Barbarian.'

effect which must lead us to a proper judgement and in making this judgement we must recall Michael Howard's view that taking Allied strategy in the round, including that part of it executed in the Mediterranean and Italy, it has yet to be shown that the war could have been won sooner or more economically. That the Mediterranean strategy was pursued at all owed much, of course, to the pressure exerted by Churchill. He was passionately anxious that the British armies which had redeemed themselves in Africa should not stand idle, but continue to engage the enemy and help fulfil his pledges to Stalin. And even though progress in Italy might have been marred by unimaginative planning, lack of speed and boldness, and a series of sluggish, slogging battles, the *mettle* was there, the quality that Churchill most admired and sought – *il dono di coraggio*. This was what mattered in the end.

Yet the Italian campaign was a mass of contradictions. It was at once opportunistic and cautious; it mixed spasmodic dash with leisurely prudence, prudence moreover which may have begun as precaution, but which continued as habit; it was to exploit a crack in Axis solidarity, yet was neither swift nor bold; it developed all the marks of a deliberate battle of attrition, yet proved so costly for the Allies that they never wore down the enemy to a point where superiority could achieve decision; it was supposed to strike at the soft under-belly of southern Europe, but was conducted over some of the most difficult terrain – ideal for the skilled defensive tactics of the German Army – that was to be found anywhere in Europe; it was thought of by some as an alternative main effort, but was in fact first and always a side-show. As for its purpose it never became the cancer to the Wehrmacht that Spain became to Napoleon's Grand Army. After Hitler's initial concern in September, 1943, concern which he quickly dissipated by establishing so swift and total a grip upon the country, the situation in Italy never again gave Hitler serious worry. Indeed he never again set foot there. And when the time came in June, 1944, for the Allies to invade France, Germany had about sixty divisions on the western front, over 200 divisions fighting the Russians, and some twenty in Italy. Such a deployment could hardly be said to constitute strategic circumstances demanding a major distraction of forces to the south.

How did the position look to Hitler on paper, on the map, as it were, at the end of 1943? He had already conceded in a talk with Jodl that victories in Russia – not that these were plentiful – were no good if he were to lose Western Europe. Such talk was almost an admission of the inevitability of ultimate defeat, as his War Directive No. 51, dated 3 November, 1943, seemed to imply:

> These last two and a half years of tough and bloody struggle against bolshevism have strained our military strength and energy to the utmost. It was appropriate to the magnitude of the danger and the overall strategic situation. Now the danger in the East remains, but an even greater one is emerging in the West: the Anglo-American invasion! The sheer vastness of the eastern spaces allows us to countenance even a major loss of territory if the worst comes to the worst, without it striking fatally at Germany's vital arteries.
>
> Not so in the West! Should the enemy succeed in breaching our defences on a wide front here, the immediate consequences would be unpredictable. Everything indicates that the enemy will launch an offensive against the Western front of Europe, at the latest in the spring, perhaps even earlier. I can therefore no longer tolerate the weakening of the West in favour of other theatres of war.

No mention of the southern front here, it will be noted, no reference to Italy. There, in Hitler's view, the Allies were being held at bay. Can his statement that there was to be no weakening of the West in favour of other theatres of war find corroboration when we take a look at what was to happen on the southern, the Italian, front? Early in December, 1943, as the Allies closed up to the Gustav Line south of Rome, the Germans had some twenty-one divisions deployed, or in the process of deploying, in Italy; there were another two divisions on the ground shortly after the Allied landing at Anzio; between then and the Gothic Line battles in August, 1944, the number of German divisions in Italy remained about the same; for the Gothic Line battle itself – *nearly three months after the Normandy landings* – the number had increased by a mere three to twenty-six divisions; and this number dropped again to twenty-three at the time of the final offensive by the Allies in April, 1945. Such juggling could hardly be called a significant weakening of the West or indeed of the East.

Curiously enough, despite his apprehensions, Hitler seemed reconciled to, seemed almost to look forward to, an Allied assault in the West. Indeed he saw in its potential defeat a solution to all his strategic problems. This notion cannot be dismissed as mere self-delusion. Former Allied amphibious operations, so he told himself, did not appal him – the very reverse rather. The landings in French North Africa had been unopposed; those in Sicily and Italy had been effected, as he saw it, with the help of traitors; the Dieppe Raid in 1942 had been bloodily repulsed. What need he fear then? 'If only they would land half a million men, and then foul weather and storms cut them off in the rear,' he consoled himself on the last day but one of 1943, 'then everything would be all right.' Although Hitler may have talked confidently about giving the Allies 'the thrashing of their lives' when they did land, he also took precautions to make things as difficult as possible: dug-in Panther tanks, concrete emplacements, pillboxes for thousands of anti-tank guns, above all the appointment of Rommel to oversee everything and plan the defensive tactics. Rommel's presence made all the difference. Unlike von Rundstedt, Commander-in-Chief, West, who favoured the traditional method of holding back powerful reserves until major incursions had been identified for counter-attack, Rommel believed that an invasion must be defeated on the beaches, since Allied air forces would never allow the German mobile reserves to intervene effectively. In February, 1944, he told his Army commanders:

> In the short time left before the great offensive starts, we must succeed in bringing all defences to such a standard that they will hold up against the strongest attacks. Never in history was there a defence of such an extent with such an obstacle as the sea. The enemy must be annihilated before he reaches our main battlefield. . . . We must stop him in the water, not only delaying him but destroying all his equipment while it is still afloat.

Rommel's conviction and energy ensured that every sort of ingenious device for defending the coastline was constructed, together with millions of mines, coastal batteries reinforced with steel and concrete, machine-gun posts, the 88 mm gun, wire, plus anti-parachute poles and booby traps. Had he had his way about putting panzer troops in the shop window he would have made the task facing Montgomery infinitely more difficult. But Hitler was not prepared to ignore the advice of General von Schweppenburg, commander Panzer Group West and a traditionalist in tactics. In fact had Rommel been in charge of defending such beachheads as Salerno and Anzio, it may be doubted whether the Allies would have obtained a foothold there at all. At Anzio it was touch and go – with Kesselring's pausing for reinforcements, the American reluctance to advance, and Hitler's own concern that Anzio's real purpose was, not so much to help capture Rome, but an Allied device to weaken the German position in France by obliging him to divert some of the newly formed SS Panzer Divisions away from France to get bogged down in an indecisive battle of attrition. This he refused to do. However desirable it might have been to eliminate the Anzio beachhead – he even commented that if it could be wiped out, there would not be an invasion anywhere else – it was more important simply to *contain* the Allies in Italy. Looking at it against the background of the crucial theatres, East and West, Hitler seemed to award the Italian part of the war the same judgment as was applied to Johnson's dictionary – interesting, but unconnected. Yet the real global nature of the conflict was admirably summed up by Brigadier Williams, Montgomery's chief Intelligence adviser. He pointed out in April, 1944, shortly before the final battles for Rome took place and just as the great Russian offensive was threatening Poland and Rumania, that Hitler was prepared to accept greater losses in the East in order to preserve the option of more significant success in the West. And although it may have been the eastern danger which caused Hitler to switch powerful panzer forces from West to East and thus ease the Allied venture in Normandy, the contribution made by the third front – the Italian front – was not to be ignored. 'A breakthrough at Lwow affects a division at Liseux,' observed Williams; 'the Russian advance was made possible by the Allied bombing of Germany, by the containing actions in the Mediterranean and by the imminence of invasion in the West. Two-thirds of the German Air Force and 100 German divisions were kept pre-occupied. Thus was the Red Army given opportunity. . . . So in their doughty turn, the Russians make *Overlord* more possible.' Compared, however, with the great battles in the East, and those which were still to come in the West, Italy in the spring of 1944 must have seemed to Hitler little more than a puny vexation.

Leaving the strategic circumstances aside for the moment, what have we to say about the conduct of the Italian campaign? Montgomery was very harsh in his condemnation of the way in which 15th Army Group had managed affairs. He was already thinking ahead to *Overlord* and having contemplated 'the mess in Italy, he had trembled at the thought of the catastrophe Eisenhower and Alexander might together make of *Overlord*'. * In a letter to Mountbatten of December, 1943, he had pointed out that the whole thing had started well. In three months

---

*Nigel Hamilton: *Monty: Master of the Battlefield 1942–1944.*

they had captured Sicily, knocked Italy out of the war, captured Naples, the Foggia airfields, and put their hands on both a third of Italy and their fleet. It had, in Montgomery's opinion, been essential to take Rome before the weather broke, and this could have been done. But to do so would have required a firm grip by 15th Army Group, which simply was not there. 'There was no "grip", no policy, no planning ahead; indecision, hesitation, ineffective command, led to a great waste of time, and we narrowly averted appalling administrative scandals. . . . Now we are faced with rain, low cloud, and mud. All this means that neither the Army nor the Air can operate properly; the whole tempo of offensive operations is cut down. You cannot operate in Italy during the rains. . . . The lesson is obvious. The high command entered on a major campaign in Europe without a clear idea as to how they were going to fight the battle. There was no clear policy, or planning ahead; the whole thing was ad hoc. . . . So I am not terribly happy about the future.'

He made himself more happy, however, by ensuring that the grip, planning and policy for the Normandy landings would be in his own hands. While he was doing so, the battle for Italy went on with Alexander still in charge of 15th Army Group; and from another fighting soldier, who played an important part in the struggle for Cassino and subsequently gave the best record of it that we have – Fred Majdalany – we have a very different account of Alexander's capabilities. Majdalany described the fourth and last battle of Cassino which began in May, 1944, as Alexander's masterpiece, 'an operation in C major with full orchestra'. He went further and in illustrating Alexander's use of Nelson's maxim that only numbers can annihilate, made it plain that this time Alexander would be able to choose the time and place of his offensive, and because of the good weather be able to deploy large numbers of complete formations. He would have more guns, tanks and aircraft, and even more important, more infantry. 'It was to be,' wrote Majdalany, 'a vindication of Churchill's Mediterranean strategy: the justification for the long winter agony: the triumphant salute of the Mediterranean veterans* to those new armies poised to strike across the English Channel and open the final chapter of the war. In the grand design of the war as a whole, the summer offensive in Italy was the prelude to the finale. But it was also a climax in its own right.'

---

*We veterans were quite happy to be classified as 'the D-Day Dodgers'.

These are extravagant claims when contrasted with A. J. P. Taylor's suggestion that with the launching of *Overlord*, the Mediterranean strategy lost all significance. It may, however, be conceded that there was some justification for Alexander's defining the strategy of his campaign at this time as being designed 'to force the enemy to commit the maximum number of divisions in Italy at the time the cross-channel invasion is launched'. It all depends on what we mean by 'maximum', and on where these divisions came from. We have already seen that it was activity on the Russian front which obliged Hitler to switch some three or four panzer divisions from West to East. Alexander's summer offensive did cause the Germans to send some divisions to Italy, one from Hungary, one from Holland, one from Denmark, one from the Balkans. But we must bear in mind that the overall difference in German deployment on the Italian front, whether we are thinking of the battles of Anzio, Cassino or the Gothic Line, and whether we are dealing with 1943, 1944 or 1945, was to be measured in a mere handful of divisions, three or four at most. It is in this sort of consideration that the real value of the Italian campaign must be gauged. It seemed to be the Allies' fate to attack and to go on attacking, no matter how slow the progress or how disappointing the results, and it was the Germans' fate to defend and to go on defending, no matter what was happening on other fronts. For many of those who took part in the campaign on the British side, there were times when it seemed to be weary, stale, flat and unprofitable.

Shortly after Mr Churchill's visit to us in August, 1944, we in the 4th Hussars sustained another visit – this time from the Commander, 8th Army. He predicted immediate and spectacular success in the forthcoming battle for the Gothic Line and even spoke of our being in Vienna in a few weeks' time. Alas, it did not turn out that way. Some *months* later we were still contesting the Gothic Line with the German parachute, panzer and panzer grenadier divisions who fought so skilfully and bravely. There was another winter of discontent to get through before we finally advanced and this time went on advancing. The perspectives then and now of someone like myself, who took part in the campaign, vary widely. The purpose of this narrative is not so much to add new facts to historical events which have commanded the attention of so many. Indeed it would be impossible to better General Sir William Jackson's definitive account of the battle for Italy, or to complement significantly the Official History, whether thinking of its volumes on Grand Strategy or on the actual Mediterranean campaigns. What is perhaps possible is to take another look at the story and present to the general reader a relatively short and digestible account of the way in which strategic considerations and tactical problems interacted in such a way as to make the whole campaign profoundly frustrating and disappointing from the Allies' point of view. The uncertainty of the Allies' strategic intentions and their sheer sluggishness of action, lack of boldness or imagination are unlikely to reflect great glory on their counsels. There is also the question of whether the Italian campaign made any significant difference to the Germans' conduct of war and whether what was intended to be a great distraction to the Wehrmacht did not in the end turn out to be an even greater distraction to the Allies. The Italians' own unhappy position in it all must not be forgotten. In her book, *War in Val d'Orcia*, Iris Origo made it clear how greatly the Italians resented the Allied call for 'Unconditional Surrender' after Mussolini's fall. After ridding their country of Fascism, they expected something more than Allied indifference to Italy's fate. To be a mere stepping stone to Germany's defeat and to be turned into a bloody battlefield in the process seemed to them a poor reward for the risks they had taken.

Perhaps one of the greatest miscalculations which Allied leaders made was their idea that attacking the Italian mainland would somehow or other turn into an easy option and yield important strategic prizes quickly. It never did! The campaign there was never more than a side-show, a mere appendage to the great game that was played out for four years on the dreadful Eastern Front and for one short, but fateful, year in the bocage of Normandy, the forests of the Ardennes and the grim flat battlefields of the Rhineland. Yet despite the relative insignificance and grave disappointments of the Italian campaign, what else could the Allies have done? And what else could Hitler do but make use of the country that had betrayed him in order to keep his enemies at bay?

2

THE UNEASY ALLIANCE

One thousand German soldiers could thrash the entire Italian
Army.

Hitler

'Now, Herr Hitler,' said the dying Hindenburg to Germany's Chancellor in August, 1934, 'don't trust the Italians.' He need not have worried. Hitler trusted nobody, not even his closest lieutenants. As Alan Bullock has pointed out, there was no one with whom he shared his private thoughts. Circumspection and secretiveness were second nature to him. He never let slip an unguarded word. All that he said was calculated. His distrust was all-embracing. Nor had he any illusions about the value of Italy as an ally. Shortly before starting the war by invading Poland, Hitler was angered by Mussolini's dithering between active support and benevolent neutrality. But anger in no way interfered with his cynically making promises of material aid to Italy, which he and everyone else knew were out of the question. When Göring remonstrated with him, Hitler simply made it clear that he was not concerned with actually fulfilling his promises, but merely 'depriving Italy of any excuse to wriggle out of her obligations'. Four months later, with Poland long since conquered, with Britain and France at war with Germany – but not with Italy – Hitler was again to receive evidence of Mussolini's readiness to take fright. Hitler's preoccupation with plans for an attack on France and Belgium had caused the Duce to write to Hitler complaining of the latter's duplicity in his dealings with the Soviet Union. It was there in the East, declared Mussolini, that Germany's *Lebensraum* was to be found, not in the Western democracies. Italy's offer of mediation with Britain and

France simply reinforced Hitler's belief that when the time came Italy would dishonour her undertakings. Weizsäcker, State Secretary at the Foreign Ministry, summed it all up when he observed that the Italians were a strange people, who at one and the same time would feign loyalty to their German allies in order to share in success, but try to keep favour with the West by passing information to them. In any case to Hitler the idea of Germany's needing military assistance from Italy was bizarre. How then had such an odd alliance come about?

Albert Speer has told us that in 1935 when Hitler would spend many autumn days at Obersalzburg, he was quite undecided as to what he should do about making alliances. He had often maintained, and indeed *Mein Kampf* is explicit here, that England and Italy were the only two possible allies for Germany. But which to choose? 'I would by far prefer to join the English. But how often in history the English have proved perfidious. If I go with them, then everything is over for good between Italy and us.' It never seemed to have occurred to Hitler that alliance with Germany would for the British have been a political non-starter. But in any case the decision was made for him by Mussolini's invasion of Abyssinia, and the consequent reaction of, and measures taken by, France and Britain. When the League of Nations, with Britain's voice very much to the fore, imposed economic sanctions on Italy, the idea of a Rome-Berlin Axis took shape. This move by the British more or less guaranteed the worst of all worlds. For it was a tragic instance of being 'willing to wound, and yet afraid to strike'. A mere show of imposing sanctions, which is what British policy amounted to, succeeded only in antagonizing Italy and robbing the League of Nations of what little authority it still had. Had Britain, on the other hand, pursued the idea of sanctions against Italy to the extreme of being prepared to go to war – and war against Italy, considering the British naval power and position in the Middle East, could have had but one result – the whole structure of collective security might have received such a boost that an effective check on both Fascism and National Socialism might have been constructed. As it turned out, it was Hitler who exploited the differences between Italy and the Western democracies.

Yet the beginnings of what Professor Deakin called *The Brutal Friendship* between Germany and Italy were not notably auspicious.

Although in *Mein Kampf* Hitler referred to his extreme admiration for 'this great man south of the Alps', his first meeting with Mussolini in June, 1934, was an unfortunate one. The very last thing that Hitler would expect or welcome was to be patronized, but this was precisely what happened. The Italian dictator, magnificently attired in uniform, actually lectured the drably dressed Hitler about both German activities in Austria and even worse the political situation in Germany itself. Albert Speer recalled how this visit reinforced Hitler's distrust of the Italians and their policy, although his belief in Mussolini remained firm. Indeed, Hitler's unwavering support for Mussolini personally throughout all the vicissitudes of a six-year war was perhaps unique, for it is hard to think of any other political or military figure whom Hitler would not either have ditched or simply removed from the scene had it suited him. It was not until the last months of the war that Hitler privately admitted that what he called his 'unshakeable friendship' with Mussolini had been a mistake. 'It is in fact quite obvious,' he observed, 'that our Italian alliance has been of more service to our enemies than to ourselves. . . . If, in spite of all our efforts, we fail to win this war, the Italian alliance will have contributed to our defeat! The greatest service which Italy could have rendered to us would have been to remain aloof from this conflict.' But, of course, it was Mussolini's determination *not* to remain aloof from conflict which brought about the German-Italian alliance in the first place.

Mussolini had long calculated that the French and British obsession with German rearmament would allow him to conduct his own territorial adventures without too much fear of interference, and it was the open declaration by Hitler of a programme already under way that gave rise to a chain of events leading to the Pact of Steel. In March, 1935, Hitler announced the creation of a new German Army, totalling thirty-six divisions in peacetime and based on compulsory service. He also revealed that the Luftwaffe already possessed 1,000 operational aircraft. So blatant a breach of the Versailles Treaty was bound to invite protest, and protests there were, but Hitler was concerned only with what action the Western Powers might take. The conference at Stresa in April was attended by the British, French and Italians. Their governments were unanimous in condemning Hitler's action and reiterating commitment to Austria's independence. They also confirmed once more their adherence to the Locarno Treaty, which ten years earlier had guaranteed the Franco-German and Belgian-German borders. Much more important than the Stresa Agreement, however, were France's pact with the Soviet Union for mutual aid in the event of unprovoked aggression, and a similar pact between the Czechs and Russians.

Hitler's answer to all this showed him at his most intuitively brilliant. His speech to the Reichstag on the evening of 21 May, 1935, did all that could be done to allay suspicious fear and bolster unfounded optimism. He deplored war, appealed to reason, redoubled his assurances for peaceful solutions to Germany's problems, offered non-aggression pacts with all his neighbours, had no intention of attacking Austria, would adhere to and strengthen the Locarno Pact, would limit armaments, and in particular agree that the German Navy should be no more than thirty-five per cent of Britain's Royal Navy. It was all that the peace-mongers were longing to hear. As Alan Bullock put it, 'His grasp of the mood of public opinion in the Western democracies was startling, considering that he had never visited any of them and spoke no foreign language. He understood intuitively their longing for peace, the idealism of the pacifists, the uneasy conscience of the liberals, the reluctance of the great mass of their peoples to look beyond their own private affairs.' The readiness of the Western democracies to be taken in was illustrated by Britain's signing a Naval agreement with Germany the following month.

Concluding a naval treaty with Britain was one thing. Finding an ally was another, and Hitler had always maintained that Great Britain was Germany's natural ally, for whereas Germany was essentially interested in continental expansion, Britain's power lay in commerce, the sea and colonies. Had it been possible before 1914 to secure an alliance with Britain, Germany's western flank would have been protected for the great crusade in the East. To have made enemies of Russia and Britain at the same time was an appalling blunder – happily a blunder that was to be repeated. It was strange that Hitler's attraction to an alliance with Britain persisted even during the war itself. But any idea that Britain would abandon its broad, traditional policy of the balance of power in Europe was bound to fail. No matter what assurances Hitler might give, a British government would never give him a free hand in Europe. Yet ironically enough, the mere conclusion of a naval treaty undermined the solidarity of the Stresa Agreement, in that neither France nor Italy had been consulted. Having on the one hand condemned German rearmament at Stresa, Britain now virtually condoned it with a private treaty. All this was not lost on Mussolini, who, however much he might deprecate the rise of German power, could not but see that its existence would distract the attention of France and Britain from his own expansionist ambitions.

'Ever since the Stresa Conference,' wrote Winston Churchill, 'Mussolini's preparations for the conquest of Abyssinia had been apparent.' From the British point of view aggression of this sort would not only be unfortunate in itself. It would signal the transfer of Italy with what was then thought to be considerable military strength from the side of France and Britain to the side of Hitler's Third Reich. At one time it was suggested that some leading British figures might go and tell Mussolini of the inevitable result on British opinion that a move against Abyssinia would have. But, as Churchill noted, nothing came of it and it probably would have done little good anyway, for 'Mussolini, like Hitler, regarded Britannia as a frightened, flabby old woman . . . incapable of making war'. It is worth recalling here Churchill's growled comment on being woken up on 9 June, 1940, with the news that Mussolini had entered the war on Hitler's side: 'People who go to Italy to look at ruins won't have to go as far as Naples and Pompeii in future'.

That event was still far off. On 3 October, 1935, the Italian armies attacked Abyssinia and the League of Nations duly applied sanctions, imports from and exports to Italy being banned by most members of the League. The exceptions were Albania, Austria and Hungary because of their close association with Italy; and the U.S.A. and Germany because they were outside the League. For the British Government the result of sanctions was far from satisfactory, for they failed to deter Mussolini and gave much encouragement to Hitler. Although Hitler regarded Italy's attack on Abyssinia premature, declaring that 'the time for struggle between the static and the dynamic nations is still some way off', he could hardly be worse off whatever the outcome. Defeat for Italy would simply strengthen Germany's position in relation to Austria and the Balkans; victory for Italy would highlight the weakness of the Western democracies and add weight to the idea of a Rome-Berlin axis. But there was more to it than just encouragement. The imposition of sanctions obliged Hitler to make a choice, and as he explained to his political and military hierarchy, he could not allow Fascism in Italy to go under. Germany would have to lend assistance to Mussolini to ensure that sanctions were as ineffectual as possible. He underlined the point that Germany too might have to stand up against opposition from outside – 'the day may come when we also begin to stake our rightful claims'.

So feeble was the opposition to Italy's aggression, so undermined the League of Nations' authority, so damaged the reputation of France and Britain, that it was not long before Hitler began to stake what he regarded as Germany's rightful claims, and in March, 1936, German soldiers reoccupied the Rhineland. This coup was an unparalleled example of military audacity and political *Fingerspitzengefühl*. Hitler was never one to jib at taking risks, but even he did not underestimate the risk he took here, admitting subsequently that the 48 hours following reoccupation were the most nerve-racking of his career. Had the French moved against him, he would have had no alternative but to withdraw. 'What would have happened,' he asked his still attentive listeners in 1943, 'if anybody other than myself had been at the head of the Reich? Anyone you care to mention would have lost his nerve. I was obliged to lie and what saved me was my unshakeable obstinacy and my amazing aplomb. I threatened, unless the situation eased, to send six extra divisions into the Rhineland. The truth was I only had four brigades.' But the French did nothing except reinforce the Maginot Line. It was, of course, not only over the French and the Western Powers generally that Hitler had triumphed. He had triumphed too over his own timid generals. And from this time forth, although these generals might give voice to their concern about the consequences of the Führer's *Vorhersehung*, his intuition, their voices grew less and less sure, as time and time again they were proved wrong and he right.

The strategic consequences of Hitler's success were profound, and as Churchill foretold in the House of Commons a month later, Germany would build a defensive barrier in the West – the Siegfried Line – which would not only give her the ability to strike strongly through Belgium or Holland, but more dangerous still would lend Germany such security on her western flank that there would be much greater freedom to threaten and act in the East. Such circumstances augured ill for such countries as Poland, Czechoslovakia and Austria. The whole strategic balance in central Europe would be changed. And as Alan Bullock has written, 'The first government to feel the effect of the change was the Austrian'.

It was the resolution of the Austrian problem which brought Hitler and Mussolini even closer together. In October, 1935, Franz von

Papen, the German Minister in Vienna, had written to the Führer suggesting that the new distribution of power in Europe would before long enable Germany 'to take up actively the question of influencing the south-eastern area', a euphemism for bringing about the *Anschluss*. Early in the following year one of von Papen's first successes was to help engineer the removal of the Austrian Vice-Chancellor, Prince Starhemberg, who was a strong opponent of the Austrian Nazis. Although Starhemberg was a friend of Mussolini, it was the latter who advised Schuschnigg, the Austrian Chancellor, to placate Hitler by arranging for Starhemberg to resign. Soon afterwards Schuschnigg, with the Duce's approval, signed the Austro-German Agreement of July, 1936, which was ostensibly to facilitate more comfortable relations between the two states, but which in fact was used by Germany to harass Austria by constantly demanding concessions and undermining her independence. It was to lead eventually to the meeting between Schuschnigg and Hitler at which the latter's shouting and bullying produced the result he wanted. But in the meantime this Agreement allowed Hitler to move more closely to Italy, and the outbreak of the Spanish Civil War in the same month, July, 1936, further reinforced this process because Germany and Italy were able to pursue a common policy in Spain, which involved far more active cooperation than had been possible during the Abyssinian crisis. Having already made it plain that Germany was ready to recognize the new Italian Empire, Hitler despatched his Justice Minister, Hans Frank, a fluent Italian speaker, to see Mussolini in Rome. Frank made a number of conciliatory declarations – Germany regarded the Mediterranean as an Italian sea, the Austrian question was settled, the Italian Empire would be recognized, the need for closer collaboration between their two countries and so on. The upshot was that a month later Ciano, Italian Foreign Minister and Mussolini's son-in-law, set off for Germany to see his opposite number, Constantin Neurath, and the Führer himself.

During their discussions – as usual most of the talking was done by Hitler – the main theme was the idea of Germany and Italy forming an alliance against the threat of Bolshevism *and* against the Western democracies. At this stage Hitler still wanted to have his cake and eat it, in that he was uncertain as to his precise policy with regard to England. The greater the strength of Germany and Italy, he argued, the more likely it would be that England would come to some accommodation with them. But in any event their two countries would be stronger, both in weapons and in attitudes. It was all very well for England to suggest that Germany and Italy were led by adventurers. When England had been led by adventurers, she had created an Empire. 'Today she is governed merely by incompetents.' As a result of all this the so-called October Protocols were signed in Berlin by the two Foreign Ministers, outlining cooperation between the two countries on issues of foreign policy. Thus, in Mussolini's words shortly afterwards, there came into being an 'axis', a centre-piece around which other similarly minded nations could rally and work for peace.

The Rome-Berlin Axis was further strengthened during the following year by frequent consultations and visits, capped by Mussolini being received in Münich by Hitler with all the trappings of military parades and manoeuvres, together with demonstrations of industrial power at which the Third Reich excelled. Mussolini was left in no doubt as to the extent of Germany's might, nor as to his own commitment, from which it was beginning to be too late to withdraw, to Hitler's intentions and methods. Hitler's speech in Berlin, with the Duce standing by his side, made it plain enough. He spoke not only of the community of views which existed between the Fascist and National Socialist states, but also of community of action. Italy, through the efforts of 'a man of constructive power', had become a great Empire. Nor was there any doubt as to Germany's strength and political intentions. These two forces together would guarantee a Europe 'which still possesses a perception of its cultural mission and is not willing through the action of destructive elements to fall into disintegration'. Mussolini could go home bewitched by Hitler's rhetoric and display of power. He would have been less content had he been present at a meeting on 5 November, 1937, when Hitler outlined to his Minister of Defence, von Blomberg, the three Commanders-in-Chief, von Fritsch, Raeder, Göring, and Foreign Minister, von Neurath, what the future direction of his policy would be. Indeed what Hitler had to say profoundly shocked even this small and devoted audience. For it was no less than the blueprint for achieving what Hitler had always intended to achieve – *Lebensraum*.

Hitler was specific about his first, main objectives – the overthrow of Austria and Czechoslovakia. Military plans for both cases were already in course of preparation, had been indeed for three or four months. While the objectives were clear, precise timing was another matter.

Hitler was often to sum up his opportunistic strategy with the words – *so oder so*, in this way or in that – so that if one course of action seemed profitless, another would be pursued. Always present, however, was one consistent element – force or the threat of force. He would always aim to get what he wanted without resort to war, by threats, profiting by others' mistakes and building up military power. After four years or more as Chancellor he was prepared to raise the stakes in the game of threatened violence, particularly as the means of employing violence was constantly growing. Yet, however opportunistic his strategy might be, the broad programme was clear. First, detach eastern Europe from the West; next neutralize or crush the West; finally, and this was always the primary goal, make war on Russia. *Mein Kampf* was explicit here: 'And so we National Socialists . . . stop the endless German movement to the South and West, and turn our gaze towards the land of the East. If we speak of new territory in Europe today, we can primarily have in mind only Russia and her vassal border states . . . . This colossal empire in the East is ripe for dissolution.'

But on the way to this Greater German Reich must come Austria and Czechoslovakia. To have Austria would deny the West opportunities to threaten Germany from the South. The Rome-Berlin Axis would help to remove obstacles here. Czechoslovakia's economic and military resources would be immensely valuable, to say nothing of its strategic position. Reassurances to Poland would smooth the way here. Besides, the incorporation into the Reich of *all* Germans was a cardinal feature of his programme. Risk? Of course, there would be risk. What would the great powers, France, Britain, Italy, Russia, actually do? It was not difficult for Hitler to convince himself, if not all his audience, that they would do nothing. Italy would be too pre-occupied with Britain and France. Russia was concerned with the aggressive power of Japan. Any idea of concerted action against Germany was absurd. The will to resist simply did not exist.

Before turning this blueprint into reality, however, Hitler took certain steps to strengthen his grip on the economic and military resources of the Reich. Blomberg, Fritsch and Neurath were all removed. Hitler himself assumed command of all the armed forces. Ribbentrop became Foreign Minister. Göring took over from Schacht in charge of Economics and War Economy. The entire war machine of the Reich was now subordinate to Hitler's will. It was on the same day,

4 February 1938, that he began to exercise supreme command of the Wehrmacht, that the Führer set in train the events which led to the *Anschluss*. Franz von Papen was recalled from Vienna, saw Hitler next day at Berchtesgaden and proposed a meeting between Hitler and Schuschnigg, the Austrian Chancellor. This meeting took place a week later at the Berghof. Hitler's combination of shouting, bullying, sending for General Keitel, threatening to order the march into Austria – 'You don't seriously believe that you can stop me,' he told Schuschnigg, 'or even delay me for half an hour, do you?' – had its effect. The Austrian Chancellor signed a protocol which agreed to far-reaching demands. His subsequent resolution to hold a plebiscite at which the Austrian people would declare whether or not they were in favour of a free, independent and united Austria, simply provoked Hitler into issuing orders for military action. But the Führer also sent Prince Philip of Hesse to Mussolini with a letter designed to secure Italy's neutrality. In it he spoke of restoring law and order in his homeland, acting in national self-defence, reminded the Duce of his steadfastness in Italy's critical hour over Abyssinia, and drew a definite boundary between Italy and Germany, the Brenner Pass, thus reassuring him about fears for southern Tyrol. While this appeal to Mussolini was under way, the move of German troops to occupy Austria continued. Before they crossed the frontier, Hitler had his answer from Mussolini. Prince Philip of Hesse telephoned to say that the Duce had 'accepted the whole thing in a very friendly manner' and sent his regards. The Führer's response was one of effusive gratitude: 'Tell Mussolini I will never forget him for this . . . never, never, never, whatever happens . . . . I shall be ready to go with him through thick and thin. . . . You may tell him that I thank him ever so much. . . . If he should ever need any help or be in any danger, he can be convinced that I shall stick to him, whatever may happen, even if the whole world were against him.' We may at least concede that, in this respect, Adolf Hitler kept his word.

The subsequent Austrian plebiscite confirmed both Germany's and Austria's approval of the *Anschluss* and of Hitler's policies. 99 per cent voted Yes. So the first of the two main objectives named by Hitler in the previous November was his, and in its realization he had been helped, or at least not hindered, by Mussolini. It was to be the same story with the second objective. But as Churchill noted in a speech to the House of Commons on 14 March, 1938, Hitler's programme had changed from one of restoring a nation's rights to one of naked aggression. Force, and force alone, had done it:

> The gravity of the event of 12 March cannot be exaggerated. Europe is confronted with a programme of aggression, nicely calculated and timed, unfolding stage by stage, and there is only one choice open, not only to us but to other countries, either to submit like Austria, or else take effective measures while time remains to ward off the danger . . . . This mastery of Vienna gives to Nazi Germany military and economic control of the whole of the communications of South-eastern Europe . . . . What is the effect of it upon what is called the balance of power?
>
> Czechoslovakia is at this moment isolated, both in the economic and in the military sense. . . . How many potential allies shall we see go one by one down the grisly gulf?

Churchill would certainly see Czechoslovakia go down the grisly gulf before the Western democracies at last nerved themselves to take a stand. And in both planning and executing the murder of Czechoslovakia, Hitler showed once more his astonishing skill in playing upon a supposed grievance in such a way that others did his work for him. Moreover, this political mastery was combined with immensely thorough military preparedness so that nothing would be left to chance. If military action proved necessary, it must be decisive within a few days. Military stalemate would promote a European crisis. Instant military success leading to *faits accomplis* would persuade foreign powers of the utter uselessness of military intervention. After some months of military preparation, during which Hitler furiously up-braided his generals for their lack of boldness, and while the West simply demonstrated their lack of either resolution or solidarity, the whole question was brought to a head by Hitler's Nuremberg Rally speech on 12 September in which he demanded justice for the Sudeten Germans. The French thereupon took fright and appealed to Chamberlain to make the best bargain he could. Chamberlain's meetings with Hitler on 15 and 22 September conceded the principle of detaching the Sudeten areas from Czechoslovakia, at which Hitler upped the stakes, insisting that the Sudetenland must be *occupied* by German troops and that the Czechs themselves must accept this by 2 pm on 28 September. Despite a good deal of bellowing that he would 'smash' Czechoslovakia, Hitler sent a letter to Chamberlain on 27 September in which he made plain his willingness to guarantee the rest of Czechoslovakia and to negotiate details with them. Chamberlain at once responded by proposing an international conference, and at the same time sending a telegram to Mussolini asking him to persuade Hitler to accept.

It was then that Mussolini's intervention was decisive. He sent his assurances of support for Hitler, but asked that the new proposals should be examined. After further furious diplomatic activity, it was agreed that the two dictators would confer with the French and British Prime Ministers at München. Hitler insisted on seeing Mussolini before the conference started, and he joined the Duce's train at Kufstein early on 29 September. It is clear that Mussolini's influence, both in convincing Hitler that the conference should at least be given a chance and in playing so important a part in the conference itself, was significant. It was he who produced a memorandum, which had previously been drafted by the Germans, but which nonetheless was brought forward as Mussolini's own draft, for the conference to discuss, and it was this memorandum which provided the essentials of an Agreement. By it Hitler got more even than he had demanded from Chamberlain – the Sudetenland and all its powerful fortifications, control of Czechoslovakia's communications and considerable economic resources. General Jodl, head of operations at Hitler's Armed Forces Headquarters, hailed the 'genius of the Führer and his determination not to shun even a world war' which in the event had produced victory without using force.

Churchill was less enthusiastic, calling it 'a total and unmitigated defeat'. He pointed out to the House of Commons that it was useless arguing what the various differences of position taken by Hitler were. One pound had been demanded at pistol point. When conceded, two pounds were required. Hitler then agreed to take £1.17.6d. with some promises of good will thrown in. An abandoned and broken Czechoslovakia would recede into darkness. Nor was this the end. It was only the beginning of the reckoning. 'This is only the first sip, the first foretaste of a bitter cup which will be proffered us year by year unless, by a supreme recovery of moral health and martial vigour, we arise again and take our stand for freedom as in the olden time'. How fitting it was that before long it would be Churchill himself who would lead and inspire this supreme recovery.

Even before this, Great Britain began to take a stand for freedom. Soon after Hitler's final destruction of Czechoslovakia by occupying Bohemia and Moravia in mid-March, 1939, the British and French governments 'guaranteed' Poland. Britain also set about putting her armed forces into better condition, and, following Italy's occupation of Albania in April, Chamberlain took the momentous decision to introduce conscription. But while the British were at last waking up to the realities of the Axis powers' intentions, these powers themselves were binding themselves even closer together. The Germans were now pressing Italy for a formal military alliance, and in order to allay Italy's fears about German intentions in Poland, Ciano invited Ribbentrop to meet him in Milan on 6 May. Ciano had with him a memorandum stressing the need for a period of peace for several years. When Ribbentrop appeared to endorse the Italian view and Ciano reported accordingly to Mussolini, the Duce threw overboard his former caution and plumped for an announcement of a military alliance with Germany. Hitler agreed. He believed that this would affect British and French resolve with regard to Poland, and so the Pact of Steel was formally signed in Berlin on 21 May. Article III contained this undertaking: 'If, contrary to the wishes and hopes of the contracting parties, it should happen that one of them is involved with another Power or Powers, the other contracting party will come immediately to its side as ally and support it with military forces on land, sea and in the air.' After the ceremony Ciano returned to Rome, where he was told by King Victor Emmanuel that as long as the Germans had need of Italy they would be courteous, but at the first opportunity they would reveal themselves as the rascals they really were. Mussolini was plagued by comparable doubts, fearing the possibility of war, and in a note to Hitler reiterated Italy's need for a period of peace lasting until at least 1942. Hitler's somewhat vague reply seemed to endorse Mussolini's view, and it was left at that.

The truth was very different. Only two days after the Pact of Steel was signed, something which Hitler regarded as a triumph of his diplomacy, he held another meeting with his senior generals and admirals. This time he showed his hand even more clearly:

> We are left with the decision: To attack Poland at the first suitable opportunity. We cannot expect a repetition of the Czech affair. There will be war. Our task is to isolate Poland. The success of this isolation will be decisive . . . . There must be no simultaneous conflict with the Western Powers. If it is not certain that German-Polish conflict will not lead to war in the West, the fight must be primarily against England and France.

In short, since *Lebensraum* was still the problem, and expansion eastwards was the solution, war was inevitable. In a war with the West, England was the most dangerous enemy. The way to defeat her was to cut off her supplies, and capitulation would follow. The German Army must therefore occupy those positions which would enable the Kriegsmarine and the Luftwaffe to strangle her life-lines. France would have to be defeated, Belgium and Holland occupied. Then the conditions for conducting a successful war against England would have been created. We must concede that, apart from the key point about capitulation, Hitler's *Vorhersehung*, his intuition as to what was going to come about, was astonishingly accurate.

As for starting the war, Hitler simply maintained that he would give a propaganda reason for it, whether plausible or no. 'The victor will not be asked afterwards whether he told the truth or not.' It was easy enough to find such a reason with regard to Poland – Danzig and the Polish Corridor. By August Hitler's campaign to exploit the alleged oppression of the German minority in Polish provinces had reached the point when the League High Commissioner in Danzig, Carl Burckhardt, was warned by the Führer that if the Poles interfered further in Danzig, he would fall upon them like lightning with all the power at his disposal. When Burckhardt replied that this could lead to general war, he was told that Germany would prefer war today than tomorrow and that it would be waged without scruple. Hitler went on: 'I want nothing from the West. . . . But I must have a free hand in the East. . . . I want to live at peace with England and to conclude a definite pact; to guarantee all the English possessions in the world and to collaborate.'

All these noises off alarmed Mussolini, who sought another meeting with Hitler. This was postponed, but Ciano met Ribbentrop instead at Salzburg on 11 August. Years later he bitterly recalled his impressions of that meeting:

> The Italian tragedy, in my opinion, had its beginnings in August, 1939, when, having gone to Salzburg on my own initiative, I suddenly found myself fact to face with the cynical German determination to provoke the conflict. The Alliance had been signed in May . . . it had a clause that for a period of three or four years neither Italy nor Germany would create controversies capable of disturbing the peace of Europe. . . . Instead, in the summer of 1939 Germany advanced its anti-Polish claims. . . . 'Well, Ribbentrop,' I asked, as we were walking together in the garden, 'What do

you want? The Corridor or Danzig?' 'Not that any more,' he said, gazing at me with his cold metallic eyes. 'We want war.'

And war they got, but not before Hitler had pulled off another astonishing coup – the Nazi-Soviet Pact of Non-Aggression signed in Moscow on 24 August. Even this remarkable event did not reassure Mussolini sufficiently for him to steel himself to make war on Germany's side, despite the Pact of Steel. He wrote to Hitler explaining his reasons. If Germany attacked Poland, and the conflict remained localized, Italy would render her ally all the necessary political and economic aid. If, however, Poland's allies attacked Germany, the Italians would be unable to initiate operations because of their unpreparedness. Only if Germany supplied them with weapons and material would they be able to counter any moves by the French or British. Hitler simply commented that the Italians were behaving as they did in 1914. Nevertheless lack of Italian support, together with the steadfastness of Britain and France induced Hitler to delay his attack on Poland from 26 August until 1 September. The final exchanges between Führer and Duce merely underlined Mussolini's craven concern – 'I leave you to imagine my state of mind in finding myself compelled by forces beyond my control not to afford you real solidarity at the moment of action' – as contrasted with Hitler's granite determination and extraordinary strategic foresight: 'If, as I have said, it should come to a major war, the issue in the East will be decided before the two Western Powers can score a success. Then, this winter, at the latest in the spring, I shall attack in the West with forces which will be at least equal to those of France and Britain.'

It all came about as Hitler had predicted. Poland was crushed in the first of many *Blitzkrieg* campaigns, and, despite Gamelin, the French Commander-in-Chief, maintaining that what had happened in Poland could not happen in France, the Wehrmacht succeeded in a matter of a few weeks in achieving what the Imperial German Army under the Kaiser, Hindenburg and Ludendorff had been unable to achieve in over four years – the destruction of the French Army and their will to resist. 'Every army is a mirror of its people,' Hitler had declared in November, 1939. He placed a low value on the French Army's will to fight. 'After the first setbacks it will quickly crack up.' And crack up it did. But France's tragedy had two profound effects. It brought Winston Churchill to power in Britain. It also brought Italy into the war. Before long Hitler's comment, made years later, that Italy would have served the Axis cause best by remaining out of the conflict was to receive some startling corroboration.

'Führer,' wrote Mussolini from Rome on 26 June, 1940, 'Now that the time has come to thrash England, I remind you of what I said to you at Münich about the direct participation of Italy in the assault of the Isle. I am ready to take part in this with land and air forces, and you know how much I desire it. I pray you to reply in order that I can pass into the phase of action. Awaiting this day, I send you my salute of comradeship.' Far from there being any direct participation by Italy in an assault on England – and even Hitler in the end jibbed at undertaking Operation *Sea Lion*, which he described as an exceptionally bold and daring idea – the mere entry of Italy into the war had created another theatre of activity where Britain would be able to damage the weaker partner of the Axis and gain great strategic advantage. This theatre, of course, was the Middle East.

There were differing views about the strategic importance of the Middle East and Mediterranean. Michael Howard has described the area as 'a centre of gravity of British forces second only to the United Kingdom itself'. It was exactly the view held by Churchill who took grave risks in boldly reinforcing Wavell's forces in Egypt with tanks at a time when others pressed for their retention at home. Churchill was never in any doubt that the Middle East base was vital for the conduct of war. Indeed winning the battle for North Africa became an obsession with him, and when it was done it led in his view logically to the so-called Mediterranean strategy, which he so eloquently and successfully persuaded the Americans to support. During nearly the first two years of the war, the Commander-in-Chief, Middle East, was General Wavell, who as early as August, 1939, was clear-sighted enough to recognize that since in war the Axis powers would enjoy the initiative, Germany would try to dominate eastern and south-eastern Europe, while Italy would aim to do the same in the Mediterranean and North Africa. Whatever use Germany made of Italy in attempting to secure advantage in the Mediterranean, Wavell was convinced that British control of the area was indispensable to successful conduct of the war. Therefore, he argued, his task was not just to guarantee the security of Egypt and the Middle East generally, but to 'take such measures of offence as will enable us and our Allies to dominate the Mediterranean at the earliest possible moment'. So successful was he in his initial operations against the Italians both in East Africa and the Western Desert that Hitler was obliged to come to the rescue of the Italian Army.

Admiral Raeder, Commander-in-Chief of the German Navy, had similar ideas and time after time tried to convince Hitler that Germany should, after their great success in France, concentrate on war against England in the Mediterranean, which was, he pointed out, 'the pivot of their world empire'. As Italy was weak, Britain would certainly try to knock her about first, and in order to attack Italy more easily would seize the whole of North Africa. Therefore, Raeder went on, Germany must prevent any such occurrence. Together with Spain and Vichy France, they must seize Gibraltar and secure French North Africa, then with the Italians take Egypt and the Suez Canal, allowing them to advance through Palestine and Syria to Turkey. 'If we reach that point,' concluded Raeder, 'Turkey will be in our power. The Russian problem will then appear in a different light. Fundamentally Russia is afraid of Germany. It is doubtful whether an advance against Russia in the north will then be necessary.' All this was sound enough, but Hitler turned the entire argument inside out. He was conscious of the need to subdue Britain, but since it was possible that direct invasion might not come about, he must seek to eliminate all other strategic developments which might operate in England's favour:

> Britain's hope lies in Russia and the United States. If Russia drops out of the picture, America, too, is lost for Britain, because the elimination of Russia would greatly increase Japan's power in the Far East. . . . Decision: Russia's destruction must therefore be made a part of this struggle. . . . The sooner Russia is crushed the better. The attack will achieve its purpose only if the Russian State can be shattered to its roots with one blow. . . . If we start in May, '41, we will have five months in which to finish the job.

Hitler made these points to his Commanders-in-Chief in July, 1940. Within a few months, however, Italy's ineffectual efforts at waging war were to create distractions in the Middle East and the Balkans, which Hitler felt obliged to take account of and which threw his Russian programme badly out of joint. On 13 September, 1940, the 10th Italian Army began its reluctant and ponderous encroachment on to Egyptian soil. They went only as far as Sidi Barrani and Sofafi. Then Graziani sat down and set about building a series of defensive positions and organizing his administrative support. As Ciano put it, never had a military commander embarked on an operation so much against his will. Meanwhile the British continued to reinforce both the Middle East and Malta, which played so decisive a role in disrupting Axis supply lines to North Africa throughout the long-drawn-out desert war. Wavell's reinforcements were timely, for not only was he planning to counterattack the Italians as soon as possible, but Mussolini was about to take a step which not only irritated and dismayed Hitler, but obliged him to divert substantial forces to the Balkans at the very time when he wished to keep that area quiet. What is more this consequent German intervention to rescue its ally turned Wavell's strategic priorities upside down, forced him to abandon success in the Western Desert and instead despatch troops to Greece and Crete, most of which were either killed, captured or evacuated.

On 4 October Hitler and Mussolini had conferred at the Brenner Pass. Hitler was full of ideas that if Spain could be persuaded into the war by promises of colonial expansion at France's expense, Italy could have Nice, Corsica and Tunis, while France would be compensated with slices of British West Africa. Little was said about Greece. But it was Greece that Mussolini had his eye on, and when the two dictators met again on 28 October at Florence Mussolini greeted Hitler with the words: *'Führer, wir marschieren!'* His armies had invaded Greece earlier that morning. This was in direct opposition to Hitler's wishes, and it had a profound effect on the conduct of the war thereafter. It was the beginning of a gigantic distraction for Axis and Western Allies alike from the two main theatres of operations which were to develop and where the fate of the Wehrmacht and the Third Reich were to be decided – the Eastern Front and North-West Europe. The magnitude of Italy's strategic blunder was such that Hitler never trusted the Italians again. Meanwhile something had to be done, and the Führer's War Directive No 18, dated 12 November, illustrated that the dissipation of the Wehrmacht over wide areas and subsidiary objectives was about to take place. It called for action by France to secure their African possessions; preparations to seize Gibraltar; employment of German forces, including one panzer division, to assist the Italians in Egypt, to be considered; plans for the occupation of Greece from Bulgaria; plans for a campaign against Russia to be continued; even reference to Operation *Sea Lion* against England was included. Here were the first signs of losing the initiative. They spelled out *re*action to what the British and Greeks were doing to the Italians. David Irving called Mussolini's invasion of Greece, for his divisions were quickly thrown back, the sowing of the first seed of later defeat.

General Wavell saw it at the time and noted on 17 November: 'I am quite sure Germany cannot afford to see Italy defeated, or even held, in Greece, and must intervene. We shall, I think, see German air assistance to Italy very shortly.' He was right on both counts, but this did not deter him from attacking the Italian 10th Army in the desert. It was General Richard O'Connor who conceived and executed the destruction of the Italian 10th Army, a campaign which lasted two months, from December, 1940, to February, 1941, and ended in the elimination of the entire enemy force opposed to him, a complete victory. Two British divisions had advanced 500 miles and had routed an army of ten divisions, capturing 130,000 enemy soldiers, 400 tanks and 800 guns. O'Connor wanted to go on from Benghazi and capture Tripoli; Wavell backed him, while warning that the Balkan situation might not allow it. On this last point he was right. Churchill insisted on 'succouring' Greece. Politically his decision could not be challenged. Militarily, it led to defeat and evacuation, but it must be remembered that after the war Jodl, Chief of Operations at Hitler's Headquarters, maintained that Germany had lost the war because she had been obliged to divert divisions to meet the British landing in Greece.

Meanwhile a new player in the game of North Africa and the Mediterranean had made his way on to the stage. On 12 February, 1941, Lieutenant-General Erwin Rommel arrived in Tripoli, and apart from other forces he would have 15th Panzer Division, 5th Light Motorized Division, Ariete Armoured Division and Trento Motorized Division. With these relatively small forces Rommel would shortly give a demonstration of blitzkrieg in the desert which left the British commanders and troops bewitched, bothered and bewildered. But before he did, a good deal more talking was done – mostly by Hitler. On 8 and 9 January he had held yet one more of his war councils and had laid down certain courses of action: Italy was to be supported both in Africa and Albania; Operation *Marita*, the attack on Greece, would start at the end of March; since Russia would not give up her claims in Eastern Europe, she would have to be crushed as quickly as possible. All this talking was turned into another War Directive, No 22, which was remarkable for the way in which it concentrated on the Mediterranean area.

One thing Hitler had already made absolutely plain – that the

Mediterranean question must be liquidated during the winter of 1940–41, for, as he put it, 'I must have my German troops back in the spring, not later than May 1st'. Directive No 22 showed the lengths to which Hitler was prepared to go to fulfil the promises he made to Mussolini at the time of the *Anschluss* to the effect that, if needed, help would be forthcoming. It was no idle boast. Some ten days after issuing it Hitler again met Mussolini, this time at the Berghof. As usual it was the Führer who did the talking, mainly concerning his forthcoming intervention in Greece and generally reviewing all strategic contingencies with what Ciano described as exceptional mastery. But one thing Hitler did not reveal to his Italian allies – his intention to attack the Soviet Union, even though the Directive for this attack had been sent out to his senior commanders more than a month before the two dictators met. It was, of course, because of the projected Russian campaign that Hitler was insisting on the return of his German troops by May.

During the spring of 1941 the war's centre of gravity was clearly in the Mediterranean. Churchill had hopes of forming a Balkan front to include Greece, Yugoslavia and Turkey, all adding up to a force of some fifty divisions – a nut, as he called it, for the Germans to crack. Alas, the nut proved to be neither large nor solid. Intervention in Greece simply robbed Wavell of sufficient strength in the Western Desert for decisive results there, while proving inadequate to stem the Germans in Greece. Hitler, on the other hand, showed how quickly and decisively the Wehrmacht could act under his direction. In order to turn the British out of Greece, he required either the cooperation or the compliance of Hungary, Bulgaria, Rumania and Yugoslavia. The first three did not hesitate to comply. Yugoslavia did, and a successful military coup in Belgrade disassociated the new government there from the Axis. Such opposition was the very thing to arouse all Hitler's fury and ruthlessness. Yugoslavia would be 'smashed with merciless brutality' and was. Orders given on 27 March had been carried out three weeks later when Yugoslavia capitulated. A week later Field-Marshal List had completed the conquest of Greece and caused yet one more evacuation by a British Army. The Germans' subsequent invasion and capture of Crete completed Axis mastery of the northern shores of the eastern Mediterranean. But even worse things were happening on the desert flank, which Churchill described as 'the peg on which all else hung'.

In late March the new player on the Middle East stage, Erwin Rommel, brought a new set of rules to desert fighting, and with a combination of speed, daring, surprise and great tactical skill, together with a *penchant*, not shared by his British counterparts, for leading from the front, had succeeded in bundling the British right out of Cyrenaica and back to Egypt, leaving only the garrison of Tobruk as the remaining prize of all O'Connor's conquests earlier that year. As Rommel put it:

> We've been attacking with dazzling success. There'll be consternation amongst our masters in Tripoli and Rome, perhaps in Berlin too. I took the risk against all orders and instructions because the opportunity seemed favourable. No doubt it will be pronounced good later and they'll all say they'd have done exactly the same in my place. We've already [3 April, 1941] reached our first objective [Benghazi] which we weren't supposed to get to until the end of May.... The British are falling over themselves to get away.

When later Rommel recorded his impressions of this first North African campaign, he severely criticized Hitler's strategy, claiming that had Germany kept her hands off Greece and concentrated on North Africa, she might have secured the entire Mediterranean and Middle East. It was Malta, not Crete, that should have been seized, for Malta was the key to lines of supply between Italy and North Africa. The prize would have been all the Middle Eastern oil, and bases from which to threaten Russia. When we think of what Rommel did achieve with relatively puny forces, it may hardly be imagined what he might have done with a tenth of the weight which was put into *Barbarossa*, the subsequent attack on the Soviet Union.

Churchill too was in no doubt about the absolutely crucial importance of Egypt and the Middle East, whose loss, he wrote in a war Cabinet directive dated 28 April, 'would be a disaster of the first magnitude to Great Britain, second only to successful invasion and final conquest!' He went on:

> Every effort is to be made to reinforce General Wavell with military and Air forces, and if Admiral Cunningham requires more ships, the Admiralty will make proposals for supplying them. It is to be impressed upon all ranks, especially the highest, that the life and honour of Great Britain depends upon the successful defence of Egypt.
>
> It is not to be expected that the British forces of the land, sea and air in the Mediterranean would wish to survive so vast and shameful a defeat as would

be entailed by our expulsion from Egypt, having regard to the difficulties of the enemy and his comparatively small numbers. Not only must Egypt be defended, but the Germans have to be beaten and thrown out of Cyrenaica.

It was to be another eighteen months before this was to come about, and had Admiral Raeder been able to convince Hitler in May, 1941 – when he renewed his proposal for 'a decisive Egypt-Suez offensive for the autumn of 1941 which would be more deadly to the British Empire than the capture of London' – it might never have come about. If the Wehrmacht had been allowed to concentrate against the British position there and then, they would have found Wavell and his fellow Commanders-in-Chief more stretched in their resources than at any other time. Although the East African campaign was soon to reach its successful conclusion in totally conquering the Italian Empire there, it was not yet over; Greece and Crete had caused grievous loss; in Iraq the pro-German revolt by Rashid Ali had to be dealt with; Syria had to be wrested from the Vichy French; and the Desert Fox was at the gates of Egypt. What might not have been achieved?

Happily the Führer refused to see it, and his Directive No 30 made it plain that the whole question of mounting an offensive finally to break the British position in the Middle East could not be decided until after *Barbarossa*. The *Official History* later made the point that 'had the Eastern Mediterranean arena not been successfully held during the lean years, in which case, for want of bases, no British fleet or air forces could have even disputed the control of the Mediterranean sea communications, the task of the Allies in gaining a foothold in Europe would have been rendered immensely more difficult; indeed it might well have proved to be beyond their powers'. But fortunately in June, 1941, Germany turned away from the Mediterranean. Hitler had achieved his immediate aims. Italy was still fighting. The Balkans were secure. The British were more or less at bay. He could turn to his great mission of eradicating the Soviet Union. He had not consulted Mussolini who heard about it only on the eve of the attack, wakened in the middle of the night by an urgent message from the Führer, which explained and justified his great decision. There was little in the letter to reassure Mussolini. 'Whatever may now come, Duce, our situation cannot become worse as a result of this step; it can only improve.'

Germany might turn away from the Mediterranean – for the time being. Italy could not. Nor could the British. Not only was it the only theatre where they could engage Axis forces on land, but as the CIGS, General Sir Alan Brooke, was to put it later that year: 'I am positive that our policy for the conduct of the war should be to direct both military and political efforts towards the early conquest of North Africa. From there we shall be able to reopen the Mediterranean and stage offensive operations against Italy.' In other words the blueprint for British strategy was becoming clear. It was to be the subject of as much controversy as almost any other great issue in the conduct of the war.

3

THE MEDITERRANEAN STRATEGY

The British were in the Mediterranean because they were there.
                                        A. J. P. Taylor

In turning away from the Mediterranean and concentrating his military effort against Russia, Hitler began to fulfil the strategic conditions which the British had always sought when waging war on a Continental power embarked on European domination and the dismantling of Britain's world position. It had for centuries been Britain's aim under such circumstances to acquire an ally enjoying the advantages of large armies and extensive territories, who would take on the bulk of the enemy's land forces and slowly but surely knock the stuffing out of them, thus leaving the British free to deploy their sea power at will, gaining more trade and overseas possessions, and, provided there was not too much risk, fiddling about on an open flank in Europe. And when Hitler committed the Wehrmacht to the limitless space and, as it turned out, almost inexhaustible reserves of the Soviet Union, Britain was once more free to indulge in her favourite strategic enterprise of seeking the open flank and making what use of it she could. During the latter part of 1941 and the first half of 1942 the British hardly made full use of their opportunities on the desert flank. Yet this persistence on the indirect approach continued even when things began to go better in the latter part of 1942.

It was often said when the war was over that its turning point had been July, 1942, with Rommel repulsed on the Alamein line, and the German Army in Russia about to be blunted on the rock of Stalingrad and so giving the Red Army its opportunity to embark on a series of remorseless offensives which never stopped until they reached the

Elbe. In the sense that until the autumn of 1942 Hitler still held the initiative, his armies, as it seemed, on the point of conquering Egypt and subduing the Soviet Union, this view might be supportable. But it might be argued that the true turning point, the point at which events occurred from which flowed the broad course of the war thereafter, was earlier. Leaving aside for the moment Japan's attack on the United States with its profound consequences, Hitler's decision to invade Russia virtually determined the outcome of the war, as it robbed him of either the means or the inclination to seek conclusive victory in the one area where it might have been available to him – the Mediterranean and Middle East.

On the eve of *Barbarossa*, Arthur Bryant made some observations in *The Illustrated London News* remarkable for their foresight and accuracy. He wrote:

> For all her glittering victories, the Third Reich is encircled by steel. And the instrument of that encirclement is the sea-power of the British Empire and its still passive but very real and potent supporter, the United States of America. Germany must break that ring or go down as surely in the end as she did in 1918.

Bryant went on to speculate as to which course of action Hitler might choose and he suggested four possibilities. First, direct invasion of England, a hazardous enough undertaking as the preliminaries of a former shot at it, the Battle for Britain in the air, had shown, but nonetheless the shortest, most direct way to victory. For, whatever Churchill might have said about carrying on the struggle from the overseas Dominions, how would Canada, Australia, New Zealand, even the United States have turned the tables on a Third Reich in possession of all Western Europe except Spain, Portugal and Sweden? The second course of action was to break the ring by concentrating on the U-boat war against our supply routes, a war which could be sharpened by surface attacks as well. We all know how near to success Raeder and Dönitz came in the Battle of the Atlantic to strangling Britain *without* Germany absolutely concentrating on this line of strategy. Thirdly and fourthly Germany could break out eastwards into Asia or southwards into Africa. Of these four options, three might have been fatal to the British position – all-out offensives on Britain itself, in the Atlantic or in Africa. Fortunately Hitler chose the fourth – to go east, *der Drang nach Osten*.

The whole argument simply reinforces the idea that, in making strategic decisions, you must abide by the fundamental rules, or you are bound to go astray. These rules are that you must first and foremost correctly select your prime objective, and, having done so, concentrate your military effort to ensure the seizure of this objective. In mid-1941 Hitler's objective should have been Britain, and if, despite all his strategic daring, he jibbed at the notion of direct assault upon these islands, then an attack on British sea power by the occupation of Egypt and the domination of the Mediterranean, which Raeder had correctly described as the pivot of the British Empire, could have yielded decisive results. Compared with all this, Russia was strategically irrelevant. Yet Bryant put his finger firmly on Hitler's dilemma when he pointed out that because the alternatives to attacking Russia, Britain itself, the Atlantic or Africa, were hedged with difficulties, Hitler might well take the 'easy' road and attempt to encircle the British position in the Mediterranean and Middle East by the very course of striking through Russia to Iran. And all this, we may recall, was written by Bryant some two weeks before the Führer committed the irretrievable blunder of invading the Soviet Union.

There was no shortage among Hitler's entourage of doubters about the wisdom of or even the need for the Russian adventure. Ribbentrop, architect of the Soviet-Nazi Pact, was consistently opposed to it, and his subordinate, Weizsäcker, made the telling comment: 'If every Russian town burned down was worth as much to us as one British warship sunk, then I would speak up for a German-Russian war this summer.' The General Staff was broadly compliant, as was shown by their meek acceptance of what Hitler had to say to them a week before the campaign began. Yet on this occasion it was Hitler himself who declared that Britain was still the main enemy, Britain who would fight on as long as there was purpose in doing so, Britain who therefore looked to the Russians to wear down Germany's military and economic strength, while the balance of power would be tilted in their favour by American help. Nonetheless, the struggle with Russia had to be precipitated for the threat would always be there to interfere with German interests, even if peace with Britain were made. But, while convincing himself, and perhaps others, of the need to strike there and then, Hitler was in no doubt about the severity of the struggle ahead. It would be 'by far the toughest . . . because for the first time we shall be fighting an *ideological* enemy, and an ideological enemy of fanatical persistence at that.'

One of the most remarkable of all Hitler's war directives had been issued some eleven days before the attack on Russia began and it laid down what was to be done *after* the defeat of Russia. Then at last the Middle East and Mediterranean question would be settled. The British position there would finally be strangled by converging attacks through Egypt from Libya, through Turkey from Bulgaria, through Iran from Transcaucasia and by seizing Gibraltar. It was a master plan all right, and ironically enough there was to occur, fleetingly but nevertheless tangibly, an opportunity when this master plan might have been put into effect – in June, 1942 – but by then the Russian campaign had Hitler in thrall, and the chance was missed, never to recur. It all reinforced the view that Hitler, despite his astonishing political foresight and strategic brilliance, could not somehow comprehend the war as a whole, and rather than exploit the promise of concentrating his efforts on the Atlantic or the Mediterranean, chose to plunge the bulk of his resouces, both in men and material, into the limitless space of the Soviet Union, so that when other fronts cried out for some of these resources, there were not enough to go round. And yet, as far as the Italian campaign is concerned, there usually seemed to be just enough of these resources to make of it for the Allies a campaign that was weary, stale, flat and unprofitable.

By the winter of 1941 the dreadful consequences of Hitler's decision to invade Russia were becoming apparent. By going for too much with too little, by trying to take Moscow, Leningrad *and* the Ukraine all at the same time, he failed to achieve decision anywhere. Moscow was not taken, nor Leningrad and, most fatal of all, the Russian armies were not taken or destroyed despite dramatic advances and hauls of prisoners. Alexander I had taken comfort in 1812 from the reflection that space was a great barrier and that, if he left his defence to the climate, he might yet have the last word. By December, 1941, the climate was doing its stuff once more, and General Guderian, perhaps the greatest exponent of blitzkrieg in the entire Wehrmacht, does much to explain why it was that in this case it was the German Army itself which began to experience the despair and paralysis that previously had been induced in others. Except for those who had been there, he maintained, it was impossible to judge what it was like – 'the endless expanse of Russian snow during the winter of our misery . . . the icy wind that blew across it, burying in snow every object in its path.' No wonder the soldiers 'who drove for hour after hour through the no-man's-land only at last to find too thin shelter', soldiers who were half-starved and insufficiently clothed and saw 'by contrast the well-fed, warmly clad and fresh Siberians fully equipped for winter fighting', felt something like despair. No wonder they wavered. Yet this setback did not turn into another rout-like retreat from Moscow. On the contrary the German Army held firm – entirely because of Hitler's willpower. 'Whatever his responsibility for the desperate situation in which the German Army now found itself,' wrote Alan Bullock, 'and whatever the ultimate consequences of his intervention, in its immediate effects it was his greatest achievement as a war leader.' Furthermore, in a step of immense significance, he assumed command of the German Army itself. Like Macbeth – King, Cawdor, Glamis – Hitler had it all now, Führer of the Third Reich, Commander-in-Chief of the Armed Forces, Commander of the German Army, Supreme War Lord. But apart from saving the Army in Russia, he was about to take a further step which would ensure that for him and the Army the war would be lost.

If Hitler's failure to subdue Britain must count as crucial mistake number one and his attack on Russia number two, then the third strategic error of incalculable proportions was surely that of gratuitously declaring war on the United States [following Japan's attempt to destroy the US fleet at Pearl Harbor]. A. J. P. Taylor has pointed out that it was Hitler who made the second war between Britain and Germany into a world conflict. Britain's defiance of Germany in 1940 left us unable to wage war strongly enough to defeat him. Thereupon Hitler presented Britain with two such powerful allies, Russia and America, that the ultimate result, short of Germany's acquiring an atomic bomb first, was never in doubt. 'So we had won after all,' was the way Churchill put it when he knew that America was now in the game as well. Yet at the time he said it Britain was not doing very well, and was about to do a good deal worse.

In August, 1941, when Churchill was visiting troops stationed in Iceland, he had predicted that the war would last for at least a further three years, and that this was one of the bleakest times in Britain's history. The Prime Minister was under great pressure from the Russians to come to their aid, but apart from providing supplies and continuing with the bombardment of Germany from the air, the only theatre of operations where such aid seemed practicable was the Middle East. 'We have certainly been very successful,' he wrote to his son, Randolph, later that month 'in tidying up the Eastern Flank.' The occupation of Persia by Anglo-Soviet forces would enable the British to hold 'the half-circle from the Volga to the Nile.' Possession of Syria, Iraq, Abyssinia, Eritrea, both Somalilands and Persia – all this constituted a very much better situation than a short time back when 'Iraq was ablaze, Palestine quaking and Syria in the hands of the Frogs'. He was even confident about the Western Desert, but was most unhappy with Auchinleck's decision to postpone his offensive there until November, when it was clear from *Ultra* that German and Italian reinforcements were reaching Cyrenaica so that Auchinleck's waiting until he was ready would give him no ultimate advantage as the enemy would be ready and stronger too. In the event, although Auchinleck did inflict defeat of a sort upon Rommel, in that he relieved Tobruk and reconquered Cyrenaica, it was a Pyrrhic victory, for within a month or so Rommel had totally turned the tables on him, put the 8th Army to flight, captured Tobruk with all its abundant supplies and threatened Egypt as it had never been threatened before.

Curiously enough, before Auchinleck's *Crusader* offensive in November, Hitler too was turning his attention back to the Mediterranean which he now again looked upon as an area most vulnerable to operations against the Axis. Russian resistance and the British occupation of Syria and Iraq had had their effect no doubt, but von Brauchitsch, at that time still Army Commander-in-Chief, had reinforced the views of both Mussolini and Rommel that there must be proper coordination of operations in the Mediterranean itself and in the Libyan desert, for both were parts of the same problem. Besides, in Hitler's view the succour of Italy was all-important. 'Let there be no mistake,' he observed, 'the Fascist régime is not as secure as the German government. Any change of government in Italy would spell the end of the Fascist régime, and Italy would unquestionably cross into the enemy camp.' We must concede that, in the business of political foresight, Hitler had few equals. So Italy had to be succoured. This meant withdrawing U-boats from the Atlantic to help regain mastery of the seas between southern Italy and North Africa and withdrawing Luftwaffe units from Russia to enable some degree of air superiority to be established over these same Axis lines of communication. At the end of November Field-Marshal Kesselring, who was to figure so largely in the battle for Italy itself, arrived in Rome to oversee this use of sea and air power in such a way that while Axis communications would be secured, British ones, particularly those to Malta, would be severed. Here at last, it seemed, was a German recipe for winning the battle for Egypt. This battle, as indeed for the whole of North Africa, had always been and would continue to be a battle for supplies. And in this battle the little island of Malta played a crucial part. Indeed the directive given to Kesselring contained two specific references to Malta – its suppression would be particularly important, and as part of this suppression, British supplies must not be allowed to reach the island. For the British, on the other hand, since Malta was an indispensable base for attacking Axis shipping either with submarines or air power, its sustenance was a cardinal feature of their entire Mediterranean strategy.

The profound importance of Malta was admirably illustrated by the circle of events which took place during and after Auchinleck's November, 1941, offensive. Because air and sea sorties from Malta had been able to savage Axis shipping, thus weakening Rommel's supply situation, Auchinleck's army had been able to advance. The further this army advanced, the closer it came to Malta, capturing airfields en route, so enabling the aircraft deployed there to give more and more protection to Malta, so that in turn the island could be reinforced with weapons, food and oil, and with these reinforcements become even more effective in renewing its attacks on the Axis supply lines. So far so good, but unfortunately the exact contrary also applied. As soon as Kesselring was able to have some success in suppressing Malta, and so allow Axis supplies to get through, Rommel's increased strength gave him just the opportunity to counter-attack, push the 8th Army away from its forward airfields and thus prevent the Royal Air Force bringing relief to Malta at the very time when that relief was crucial to its survival. The truth was that just as Malta's ability to sink Axis shipping was a necessary ingredient to the 8th Army's success against Rommel, so was the 8th Army's success indispensable to Malta's continued campaign to rob Rommel of the sinews of war. It was a vicious circle indeed.

British sea power, supported from the air, might do very well for sustaining Malta and aiding the 8th Army's advance against Rommel – to say nothing of its vital roles in preserving Britain's integrity, fighting the Atlantic battle and supplying Russia – but this same sea power could do little to unseat Hitler from his almost impregnable position on the continent of Europe, despite what Arthur Bryant and other historians might maintain. Bryant was very fond of extolling the virtues of sea power, about which there is no doubt in principle, but he perhaps went a little far when he wrote in *The Illustrated London News* that because of our sea power and our consequent control of sea communications

> we shall be able to attack wherever and whenever we like on a wide circumference. And the wider that circumference, other things being equal, the better. The further the enemy has to fight from his own central bases, the easier for us and the more costly for him. Obviously a blow close to his heart is the best offensive weapon of all, but only – and this is an important point – if and when it can be pressed home. If it cannot be, such a blow is likely to be less damaging to the enemy than an attack on some outlying limb, since it can be parried with comparative ease and at moderate cost. *It is the wasting campaign at the remote circumference which most speedily and surely drains the strength of a military giant still too strongly entrenched to be destroyed at close quarters.* *

Here in a nutshell lay the strategic conundrum which puzzled the Allies and gave rise to more disagreement between the British and the Americans than any other single issue. In a sense it reveals the core of all the controversy about the Mediterranean strategy and the campaign in Italy itself. Yet at first there was little disagreement between the Western Allies as to how the war against Germany and Japan should be conducted. When Churchill, Roosevelt and their respective Chiefs of Staff first met in Washington in December, 1941, and drew up a memorandum on Allied Grand Strategy, the Americans largely accepted the British point of view. In essence this strategy was that Japan would be denied the means to wage war while the Allies would concentrate on Germany's defeat, tightening the ring round her by sustaining Russia, strengthening the Middle East and getting hold of the entire North African coast. In one section of this Memorandum appeared some significant sentences concerning the development of land offensives on the Continent:

> It does not seem likely that in 1942 any large-scale land offensive against Germany except on the Russian front will be possible. . . . In 1943 the way may be clear for a return to the Continent, across the Mediterranean, from Turkey into the Balkans, or by landings in Western Europe. Such operations must be the prelude to the final assault on Germany itself.

---

* Author's italics.

There is some irony in the reflection that while the British and Americans are putting the finishing touches to their 'Germany First' policy, the Führer is asking Raeder whether there is any chance that the United States and Britain will abandon East Asia for a time in order to crush Germany and Italy first. Raeder reassures Hitler that the British cannot afford to risk the loss of India nor the Americans allow the Japanese Navy a free run in the Pacific, and then, because of these Allied preoccupations elsewhere, urges his master once more to divert forces to seize Malta and the Suez Canal, thus preparing the way for a great link-up with the Japanese in the Indian Ocean. 'The favourable situation in the Mediterranean, so pronounced at the present time,' he argues, 'will probably never occur again.' It was to occur once more in fact, but in neither case could Hitler be persuaded. Had he been so persuaded, much of the Anglo-American controversy about what to do in 1942 would never have occurred. As it was, this controversy dominated Allied counsels, and was not only about the where and how to employ resources. It concerned broad attitudes as well.

This difference of attitudes has been admirably summarised by Michael Howard in the Lees-Knowles lectures which he gave about the Mediterranean strategy. He pointed out that whereas the British deployed their forces both where they could, and it seemed, must – for example armies in the Middle East and navies in the Atlantic – assuming that circumstances would then dictate where decisive battles would occur, the Americans preferred to decide first where decision was to be sought and then determine where to deploy what sort of resources. Each of them thought the other wrong, the Americans instinctively distrusting the British preference for what they saw as indirect, indecisive strategies; the British, made weary by their experience, unconvinced that the direct approach could be successful without a good deal of preparatory skirmishing elsewhere beforehand. In the preface to his brilliant book on *Grand Strategy* Michael Howard reviewed problems facing the Allies during 1942 and 1943 as to how the various resources for making war on the Axis should be employed, and he concluded this review by asking: 'Above all, should Allied resources be used to extend the conflict in the Mediterranean, or concentrated in preparation for a cross-Channel attack?' It was the resolution of this question which so vexed Allied counsels, and it is well illustrated by the respective positions taken up by General Sir Alan Brooke, Chief of the Imperial General Staff, and General George Marshall, Chief of Staff, United States Army.

When the two men met in London in April, 1942 – it was their first meeting – there was much about which they agreed. Germany must be invaded by the Western powers in order to bring the war against her to a successful conclusion. An absolute prerequisite to such an invasion was that Russia should be sustained so that the Red Army could continue to engage and weaken the Wehrmacht. These points were not in doubt. What was in doubt was the extent to which the German armed forces should be distracted elsewhere, that is other than on the Eastern front, before invasion from the West; and also the military conditions – land forces, sea and air power, shipping, logistics – necessary to ensure that this invasion would work. In a sense the whole argument revolved around how the two men regarded with suspicious or favourable eyes the concept of 'distraction'. To Marshall any dispersion of Allied effort would delay and jeopardize the decisive enterprise on which he had set his heart – the cross-Channel operation; to Brooke some activity elsewhere, particularly in the Mediterranean, was an indispensable pre-condition for this great enterprise.

Before we see how these differences were, if not reconciled, at least amenable to compromise, we may take a look at the other side of the hill. In the same month, April, 1942, Hitler and Mussolini met at Salzburg. Both were concerned at Germany's setback in Russia, but Hitler was bent on squeezing more divisions from his ally in order to renew the offensive there. 'Hitler talks, talks, talks, talks,' wrote Ciano in his diary, 'Mussolini suffers – he, who is in the habit of talking himself, and who, instead, has to remain silent.' Despite this deprivation, Mussolini agreed to provide nine divisions. What was Hitler's intention this time? He set himself formidable tasks:

> Our aim is to wipe out the entire defence potential remaining to the Soviets, and to cut them off, as far as possible, from their most important centres of war industry. All available forces, German and allied, will be employed in this task . . . the armies of the Central sector will stand fast, those in the North will capture Leningrad and link up with the Finns, while those on the southern flank will break through into the Caucasus . . . forces will be concentrated on the main operations in the Southern sector, with the aim of destroying the enemy before the Don, in order to secure the Caucasian oilfields and the passes through the Caucasus Mountains themselves.

With such undertakings in hand it was hardly surprising that Hitler was cool to the Italians' pleading that Malta should be captured as soon as possible. While conceding that if the British hold on the Middle East could be broken, the Axis would greatly benefit, Hitler's lukewarm attitude to Operation *Hercules*, seizing Malta, was not only because it would be primarily carried out by Italian troops. He continued to maintain that the war could be won only in the East. The Mediterranean was a 'sideshow' whose value could be measured in terms of 'tying down enemy forces'. [Thus we have the singular circumstance that both sides in the world conflict are arguing that operations in the Mediterranean are essentially conducted in order to distract the other side from more important activities elsewhere.] Hitler did, however, promise to supply German parachute troops to assist in capturing Malta, but only after Rommel's forthcoming summer offensive had driven the British from Cyrenaica and taken Tobruk. To this extent Hitler was prepared to humour Raeder's 'Great Plan' for a gigantic pincer movement, left-handed through the Caucasus and Persia, right-handed through the Suez Canal, designed to link up with the Japanese in the Indian Ocean. Meanwhile the Allies were making some plans of their own.

Following the Brooke-Marshall discussions in April, 1942, it had been agreed that the 'only means for quickly applying available force against the German war machine' was the 'use of the British Isles as a base area for an offensive to defeat the German armed forces'. Therefore, it was further agreed that United States forces should at once begin to concentrate in the U.K. – codename *Bolero* – and that *Round-Up*, the invasion of Western Europe, should be mounted in 1943. This still left open what was to be done in 1942, and by a curious chain of circumstances it was eventually decided that the first joint Anglo-American military operation should be undertaken *in the Mediterranean*, not because it was the decisive theatre, but because it was not. It all came about like this.

Although in the early stages of planning the British and Americans were in full agreement that nothing must be allowed to interfere with Operation *Round-Up*, what the Americans had really been hoping for was an invasion of Western Europe *in 1942*, codename *Sledgehammer*. General Marshall himself had talked of it as an emergency attack, one which would only be justified if 'the situation on the Russian front became desperate' or if 'the German situation in Western Europe becomes critically weakened'. At the same time the U.S. Chiefs of Staff were under pressure from their own President to do something soon in view of the enormous burden being borne by the Russians. 'The necessities of the case,' declared Roosevelt, 'called for action in 1942, not 1943.' So strongly did Roosevelt hold this view that when Molotov visited him at the end of May, 1942, he received an assurance from the President which in the language of the communiqué issued later stated that 'in the course of conversations full understanding was reached with regard to the urgent task of creating a Second Front in Europe in 1942'. In other words the Americans pledged themselves to send their ground trooops into battle against the Germans on land somewhere before the end of that year.

Once Roosevelt had given this undertaking it gradually became clear that, if it were to be honoured, there was only one sound course of action – to revert to an idea which Churchill had put forward as early as December, 1941, a landing in French North Africa, Operation *Gymnast*. The route to this decision was a devious one. At first the Combined Chiefs of Staff were unanimous in their opposition to *Gymnast*, which, they pointed out, would represent a dangerous dispersion of the whole Allied strategic activity. Therefore, they argued, it should not be undertaken, but rather they should concentrate on speeding up *Bolero* and continue to study the possibilities of a Continental operation in 1942 if conditions favourable for such a thing arose. Indeed what the Chiefs of Staff were really saying was that there should be no operation in 1942 at all. Here, however, they fell foul of their political masters, for when Churchill flew to Washington in June his eloquence had a powerful effect upon Roosevelt. He pointed out that *Sledgehammer* was impossible – and after further study this view was shared by all the military men both British and American. Churchill made it plain that to try and effect a foothold in Europe and fail 'would not help the Russians whatever their plight, would compromise and expose to Nazi vengeance the French population involved and would gravely delay the main operation in 1943. Ought we not,' he went on, 'to be preparing within the general structure of *Bolero* some other operation by which we may gain position of advantage and also directly or indirectly take some weight off Russia.' It was in this light, he concluded, that *Gymnast* should be looked at again.

The Combined Chiefs of Staff did look at it again and came to the unwelcome conclusion that *Gymnast* would certainly mean that there could be no *Sledgehammer* in 1942 and would probably mean too that

Round-Up could not be carried out in the spring of 1943. Such conclusions were hitting at the very heart of American strategy for pursuing the Germany First policy. Moreover, their report actually suggested that *Gymnast* would be ineffectual. 'We are strongly of the opinion that *Gymnast* would be both indecisive and a heavy drain on our resources and that, if we undertake it, we would nowhere be acting decisively against the enemy and would definitely jeopardize our naval position in the Pacific.' This very firm stand was, however, to be undermined by two further developments. The first was a clear direction from the President to his Joint Chiefs of Staff that they could not wait until 1943 to strike at Germany. It had to be done in 1942, and, if it could not be in Western Europe, it must be elsewhere. Therefore they, the Joint Chiefs, would go to London to determine with the British where it was to be. The second development was a change in the position of the British, who were now looking at *Gymnast* with new eyes. It would be a means both of securing the Middle East, with its oil and strategic importance, and of opening the Mediterranean sea routes which would have a profound effect on shipping resources released from the long haul round the Cape. Furthermore, this closing of the ring round the Third Reich would enable them not just to stand there defensively, but begin the process of tightening the noose in order to throttle the Axis. It is never difficult to find good reasons for doing what seems to be the only thing you can do, and the British Chiefs of Staff were no exception to the rule:

> In respect of action in 1942, the only feasible proposition appeared to be *Gymnast* . . . which would, in effect, be the right wing of our Second Front. An American occupation of Casablanca and district would not be sufficient. The operations would have to extend to Algiers, Oran and possibly further east.

Moreover, if the Americans were unable to supply all the land and sea forces required for the operations, the British would do so, in particular for the more easterly objectives.

By the time the U.S. Joint Chiefs of Staff met their British colleagues in London in July, therefore, they found the latter firmly of the opinion that the only practicable option for 1942 was *Gymnast*. It was with the greatest reluctance that they accepted this view, and they insisted that, if it were undertaken, there would be no question of mounting *Round-Up* in 1943. While the British military people did not argue the point, the Chief of Air Staff, Portal, maintained that *Gymnast* might so distract the Wehrmacht that it might be necessary for them to occupy Italy and Spain, and so disperse German forces that *Round-Up* would after all be impossible. In any event the Combined Chiefs of Staff recommended that the invasion of North West Africa – now renamed Operation *Torch* – should be launched, if a collapse of Russian resistance meant that *Round-Up* could not be mounted in 1943. They further stated that a decision should be made by mid-September. Neither of these last two conditions suited either Churchill or Roosevelt. Indeed the Prime Minister, in a minute notable for its grasp of how Allied Strategy would develop in the years to come, took exception to the notion that the African invasion would prejudice the invasion of Western Europe. It was not a defensive move, but one which would yield new potential for attack. Indeed, by moving northward into Europe from Africa, a totally new situation would be created. In some memorable sentences, which later had great relevance to the Italian campaign, Churchill wrote:

> The flank attack may become the main attack, and the main attack a holding operation in the early stages. Our second front will in fact comprise both the Atlantic and Mediterranean coasts of Europe, and we can push either right-handed, left-handed, or both-handed, as our resources and circumstances permit. Meanwhile, we shall pin down the largest number possible of enemy troops opposite *Bolero* .... In so vast and complex a scene above all it is specially desirable to have options open which allow of strategic manoeuvres according as events unfold.

When Roosevelt received a telegram from Churchill on these lines, he agreed that *Torch* should be carried out as soon as possible and gave the necessary instructions to his Joint Chiefs of Staff.

It was while all these deliberations had been in progress that Hitler had got closer to wrecking the British position in the Middle East once and for all than he ever had before or would again. General Erwin Rommel, in a devastating display of how to bring about a pell-mell battle and then win it hands down, had defeated the 8th Army, sent them scurrying back to the Alamein line, and had on 21 June *taken Tobruk*. Egypt beckoned him. Had he then remembered his own previous warning that 'without Malta the Axis will end by losing control of North Africa', Egypt might have been his, the Canal, the Levant, Iraq, the Gulf oil, everything. Mussolini, not always renowned as a strategist, saw what had to be done. He at once advised Hitler that this was the moment to launch Operation *Hercules*, the assault on Malta, and that Rommel should pause until after its capture. In giving this advice Mussolini showed a proper understanding of what the real strategic and supply situation was in North Africa and the Mediterranean. But Rommel was riding high and the sheer abundance of supplies which fell into his hands at Tobruk – apart from other things, more than 2,000 tons of fuel and 2,000 vehicles, his two principal needs – closed his eyes to logistic realities. Besides, he thought the British were beaten. Delay would simply allow them to recover. The arch opportunist, he refused to acknowledge that there are times when opportunity must be foregone in order to create an even greater one. His sentiments were matched exactly by the Führer, a gambler if ever there was one. To Hitler the prospect of Rommel's further success persuaded him that *Hercules*, an operation he had never favoured, would now be unnecessary. He could not see that it was an indispensable preliminary to Rommel's continued success.

He therefore telegraphed to Mussolini in Rome in suitably dramatic language, talking of Rommel's victory with German and Italian troops as a turning point, arguing that the 8th Army had been shattered and that the supply problem could be eased by using the British railway from Tobruk to Egypt. He ended his telegram in extravagant style. There is no record as to whether Hitler was a student of Shakespeare. Nietzsche, Wagner, Schopenhauer and Hegel seemed more to his taste. Yet in this ending he gave a fair paraphrase of the comment which Brutus made to Cassius before Philippi: 'The battle's Goddess of Fortune draws nigh upon the commanders only once; he who does not grasp her at that moment will seldom come to grips with her again'. In short, Rommel, promoted to Field-Marshal, was told to get on and take Egypt. *Hercules* would have to wait. In allowing himself to be persuaded from his former prudence, Mussolini took comfort in the alluring idea of riding in triumph through Alexandria mounted on a white charger. Two days after capturing Tobruk Rommel and his *Panzerarmee* crossed the frontier into Egypt.

The British, however, never more dangerous than when everyone else thought they were beaten, were preparing to stand at the Alamein line, which could not be outflanked, and where a battle, not of manoeuvre at which the Afrika Korps excelled and the 8th Army did not, but of attrition would have to be fought. For such a battle the British already enjoyed considerable advantages. In the first place

Auchinleck, confident of himself and his army, had taken personal command; secondly, Malta had been reprieved and was already doing great harm to Axis supply convoys; thirdly Churchill had extracted 300 Sherman tanks and a hundred 105mm self-propelled guns from Roosevelt; fourthly the air situation was turning to favour the British; lastly the 8th Army would be fighting near to its sources of supply with secure lines of communication, while Rommel would be at the very end of extremely long and *in*secure supply lines. Never was the notion that the battle for North Africa was a battle of supplies to be more strikingly demonstrated. In the event Auchinleck was successful not merely in stopping Rommel. He began to mount his own counterattacks, causing Rommel to comment:

> 15th Panzer Division was pulled out to parry this attack and its armour was soon involved in violent fighting with the British. 21st Panzer Division's units were also forced increasingly on the defensive until by evening [2 July] the whole of the Afrika Korps were locked in violent defensive fighting against a hundred British tanks and about ten batteries. . . . General Auchinleck was handling his forces with very considerable skill. He seemed to view the situation with decided coolness, for he was not allowing himself to be rushed into accepting a second-best solution by any moves we made.

Yet for all Auchinleck's staunchness in holding the Alamein line and beginning to hit back, he had not *defeated* Rommel, and victory was what Churchill wanted, particularly at a time when his political position at home had been weakened. In August, therefore, during his visit to Egypt, he appointed the new brooms, Alexander and Montgomery, as Commander-in-Chief, Middle East, and Commander 8th Army respectively, and gave them their prime duty of taking or destroying Rommel's *Panzerarmee Afrika*. By the beginning of September Montgomery had successfully repulsed the Afrika Korps at Alam el Halfa in a battle which Rommel correctly described as one without hope. Montgomery then began to prepare for his own offensive, which would take place in the latter part of October. Well before this came about, Churchill had been turning his attention to what was to happen *after* Rommel's defeat, at a time when *Torch* would have been successfully carried out and further exploitation of the Allied position in North Africa and the Mediterranean would be appropriate.

Churchill's vision of *Torch* was often very different from that of his American allies and sometimes at odds too with that of his own Chiefs of Staff. As we have seen, he looked upon it not simply as a kind of blocking operation as part of the general ring-closing strategy, but as a prelude to the actual business of assaulting Hitler's *Festung Europa*. The right-fisted bit of it might be secondary, or might be primary, but there was no doubt in his mind that *Torch* and what would follow from it was all to be part of the Second Front against Germany. To the Americans, however, *Torch* had always been a dissipation of resources away from the decisive theatre of operations. Marshall and Eisenhower, who had been appointed to command the Anglo-American forces, saw it as an acceptance of the concept of establishing a defensive circle round Europe. There was, therefore, bound to be a renewal of controversy between the Western Allies as to what the proper Grand Strategy for conducting the war should be. In preparation for the inevitable argument with the Americans the British Chiefs of Staff instructed their joint planners to produce an appreciation of the situation – a time-honoured recipe for arriving at a choice between options of difficulty. The answers they came up with were certainly acceptable to Churchill and in fact were a foretaste of what was later to become known as the Mediterranean strategy. Yet these conclusions were hardly sanguine.

In the first place there was a continuing drain on resources for security purposes alone. To ensure the integrity of the United Kingdom, to guarantee control of the Middle East, to maintain the Atlantic communications – all these requirements demanded much. But the joint planners' document went on to make a statement which, however unpalatable it might have been to the Americans, rang true to the British. It said that only the Russian Army was capable of defeating, or even containing, the German Army, and that the British and American forces were simply not powerful enough to take on the '*bulk* of the Axis forces on land'. Indeed it was doubtful whether they would have mustered a sufficient number of divisions to do so in 1943. What this meant was that American predictions that *Torch* would prejudice *Round-Up* looked perilously like coming true. The only alternative, went on the joint planners, was to wear down the German war-machine, in short a policy of attrition. While this wearing-down process could obviously be pursued by bombing and by blockade, there was no possibility of grand Continental adventures. The best follow-up to *Torch*, they concluded, would be to make the Mediterranean area as great a distraction to the Germans as possible. This might be done by seizing Sardinia or Sicily or Crete and by 'forcing the Axis to lock up increased forces for the holding down of Italy as well as for the defence of all threatened points'. A strategy which called for a major bombing campaign, increased activity at sea *and* the exploitation of *Torch* by landing somewhere in southern Europe was bound to create a battle of priorities. In countering the arguments of the Chief of Air Staff, Portal, for the entire bomber force to be used against Germany, Brooke, the CIGS, insisted that apart from exerting pressure on the German military and economic machine, and backing up the Russians:

> We should take full advantage of the sea and air bases in North Africa to exert a heavy pressure on Italy with a view to turning her into a serious liability for Germany. . . . At the same time we should intensify our bomber offensive from this country against Germany.

In this first requirement he was echoing Churchill, who had already called for the results of studies made for the exploitation of *Torch*. 'Sardinia, Sicily and Italy itself have no doubt been considered. If things go well we should not waste a day, but carry the war northwards with audacity'. The war was eventually carried northwards. But, alas, not with audacity.

In considering where to strike northwards the British Chiefs of Staff ranged wide. Southern France, the Balkans and Italy were all looked at. The first two were discarded as presenting too many political problems, for southern France was still not occupied – although it would be as soon as *Torch* was launched – and Turkey was still wavering. Besides, the logistic difficulties of sustaining forces in either area were formidable. Threatening Italy, however, might produce valuable dividends by diverting German forces both from Russia and the Atlantic. 'Our main effort in the Mediterranean,' they concluded, 'should be directed against Italy. Threats against the south of France and the Balkans will also extend the enemy.' What was not immediately foreseen by all those concerned in these appreciations was that a strategy of this sort would probably lead to a campaign of fighting on land in Italy with all that this might mean in terms of taking on the German Army in difficult, easily defensible country. Churchill's view, expressed on 15 November, was that:

> The paramount task before us is, first, to conquer the African shores of the Mediterranean and open an effective passage through it for military traffic; and secondly, using the bases on the African shore, to strike at the underbelly of the Axis in effective strength in the shortest time.

By the time this view was made known to the Chiefs of Staff, *Torch* had begun and the Germans had occupied southern France. This in no way altered Churchill's decision – and in this he was supported by his military advisers – that the next step in the Mediterranean should be to knock Italy out of the war. Just how this would be done was still to be determined, but Churchill's telegram to Roosevelt was clear about the aim itself.

Torch itself had gone well – initially. Landings at Casablanca, Oran and Algiers had been made on 8 November, no small achievement for 110 cargo and troop ships with more than 200 warships to have run the gauntlet of enemy U-boats and within range of enemy aircraft. Algiers had been occupied the same day; Oran surrendered on 9 November and Casablanca two days later. The second task for Eisenhower's forces could now be undertaken – to drive on to Tunis. But any idea that this could be done quickly was put out of court by Hitler's characteristically violent and prompt reaction. His occupation of southern France was rapidly effected, even though it led to the scuttling of the French fleet at Toulon, and even though the Italian Army's behaviour in occupying the Riviera and Corsica created such hostility in France that Laval threatened to declare war on Italy. But Hitler was too concerned with consideration for his Italian ally to make much of it. As Jodl reported: 'The Führer believes it absolutely vital to bolster the Duce in every way we can, and this is why he categorically refuses to oppose Italy's claims to leadership in the Mediterranean, including the coast of southern France.' Italy's leadership was shortly to undergo a sea-change, but for the time being Hitler continued to bolster the Duce by despatching troops in large numbers to Tunis. By the end of November there were no fewer than 15,000 German soldiers, with some highly experienced and skilful parachute, panzer and panzer grenadier regiments among them, together with the new and formidable Tiger tank, mounting the renowned 88mm gun. General von Arnim took command of the German and Italian divisions there on 8 December. It was to be five months before the Allies captured Tunis and so made themselves masters of the North African shores.

In Britain the War Cabinet was still debating how to knock Italy out of the war. Eden, the Foreign Secretary, had pointed out that however successful the Allies might be in conquering North Africa and lowering Italian morale by bombing cities, the Fascist régime was unlikely to sue for peace and the Germans would not allow its removal. Indeed, if such a thing were likely, the Germans would simply occupy Italy and prevent any such peace move. But if the bombing, combined later with the capture of Sardinia and Sicily, could so destroy Italian morale that there would be a collapse internally, then the Germans might be compelled to take over Italy both to defend it and also assume all the other Italian commitments in the Balkans. Churchill, on the other hand, felt that the Fascist régime might suddenly disintegrate, and that the Italian people would have to choose between 'setting up a government under someone like Grandi to sue for a separate peace' or submit to a German occupation, which would not be in Allied interests and would 'aggravate the severity of the war'. But he could not rule out the possibility of Italy wanting a separate peace and therefore he agreed with the United States policy of attempting to divide the Italian people from Mussolini's government. The Joint Planning Staff then produced a report which would outline how the Allies should achieve the dual aim of inducing the Italians to give up *and* oblige the Germans to occupy Italy, so stretching her resources still further. This was to be done by continuing the bombing, raiding the coasts, including shipping, seizing either Sicily or Sardinia, threatening Crete and the Dodecanese, and stepping up subversion in the Balkans. The conclusion of their paper amounted to a definition of the so-called Mediterranean Strategy:

> The prizes open to the Allies in the Mediterranean in 1943 are very great. They include the severe reduction of German air-power, the reopening of the short sea route, the denial to Germany of oil, chrome and other minerals, the elimination of one of the Axis partners and the opening of the Balkans.
>
> If we decide to exploit the position which we have gained, our first object should be to induce the Italians to lay down their arms everywhere; our next should be directed against the Balkans.
>
> Unless Italy collapses far more quickly than we expect, this exploitation must, however, be at the expense of *Round-Up* in 1943.
>
> We are therefore faced with the alternatives of:
>
> (a) Concentrating resources in the United Kingdom for a *Round-Up* which may, in any event, be impracticable for 1943; and this at the cost of abandoning the great prizes open to us in the Mediterranean and of

remaining inactive for many months during which Germany would recuperate;

or

(b)   Pursuing the offensive in the Mediterranean with the knowledge that we shall only be able to assault Northern France next year if there is a pronounced decline in German fighting power.

We cannot have it both ways. In our view (b) is the correct strategy and will give the Russians more certain, and possibly even greater relief.

The Chiefs of Staff endorsed this paper which became the British brief for their planned consultations with the Americans in Casablanca in January, 1943. If the strategy outlined were to be adopted it would mean that *Torch* and its consequences *had* been at the expense of *Round-Up*, an idea which would be most unpalatable to the Americans, confirming all their worst fears about British reluctance to take the direct route to victory. While the Allies were preparing to discuss their plans to do great harm to the Wehrmacht, however, the Red Army was actually doing it.

At the same time as Hitler was pouring troops into Tunisia, all of whom were to become hostages to fortune, the Russians were preparing a shock for the German Army at Stalingrad from which it never really recovered. It began on 19 November and within two days the armies of General Vatutin and General Eremenko, advancing respectively from the north and south, had joined hands at Kalach, encircling the entire German 6th Army of some 300,000 men. By 23 November Hitler was back at his East Prussian headquarters to hear the unwelcome advice from Zeitzler, Army Chief of Staff, and von Weichs, the Army Group Commander, that unless the 6th Army was withdrawn, it was doomed. This appeal was echoed the same evening by the Commander of 6th Army himself, Paulus. Hitler would not hear of it – 'We are not budging from the Volga!' He had been right to stand firm in December, 1941, and he would prove right again a year later. It might indeed have come about had not von Manstein's great drive from the south to relieve Stalingrad been checked by Malinovsky, and had not the Italian 8th Army, responsible for the Don sector to the north-west of the city, simply collapsed. Such an event did not make things easy for Ciano when he met Hitler at his headquarters, *Wolfsschanze*, the Wolf's Lair, on 18 December. Whereas the Führer demanded a real Italian effort to maintain supplies to North Africa, tactfully making no reference to the Italians' poor showing on the Eastern front, the one place where Hitler sought decision, Ciano had come to seek Hitler's views on Mussolini's hypothesis that if 1943 were to be the year in which the Allies mounted operations in both southern Europe and the West, to say nothing of North Africa, would not some political 'accommodation' with Russia be worth considering. Such notions were brushed aside by the Führer who made it plain that he would never agree to stripping the Eastern front in order to prop up positions in the Mediterranean. After Ciano had left, Hitler observed that he had no trust in the Italians, and Admiral Canaris, head of the *Abwehr*, the German secret service, was instructed to 'keep an eye on Italy' for possible signs of defection.

Even before the final tragedy of Stalingrad – Paulus capitulated at the end of January, 1943, and a quarter of a million German soldiers went into captivity – it was clear that Germany's possession of the initiative had gone, never to return except for one brief and final gamble in the Ardennes at the end of 1944. Hitler's War Directive No 47, dated 28 December, 1942, is full of the word 'defence' and of the need to prepare for defensive battles. It goes on: 'The situation in the Mediterranean makes it possible that an attack may be made in the foreseeable future on Crete and on German and Italian bases in the Aegean Sea and the Balkan peninsula.' In fact, although the Allies, and particularly Churchill, had long had their eye on Crete, the principal argument which sprang up before the Casablanca Conference started was whether to go for Sardinia or Sicily, after the North African coast had been cleared of Axis forces. This argument revolved around timings, the ground forces required, the consequent demands on shipping and the question of air cover. It was also clear that the final clearing of Tunisia and the rest of North Africa was going to take much longer than had been hoped. Churchill was strongly in favour of Sicily, codename *Husky*, as it alone 'gives a worthwhile prize, even if we have to wait till May. Moreover the PQ convoys [to Russia] can then be run regularly at least till the end of March'. The Joint Planning Staff did not agree because of the large requirements of escort vessels and landing craft which might be impossible to muster. Moreover, if German Army formations were in position in Sicily before *Husky* was mounted, it might fail. On the eve, therefore, of the Casablanca Conference, they produced a paper which stated:

Much as we would like to take Sicily, we feel that, against the odds for which we must at present allow, the operation is not practicable.

We therefore recommend the capture of Sardinia to be followed by the capture of Corsica as soon after as possible.

This would be but one of the questions to be resolved at Casablanca. To do either would seem to imply that the Allies would embrace a policy which chose to seek decision in a theatre of war, the Mediterranean and more particularly Italy, where decision against the German armed forces – the only ones in Europe which really mattered – would be extremely difficult to obtain. Hitler himself had declared the theatre to be a sideshow, suitable only for distracting and dispersing enemy resources. Whom would it distract more? That was the question. But until the two Allied leaders had met at Casablanca – and for security purposes Roosevelt was to be known as Admiral Q and Churchill Mr P – the policy of pursuing the offensive in the Mediterranean still had to receive a certificate of legitimacy. And since such a policy would have a profound effect on the future conduct of the war as a whole, it would be necessary, as Churchill put it 'to mind their P's and Q's'.

4

CASABLANCA

Play it again, Sam.
Humphrey Bogart

The tune played by Churchill at Casablanca was one he had often played before and was to play time and time again. Its theme was essentially that Germany must be defeated first and the proper way to set about it was by a maximum effort in the Mediterranean, which would keep pressure on the Germans and draw forces away from the Russian front. It was not merely expedient that this should be done. Early in 1943 there was no alternative. This was the theme. The instrument for putting it over was the CIGS, General Sir Alan Brooke. Brooke had noted in his diary on New Year's Day, 1943:

> We start 1943 under conditions I would never had dared to hope for. Russia has held, Egypt for the present is safe. There is a hope of clearing North Africa of Germans in the near future. The Mediterranean may be partially opened up. Malta is safe for the present. We can now work freely against Italy, and Russia is scoring wonderful successes in Southern Russia.

Underlying this desire to concentrate on the Mediterranean was the British concern to detach Italy from the Axis, a goal on which Churchill's eye had been as far back as his meeting with Roosevelt in December, 1941. Brooke had set himself three main tasks for the conference at Casablanca – to ensure that the Germany First policy was endorsed; to get agreement that the best way of attacking Germany for the present would be through 'the medium of Italy'; and that this in turn should be done by operations against Sicily. He was successful in all three.

The first meeting of the Combined Chiefs of Staff was on 14 January and it was then that Brooke presented the British position. The first crucial point he made was about shipping. Unless the battle against the U-boats was won, he maintained, the war itself could not be won. Only if the Allies could overcome the shortage of shipping would they be able to mount offensive operations.* Yet it was in this respect alone that the Germans were still in possession of the initiative. Everywhere else they were defending, rather than attacking. Above all they were on the defensive in Russia, and therefore Russia had to be given maximum support. One way of doing so would be to mount amphibious operations. In suggesting where these might be mounted, Brooke illustrated the extent to which military prudence dictated British strategic thinking, a prudence which the Americans frequently took to be an unwillingness to launch a bold, concentrated and telling blow against the heart of the Third Reich. Brooke argued that since for Germany east-west communications were so much easier and quicker than north-south routes, and since also the Mediterranean offered so many different and widely separated striking points, it was here rather than in France that the Germans would find it most difficult to counter an Allied incursion. His idea was not so much how to strike a decisive blow, but how to strike one which the Germans could not instantly and effectively parry, and which at the same time would bring some relief to the Russians, because the Germans would be obliged to react. The build-up of British and American divisions in the United Kingdom would in any event continue, so that operations in North-West Europe could be mounted when the Germans had been sufficiently weakened in France.

Quite apart from the respective demands of North-West Europe and the Mediterranean, another major issue which divided the British and the Americans was what was to be done in the Pacific. They could

---

* The soundness of this absolute priority was endorsed by Hitler himself, when as a result of Allied action to win the Atlantic battle by using aircraft carriers, long-range shore-based aircraft and radar with surface escorts, the Germans lost eighty-seven U-boats between February and May, 1943. When Doenitz withdrew his submarines from the North Atlantic, Hitler ordered them back again. 'There can be no talk of let-up in submarine warfare,' he bellowed at Doenitz. 'The Atlantic is my first line of defence in the West.'

not allow the Japanese so to consolidate their gains in the South-West Pacific that it would be almost impossible to turn them out again. American supply lines to Australia would be permanently threatened. Pressure on the Japanese had to be kept up somehow, but whether it should be in Burma, the Dutch East Indies or towards the Philippines from the east was not certain. What was certain – and about this Admiral King and General Marshall were adamant, nor did the British dissent – was that the forces at present available in the Pacific were not adequate to do the job. What worried the British was that if substantial resources were detached to the Far East, there would be insufficient forces left in the West to fulfil the agreed strategy of defeating Germany first. Inability by the principal military men to agree led, as it usually does in such cases, to the preparation of 'position papers' by their subordinates. Happily, subsequent discussion of these papers did lead to a reconciliation and thus a blueprint for the conduct of the war in 1943.

Yet one of the disagreements which persisted was about the importance to be attached to operations in the Mediterranean. Brooke favoured a major effort there as the means of defeating Germany as it would draw forces from the Russian front; Marshall was concerned that the Allies should not become involved in endless operations in the Mediterranean which would be at the expense of both security in the Pacific and decision elsewhere against Germany. Indeed Marshall has been commended by some historians for having the perception to wield the Pacific card in such a way as to ensure that forces in Europe would be balanced in order to allow both Mediterranean operations *and*, more importantly, the cross-Channel assault which he had always favoured. By abandoning the dangerous nettle of absolute priority for Europe, however, the British were able to pluck the safe flower of compromise, and the Memorandum drawn up by the Combined Chiefs of Staff on 19 January satisfied both the British and the Americans. Churchill had got his way and in his report to the War Cabinet next day he reported:

Admiral Q and I called a plenary conference this afternoon, at which the Combined Chiefs of Staff reported progress. It was a most satisfactory meeting. After five days' discussions and a good deal of apparent disagreement the Combined Chiefs of Staff are now, I think, unanimous in essentials about the conduct of the war in 1943. . . . The security of sea communications was agreed to be the first charge upon our combined resources, and the principle reaffirmed that we must concentrate first on the defeat of Germany. Full preparations for taking Sicily are to go ahead at once with a view to carrying out the operations at the earliest possible moment. In addition we hope to mount the Burma plan towards the end of this year.... At home *Bolero* is to go ahead as fast as our commitments allow, with a view to a *Sledgehammer* of some sort this year or a return to the Continent with all available forces if Germany shows definite signs of collapse. In the Pacific, operations for the capture of Rabaul and the clearing of New Guinea are to continue in order to retain the initiative and hold Japan.

Agreement to take Sicily appeared to give the British what they wanted as far as their Mediterranean strategy went. But the Americans were far from convinced that this was the way to win the war. Only by engaging major German forces in North-West Europe, they still maintained, could this be done. But, as so many Allied forces were in the Mediterranean, it would be sensible to use them there. Moreover, Sicily seemed to be the best bet among the various options. Yet there were two very important, unanswered questions. To go from North Africa to Sicily in order to increase pressure on Italy and distract the Germans from Russia was all very well, provided it was recognized as being merely opportunistic and in no way part of some master strategic plan. What was to happen after that? This was the first question. The second concerned its effect on the invasion of North-West Europe, for, as everyone at Casablanca was now beginning to acknowledge, Mediterranean operations on the scale envisaged would delay this other and crucial invasion for at least a year. Was such delay acceptable? The British answer was that even if there were no Mediterranean operations, it would still not be possible to invade North-West Europe in 1943. Better therefore to exploit success now in the south and guarantee proper action in the west in 1944 – in other words, Churchill's words in fact, push right-handed now, then left-handed later, and finally both-handed 'as our resources and circumstances permit'. On this point Roosevelt agreed with Churchill. The invasion of Sicily was thus decided upon. At this time, however, no one had admitted that it was likely to lead inevitably to a land campaign in Italy itself. The purpose of occupying Sicily was, in the words of the Combined Chiefs of Staff memorandum, to make the Mediterranean line of communications more secure; to divert German pressure from the Russian front; and to intensify the pressure on Italy. There was to be little doubt about achieving the first and third of these two objectives. The extent to which the second one would succeed was less certain. Nothing could be done, of course, until the whole of North Africa had been conquered.

To what extent had *Torch* created a Second Front as the Allies had hoped it would? One answer to this question was given by the C.-in-C. of Germany's Replacement Army, General Fromm, who as early as 18 November, 1942, ten days after the Allied landings in North Africa, had observed to Field-Marshal Keitel, Chief of Hitler's Armed Forces HQ, that Rommel's defeat at Alamein and these landings *had* created a Second Front. He went on to say that the threat to the Southern Front would make it 'necessary to create a new German army for South Europe'. Yet this threat was slow in making itself felt. Far from *Torch* diverting substantial German forces from the Eastern front, only three divisions were sent to Tunisia from there, while at the same time the demands of Stalingrad had resulted in no fewer than seventeen divisions being sent to Russia from the West. Yet just as the Allies were anxious to open up the Mediterranean for their shipping by indulging in and exploiting *Torch*, so Hitler was determined to deny the Allies this freedom of sea communications as long as possible. Hence his reinforcement of Tunisia and determination to hold the bridgehead there as long as possible. It was a supreme example of the classic strategic error of reinforcing failure, and was in the end to cost the Axis as many men as had been lost at Stalingrad. In this way, therefore, the Mediterranean strategy *did* bring some relief to Russia.

At first, however, Allied operations to finish off the Axis forces in North Africa and take Tunis were depressingly slow, despite some new command arrangements which had been agreed at Casablanca. Eisenhower became Allied Supreme Commander, North Africa; his deputy, Alexander, would also command a group of armies; Tedder became Air C.-in-C.; Cunningham controlled all naval forces. The Axis too had made changes, one of which was to have a profound effect on the German conduct of operations in the Mediterranean. Kesselring became Commander-in-Chief, South, and one of the things Kesselring wanted to do, and before long did, was to get rid of Rommel. Yet before Rommel went he once more behaved like an eagle in a dovecote and fluttered the Allied armies at the Kasserine Pass. After he had withdrawn from Tripoli and had established a further defensive position at Mareth, Rommel was so confident that

Montgomery's advance would as usual be slow and sure that he felt there was time for him to nip another danger in the bud. If the Americans should advance successfully from Sbeitla or Gafsa, they could cut off his withdrawal from the Mareth Line. He thereupon determined to attack the two Allied armies in turn, 1st Army in the West to begin with, then 8th Army. In this way he might impose further delay on them and keep things going in North Africa for a bit longer. On 14 February Rommel attacked the Americans with 10th and 12th Panzer Divisions. In spite of initial successes the German thrust was held by a series of uncoordinated reactions by British and U.S. forces. Yet, as that best of historians about the North African battles, Ronald Lewin, has written:

> Had Rommel and General von Arnim, who commanded 5 Panzer Army within the bridgehead, felt less than detestation for one another this combination might have been disastrous against an Allied command set-up which has itself been described as 'a tangled skein of misunderstanding, duplication of effort, over-lapping responsibility and consequential muddle' . . . might have resulted in a breakthrough as significant for the Tunisian campaign as that at Sedan had been in the Battle of France.

It was to be hoped that what the Allies learned about command arrangements in North Africa would be put to good effect when they began to embark on military adventures in Europe. On the whole it was, although before long Patton and Montgomery were to initiate a rivalry and distrust which were to survive, indeed to flourish, until the end of the war. Hitler was not prepared to allow any comparable rivalry between von Arnim and Rommel to tarnish the latter's reputation, which by itself alone was of such infinite value to him and to the German Army.

Hitler was not in any doubt about the inevitable end in Tunis. He saw as clearly as any that the Axis failure to protect supply ships must mean that holding the bridgehead there could not be carried on much longer. But he hung on simply because of the political repercussions which Tunisia's fall would have on Italy. And although he was beginning to have doubts about Rommel's attitude – for while conceding that the Desert Fox was 'an extraordinarily bold and clever commander' he considered that he lacked optimism and staying power – despite this, he appointed Rommel to command Army Group Africa in the hope that this would provide just the pepping-up to induce one more decisive blow against the Allies. But Rommel was nothing if not a realist. 'If only we could win a major victory here,' he wrote to his wife three days after assuming his new command. 'I rack my brains night and day to find a way. Unfortunately the conditions for it don't exist. Everything depends on supplies, and has done for years.' To improve his situation Rommel proposed further withdrawals to shorten the front. Hitler would not hear of it, and when Rommel's final attack on the 8th Army at Medenine failed, as it was bound to fail given the depth and strength of Montgomery's defences, Hitler recalled Rommel for consultation. He never returned to Africa, but was still a power to be reckoned with as the grip he helped to impose on Italy later that year was to illustrate, to say nothing of the work he did to strengthen the Atlantic Wall in 1944. Had he been appointed to this task from the moment he left Africa, it may be questioned whether the Allies would have gained a foothold in Normandy a year later.

As it was, when Rommel met the Führer at Vinnitsa on 9 March, his pessimism was overruled by his master, who was strongly supported by Göring, Kesselring and Dönitz. For the present Hitler was determined to hang on in Tunis and would therefore increase supplies to the bridgehead there. This, of course, would demand the agreement and collaboration of the Italians, and in despatching Kesselring and Dönitz to see Mussolini in Rome, Hitler left the latter in no doubt as to what he required. Sea transport of supplies must be stepped up to the maximum possible. In his message to the Duce, Hitler emphasized that it was only because of logistic problems that Rommel, a feared opponent to the enemy, well loved by his own troops, 'one of my most courageous officers and distinguished by exceptional capability', had come to grief. But Hitler had more serious matters on hand than Tunis and its logistic or command problems – the Eastern Front. What was to be done in 1943?

One thing was plain. Although 1943 might have to be a year of German defensive strategy – and with North Africa going wrong, the Russians preparing for another offensive, British and American bombers raiding towns like Wilhelmshaven and Berlin, there seemed little alternative – the fight would go on. Hitler's response to Roosevelt's unscheduled call for 'Unconditional Surrender' during the Casablanca Conference* was to proclaim that Germany would have

* Hitler did not know until later that Churchill and Roosevelt had met at Casablanca. Such were the shortcomings of Canaris's intelligence network.

the Almighty on their side. 'We will not shy from shedding our own blood, because one day a new land will blossom from the sacrifices of the fallen. And our teutonic state, our German nation, shall emerge victorious.' He followed this up by an exhortation to the soldiers and airmen of Manstein's Army Group South and Richthofen's 4th Air Force, who took part in the successful counter-attack to restore the line between the Dnieper and Donetz. They were about to take part in a crucial battle. Germany's fate was in the balance. At home everything and everyone had been mobilized. More divisions and more weapons were on their way. 'This is why I have flown to you, to exhaust every means of alleviating your defensive battle and to convert it into ultimate victory'. The attack did succeed in closing a dangerous gap, and when Hitler was asked by von Kluge, commanding Army Group Centre, during a visit to the latter's headquarters on 13 March, what the plan for the coming summer was, he replied to everyone's surprise that it would be to 'hold the Eastern front'. It was not long before he changed his mind, however, too impatient to be sitting on the defensive, and gave orders that plans should be prepared for an attack on the Red Army's salient at Kursk by two Army Groups, Centre and South. Meanwhile he would return to Obersalzburg to rest, and once more confer with Mussolini, for Canaris had forecast that before long the Allies would invade Sicily, Sardinia and Corsica. How, in fact, were the Allied plans for taking Sicily getting on?

After Churchill and Roosevelt had accepted the Combined Chiefs' of Staff proposals at Casablanca, a directive had been given to General Eisenhower:

> The Combined Chiefs of Staff have resolved that an attack against Sicily will be launched in 1943, with the target date as the period of the favourable July moon (Code designation 'Husky').

Eisenhower was to be the Supreme Commander, with Alexander as his Deputy, and he would be responsible for all the planning, preparation and execution of the operation. Cunningham and Tedder were respectively Naval and Air Commanders. Eisenhower was further instructed to nominate commanders for what were described as Western and Eastern Task Forces – for the directive included an outline operational plan featuring two such forces. Details of forces to be made available and their training were also included. Eisenhower's instructions concluded with a requirement to report by 1 March as to whether there would be any cause to delay the assault beyond the July moon period, insisted that August must be absolutely the latest date, and urged that if possible the whole thing should be brought forward to June. Such vagaries – unthinkable in any directive issued by Hitler – were matched by comparable indecision in the command and staff machinery which was set up to give effect to the ideas contained in the Combined Chiefs' of Staff instructions. There was no difficulty in establishing staffs to plan the operation. The trouble was that there was no firm and authoritative plan for the staffs to get their teeth into. And all the top commanders who sooner or later would be intimately involved – Eisenhower, Alexander, Montgomery and Patton – were far too busy finishing off the battle for Tunis to give Sicily much attention. As the *Official History* has pointed out: 'Eisenhower and Alexander had the outline plan of the Combined Chiefs of Staff, but neither, because he was preoccupied with operations in progress, was able closely to study this plan for himself and discover the points that he must resolve. Instead the document was issued as an outline, and was treated as a proposal for debate, and not as a commander's fiat.' If there were going to be a debate, then it was certain that Montgomery's voice would be both raised and heard. It was just as well that it was.

As planning began it soon became clear to the planners that the capture of Sicily would be a far more hazardous and complicated operation than had at first been thought. Any such operation called for the ability to establish and maintain substantial superiority of resources and fire power in its three crucial phases – getting there, getting ashore and the momentum of build-up. There was not too much difficulty about the first of these, getting there, in that sufficiently powerful Allied sea and air forces could more or less guarantee it. On the other hand, concern about the other two was justified by virtue of the enemy's ability to reinforce Sicily with both air and ground forces relatively quickly, and this consideration led the planners initially into aiming for the capture of too many ports and too many airfields – with the inevitable consequence of violating one of the principles of war which should never be violated, concentration of force. In the end the limiting factor which was decisive was the number of landing-craft available, for this would determine the number of assault forces. The same point applied to transport aircraft and airborne troops. If, therefore, the *number* of assaulting troops was invariable, the only flexibility applicable to their use would be *where* and *when*. It was in these areas that the main differences of opinion in Allied counsels lay.

The first plan, proposed by a special planning staff under Major-General Gairdner, was so obsessed with the aim of seizing major ports early, ie. Catania by the Eastern Task Force and Palermo by the Western, that it not only required these forces to try to do things quite beyond their capacity, it also separated them so much that they would be unable to support each other and risked defeat in detail. This plan therefore found no favour with anyone, nor did an initial modification of it which proposed that the Western Task Force should await the success of the Eastern before being launched. Again concentration of force leading to rapid seizure of important objectives, like airfields, was not the main theme. It was then that the intervention of General Montgomery was decisive. In a remarkable signal to Alexander, he stated what it was he was prepared to do, and it was this statement which shaped the final plan:

1. The fact that I have not been able to devote my SOLE attention to the Eastern Task Force problem has affected all the work here.

2. Planning so far has been based on assumption that opposition will be slight and that Sicily will be captured relatively easily. Never was there a greater error. Germans and also Italians are fighting desperately now in Tunisia and will do so in Sicily. To go ahead on this assumption with all the consequent tactical repercussions such as dispersion of effort which is a feature of all planning to date will land the Allied Nations in a first class military disaster.

3. We must plan the operation on assumption that resistance will be fierce and that a prolonged dogfight battle will follow the initial assault.

4. I am prepared to carry the war into Sicily with the Eighth Army but must do so in my own way. The fight will be hard and bitter.

5. In view of above considerations my Army must operate concentrated with Corps and Divisions in supporting distance of each other. Pozallo and Gela landings must be given up and the whole initial effort be made in the areas of Avola and Pachino. Subsequent operations will be developed so as to secure airfields and ports and so on. The first thing to do is to secure a lodgement in a suitable area and then operate from that firm base.

6. Time is pressing and if we delay while above is argued in London and Washington the operation will never be launched in July. . . .

7. I have given orders that as far as the army is concerned all planning and work as regards ETF is now to go ahead on lines indicated in para. 5. . . .

8. Admiral Ramsay is in complete agreement with me. . . .

9. I want to make it clear that I shall require for this battle the whole of

Eighth Army. . . . I also want to make it clear that the above solution is the only possible way to handle the ETF problem with the resources available. I am not able to judge the repercussions of this solution on the operation as a whole. . . . I must emphasize that the success of this operation depends on obtaining supremacy in the air . . . and that the operation will NOT be possible if Sicily is developed before July into a heavily defended island strongly held by German troops.

Montgomery's views as to his, that is the Eastern Task Force's, part in the operation had so profound an effect that the Western Task Force's role, ie. General Patton's 7th Army, was completely recast to concentrate on the left flank of Montgomery's Army and to take the Gela airfields. Then, while Patton provided a firm base, the British would push on to take Catania. It was this plan which Eisenhower persuaded his military colleagues to accept. The timing would be early in July.

There were two aspects of the whole thing which gave rise to immense exasperation and wrath on the Prime Minister's part. Passionately committed to the relief of Russia from German pressure, he could not stomach the idea of being inactive at the height of the campaigning season. 'It is absolutely necessary,' he declared, 'to do this operation in June. We shall become a laughing stock if, during the spring and early summer, no British and American soldiers are firing at any German and Italian soldiers.' Churchill at length was reconciled to a date early in July, but was even more vehemently irritated by the suggestions, implied in Montgomery's signal and further aired by Eisenhower, that any substantial German presence in Sicily would render the whole operation impracticable. When moreover he learned that anything more than two divisions was regarded by the military commanders as 'substantial' his discomposure knew no bounds:

If the presence of two German divisions is held to be decisive against any operation of an offensive or amphibious character open to the million men now in North Africa, it is difficult to see how the war can be carried on. Months of preparation, sea power and air power in abundance, and yet two German divisions are sufficient to knock it all on the head. . . . We have told the Russians that they cannot have their supplies by the Northern convoy for the sake of *Husky*, and now *Husky* is to be abandoned if there are two German divisions in the neighbourhood. What Stalin would think of this, when he has 185 German divisions on his front I cannot imagine.

In addressing this minute to his Chiefs of Staff, Churchill exhorted them to have nothing to do with such 'pusillanimous and defeatist doctrines'. They did not. Nor did the U.S. Joint Chiefs of Staff. The operation would go ahead. Before it did, however, Allied leaders were to confer again – in Washington.

In preparation for this meeting Churchill had set down his views as to what should be done to exploit the anticipated success of *Husky*. These views, recorded at the beginning of April, have as their underlying theme that the mere capture of Sicily could not be regarded as a fitting objective for the Allied armies' campaign of 1943. This would be too modest, petty even. Something far grander must be conceived. Much would depend on the enemy's reaction to their loss of Sicily:

> If large German forces are brought down into Italy and Italian morale and will to fight is thereby enhanced, the scale required for the taking of Rome and Naples might be beyond our power. In that case we must be ready with our plans in the Eastern Mediterranean. . . . If, however, the Germans do not come, and the Italians crumple, there is no limit to the amount of Italian territory we may overrun. Italy may be forced out of the war. We may become possessed of Sardinia without fighting. Corsica may be liberated. All our available forces . . . will have to be moved northwards into Italy till they come into contact with the Germans on the Brenner or along the French Riviera. . . . Even if Italy remains in the war with a certain amount of German help, we ought, the moment we are masters of *Husky*-land, to try to get a footing both on the toe and heel of Italy.

It will be seen that the one contingency Churchill did not foresee was that which actually transpired – the crumpling of Italy and its swift occupation by the Germans in strength. Nevertheless as a direction to the Chiefs of Staff to study the problems before the Washington Conference, it served very well. Before we see what happened at this conference, we must examine in what light Hitler and Mussolini were contemplating the same set of strategic circumstances.

However fanciful many of Hitler's military ideas might have been, politically he remained coldly and calculatingly realistic. During the meetings between himself and Mussolini which took place at Klessheim, near Salzburg, from 7 to 10 April he observed quietly to his own staff that Germany's neighbours and allies were all potential enemies. Therefore everything that could be had to be squeezed out of them. But no promises must be made. It was with this sort of realism in mind that Hitler listened to Mussolini's oft-rehearsed view that if the Axis position in the Mediterranean area were to be held together, the war's centre of gravity would have to be shifted there, and thus away from the Russian front. Only by such a shift in concentration could the course of events in the Mediterranean be changed. Italy's understandable concern was that, with the Tunisian front on the brink of collapse, the Italian mainland would before long be in the front line, and given the current position there – a bankrupt economy, low morale, a dearth of weapons and supplies, and a general disillusionment with their German ally – what prospects were there for successful resistance against an Anglo-American assault? We may reflect here that had Hitler taken Mussolini's advice seriously, patched up some sort of truce with the Russians, and transferred powerful air and ground forces from the East to the Mediterranean theatre, he would have given the Western Allies much food for thought. Indeed it is doubtful whether a successful landing by them could have been effected at all in southern Europe during 1943.

But it was not in Hitler's nature to draw back from his great mission – the destruction of Russian Bolshevism. Besides he had never been reconciled to surrender or compromise. *Weltmacht oder Niedergang*, world power or ruin, summarized his nihilistic philosophy, and he was certainly successful in bringing about the latter. And even if he had been inclined to compromise in Russia, he no longer held the initiative there, although he was about to embark on yet one more offensive in order to regain it. So, instead of acknowledging that there was anything in what Mussolini had to say, he gave reassurances about Tunisia, agreed to supply oil for the Italian Navy, and resolutely refused to contemplate disengagement on the Russian front.

Yet despite these bolstering-up reassurances which sent Mussolini back to Rome in better spirits, Hitler knew that the Axis alliance was, as David Irving put it, 'a myth'. Before long he made his arrangements accordingly. Whether he recalled Hindenburg's warning never to trust the Italians may be doubted. That in fact he no longer did trust them need not. He had for long been receiving the frankest reports from his Military Attaché in Rome, General von Rintelen, who made no bones about the gravity of the situation as early as March, 1943:

Since the American landings in North Africa and the loss of Libya, military circles in Italy, and all civilians as well, regard the situation there as practically hopeless . . . the Italians regard the expected loss of the African theatre of war as a turning point . . . as a sign of having been finally thrown back on the defensive.

Individual Italians [officers in the army and the militia] have felt obliged to express their concern about possible future domestic political developments in Germany . . . there was also a lack of understanding of German policy in relation to Catholicism, while in Italy the importance and influence of the Church was increasing . . . in order to improve the morale of Italian troops.

Italians actually say that it would be better for Italy for the British to come into the country before the possibility of further unfavourable developments in the East brought Bolshevism to the gates of Italy.

A general cooling off in the attitude to German troops committed to the Mediterranean area is becoming noticeable in Italy. . . . Italian officers . . . because of setbacks in Russia and Africa have grave doubts whether Germany can win the war by force of arms.

With such reports as this in front of him, it was small wonder that Hitler made his preparations for dealing with either an Italian collapse or Italian treachery. He gave his orders for any such eventuality shortly after the end of the Axis position in North Africa.

The final battle for Tunisia, like other successes which the British had enjoyed in North Africa, was won because the battle for supplies had previously been so totally lost by the Axis. During March and April, 1943, when the minimum supply tonnage per month required by the Germans and Italians in North Africa was something approaching 200,000, the amount getting through was less than a quarter of this total. The Allied air forces and submarines ensured that only a small fraction of Axis shipping got through. On the other hand Allied supplies, soldiers, weapons and all the ironmongery of war were in abundance. The result could not have been other than it was. Alexander's 18th Army Group simply overwhelmed Army Group Africa, and on 13 May two signals were despatched, one by Alexander to Churchill, one by the Headquarters Afrika Korps to their superior HQ. The first signal announced the end of the campaign and stated that the Allies were masters of the North African shores. The second was less triumphant. With all ammunition expended, with arms and equipment destroyed, the Deutsches Afrika Korps had fought itself to a state in which it could fight no more. The signal ended on a defiant note: 'The German Afrika Korps must rise again.' Its gallant members need not have worried. Whenever the desert war is talked of or written about, whenever the illustrious name of Erwin Rommel is mentioned, whenever the extraordinary feats of the German Army are wondered at, this famous fighting formation *does* rise again.

For Churchill the victory in Tunis was the redemption of all that he had been striving for in Africa. It was he who was the architect of that victory. The question facing him now was what to do with it. 'Were its fruits to be gathered only in the Tunisian tip, or should we drive Italy out of the war and bring Turkey in on our side?' Such questions demanded urgent consultation and the Prime Minister had already anticipated this need by telegraphing Roosevelt on 29 April:

> It seems to me most necessary that we should all settle together, now, first Sicily and then exploitation thereof, and secondly the future of the Burma campaign in the light of our experiences and shipping stringency. There are also a number of other burning questions which you and I could with advantage bring up to date.

In this way the second great Washington Conference, codename *Trident*, was convened, and Churchill with the British Chiefs of Staff actually set sail for Washington in the *Queen Mary* a week before the Axis surrender in Tunis. As Michael Howard has explained in his *Grand Strategy*, the British Chiefs of Staff were quite clear that Mediterranean successes *must* be exploited. They had not yet decided how. Nor did their discussions in Washington do much to fix their minds. There was no shortage of options to consider – the invasion of Italy; the seizure of Sardinia and Corsica; operations in the eastern Mediterranean.

Of these options that of invading Italy – while it offered certain attractions, such as knocking Italy out of the war and providing important new bases for giving direct support to Yugoslav partisans and for stepping up the bombing of Germany – could have one grave strategic drawback. It could, as Michael Howard wrote, 'involve the Allies in a prolonged campaign which might impose a greater strain on their resources than on those of the enemy'. Here in a nutshell is the criterion by which the effectiveness of the Italian campaign must be gauged.

As usual when presented with a variety of difficult options, the British Chiefs of Staff invited their joint planners to examine possible courses of action and make recommendations. Although the Chiefs of Staff stuck firmly to their previous view that operations in the Mediterranean were designed to assist Russia to defeat Germany by forcing a diversion of German divisions from the Eastern front and that this was to be achieved by knocking Italy out of the war, when they were obliged to consider the likely course of events as a result of this policy, there were many areas of uncertainty. What would it take to eliminate Italy? Would a mere landing there in the south be enough? And would Italy's collapse in itself oblige the Germans to withdraw? Was it not more probable that the Italians would require massive assistance to throw the Germans out of their country? All these considerations were examined and discussed during the voyage to Washington and led the planning staff to make proposals on which the forthcoming talks with the Americans could be based. Two circumstances dominated their thinking. One was their belief that the low Italian morale must be exploited; the other concerned the Germans' willingness and ability to prop up their ally. Since Italy's imminent collapse was almost a foregone conclusion, alternative courses of action depended not on what Italy, but on what Germany, did. Non-reinforcement of Italy by the Germans would allow the Allies a free hand; reinforcement would both relieve the Russians and present the Allies with alternative goals, such as Sardinia and Corsica.

Such plans were relatively circumspect. But the joint planners toyed with one other possibility – Italy's collapse *before* either the Allies invaded or the Germans reinforced. And here they let their imaginations soar. The occupation of southern Italy; seizure of airfields at Rome and Naples; a bridgehead to be established at Durazzo [Albania]; Ploesti, some 40 miles north of Bucharest, to be seized by air; Corsica and Sardinia to be occupied; and enough troops landed in central Italy to prevent Germany moving their own forces south. Here was the very sort of boldness which had in the past to often characterized Hitler's blitzkrieg methods. Had these ideas been taken seriously and prepared for thoroughly, the Allies would have found a few months later that they were offered an opportunity which would have yielded great prizes, and – foregone as it was – would never again recur. The one thing the joint planners never seemed able to grasp was that Hitler's conduct of war cared nothing for military logic and likelihoods. It was driven solely by his will, and this will was inexorably supported by the skill, dedication and fervour of the Wehrmacht. In stating their belief that the Germans would be unable to hold both northern Italy and the Balkans without hazarding the Russian front, the joint planners were wide of the mark. Their conclusion, however, highlighted one of the major strategic controversies of the war, even though it ended with a further misreading of the Wehrmacht's power and its absolute subordination to the Führer's total grip on the resources of the Third Reich:

> Our final conclusion is that the Mediterranean offers us opportunities for action in the coming autumn and winter which may be decisive, and at the least will do far more to prepare the way for a cross-Channel operation in 1944 than we should achieve by attempting to transfer back to the United Kingdom any of the forces now in the Mediterranean theatre. If we take these opportunities, we shall have every chance of breaking the Axis and of bringing the war to a successful conclusion in 1944.

In commenting on this paper, Michael Howard made the point that its spirit of hope and resolution had nothing to do with commitment to 'peripheral strategy' – so bewitching to some British minds, so disagreeable to the Americans – and certainly had no origin in ideas about political influences to be exercised when the war was finally won. It was simply that victory in North Africa had to be followed up. Churchill himself had declared that he would in no circumstances allow the powerful British and British-controlled armies in the Mediterranean to stand idle.

The British might be able to convince themselves. Convincing their American allies was another matter. The United States' stance was still greatly influenced by General Marshall's continued fears that Mediterranean operations would jeopardize, even prevent, the invasion of North-West Europe in 1944. As there were by this time nearly 400,000 U.S. servicemen in the Mediterranean area, and a mere 60,000 men of the U.S. Army in the United Kingdom, his fears seemed justified. To Marshall the whole idea of major exploitation of Allied progress in the Mediterranean was completely at odds with his longed for cross-Channel operation. Small wonder, therefore, that the question of how these conflicting demands would affect what was to happen in the Pacific once more loomed large in American eyes.

At the same time the Americans were prepared to concede that there might be some advantage in exploiting success in Sicily. It was all a matter of degree. In essence the difference of attitude was this. The principal British concern was to take the Mediterranean tide at the flood, squeeze every possible dividend from it, while still remaining committed to the invasion of North-West Europe in 1944. The

Americans turned the thing inside out. They put the cross-Channel venture first and foremost, looking askance at any Mediterranean operations which might interfere with it.

The arguments at Washington went to and fro, but what mattered was broad agreement both as to the cross-Channel operation *and* as to what should happen in the Mediterranean. This agreement went so far as to specify the *numbers of Allied divisions* which should or should not be used. The combined Chiefs' of Staff conclusions were these:

(a) That forces and equipment shall be established in the United Kingdom with the object of mounting an operation with target date 1st May, 1944, to secure a lodgement on the Continent from which further offensive operations can be carried out. The scope of the operations will be such as to necessitate the following forces being present and available for use in the U.K. by 1st May, 1944:

  Assault 5 Infantry Divisions [simultaneously loaded in landing-craft]
       2 Infantry Divisions – Follow up.
       2 Airborne Divisions.
    Total 9 Divisions in the Assault.
  Build-up 20 Divisions available for movement into lodgement area.
  Total: 29 Divisions.

(b) That the Allied Commander-in-Chief, North Africa, should be instructed to mount such operations in exploitation of *Husky* as are best calculated to eliminate Italy from the war and to contain the maximum number of German forces.

The paper went on to say that the C.-in-C., North Africa, could use for his operations all forces available in the Mediterranean area *except* for four American and three British divisions which were to be held in readiness from 1 November for withdrawal to take part in operations from the U.K. All this talk of numbers of divisions was the very nub of the subsequent argument about the efficacy or otherwise of the Italian campaign. Such argument revolved essentially around how many German divisions were diverted to the Italian theatre from the Russian, and later from the Normandy, front; it revolved too around where Allied divisions should be committed – to France or to Italy, whether in Churchill's words they should push left-handed, right-handed or both-handed?

In agreeing a joint policy the Allies may have compromised, but it was a compromise which satisfied both parties, brought about as it was, not by either partner abandoning a cherished strategic idea, but by a limitation of landing-craft available for *Overlord* [codename for the cross-Channel assault]. Thus with only seven assault divisions, not counting those to be delivered by air, committed to *Overlord*, there would be enough left in the Mediterranean area to allow the British to pursue their objectives of savaging Italy and distracting Germany. Accordingly General Eisenhower was instructed 'to submit proposals for operations in the Mediterranean Area, to be carried out concurrently with or subsequent to a successful *Husky*'. At the same time a directive was given to the Chief of Staff, Supreme Allied Commander, for *Overlord* to plan the cross-Channel attack. At this time Eisenhower was given no precise guidance as to what to do after capturing Sicily. This did not greatly matter, for it was what Hitler said and did that largely determined the course of events in the Mediterranean area from July, 1943, onwards.

Hitler's strategic dilemma as a result of defeat in North Africa was admirably summed up by himself in a speech he made to his generals on 15 May at his East Prussian headquarters, *Wolfsschanze*. The enemy had opened up the Mediterranean, and had powerful naval and air forces, plus some twenty divisions, available to exploit the situation and persuade Germany's weaker allies to defect. Italy was a particular danger. Only Mussolini himself could be trusted, and he might well be got rid of. Real power in Italy lay elsewhere. They could not expect a neutral Italy – it would defect to the enemy camp. This would mean a Second Front in Europe, and that was to be avoided at all costs. Moreover the Western flank of the Balkans would be at risk. It was therefore just as well that the planned offensive in the East had been postponed, for forces available there could be rushed to Italy if there were a crisis. Eight panzer and four infantry divisions from the mobile reserve in the East would take a firm grip on Italy and defend her against any Anglo-American incursion. No resistance could be expected from the Italians. Hungary would have to be occupied. All this would have serious consequences on the Eastern front. There would be risk in the Donetz region; the Orel bend might have to be evacuated; it might even be necessary to withdraw to the Luga Line in the North.

In commenting on this speech, David Irving makes the important point that it 'destroys the myth that Hitler always refused to abandon territory voluntarily in Russia, when it was strategically necessary'. In this respect alone the Allies' Mediterranean strategy was paying off.

David Irving also draws attention to the fact that the dangers in Italy and neighbouring countries had a profound effect on Hitler's planned offensive in the East. Despite all the emphasis he had previously been putting on this attempt to wipe out the Kursk Salient, Operation *Zitadelle*, it was, Irving writes, 'subordinated to the need to prop up a crumbling dictatorship in a country whose military value was nil'.

A week after making this speech Hitler gave Rommel his orders to deal with the situation which would arise from Italy's collapse or defection. Half a dozen panzer or panzer grenadier divisions would be quickly moved from the eastern front and positioned on Italy's northern frontiers ready to cross over and take control of the country. It will be seen, therefore, that during the month of May, 1943, we have the interesting circumstances that both the Allies and the Germans have laid plans for taking over Italy. The Germans plans would be put into effect *blitzartigschnell*, at lightning speed, at the whim of a single man, whose political instincts were in no way unsharpened by four years of war. And once the order was given, it would be executed with all the ruthless efficiency and thoroughness of the German Army. On the other hand, any idea that the Allies would act with speed and boldness, or indeed would act at all without endless discussion, equivocation or taking counsel of fears – all the superhuman courage and imagination of Churchill notwithstanding – was soon to be dismissed. In any event the Allies had to take Sicily first.

5

AN HONEST TRIFLE

And oftentimes to win us to our harm,
The instruments of darkness tell us truths,
Win us with honest trifles, to betray's
In deepest consequence.

Shakespeare

The campaign in Sicily was memorable for four things – the valuable experience gained by the Allies in executing an amphibious operation of unprecedented scale; the ease with which the German divisions there evaded capture; the birth of furious hostility between Montgomery and Patton, which was to vex Allied military cooperation for the next two years; and a complicated deception plan which was almost wholly successful and which pointed the way to further such measures of incalculable importance. Otherwise, as Alexander's despatch put it, operations proceeded according to plan. That this was so owed much to an imaginative deception operation, *Mincemeat*, whose purpose was to persuade the Germans into believing that the Allies were *not* going to invade Sicily.

In his admirable book, *The Man Who Never Was*, Ewen Montagu has explained that if the idea of a document to deceive the Germans were to have any chance of being taken seriously enough by them to act on it, it would have to be at an extremely high level. As he put it: 'If the German General Staff was to be persuaded, in face of all probabilities, to bank on our next target being somewhere other than Sicily, it would have to have before it a document which was passing between officers who *must* know what our real plans were, who could not possibly be mistaken and who could not themselves be the victims of a cover plan.'

Another important consideration, stressed by Ronald Lewin in his book about *Ultra*, was that of trying to reinforce the enemy's belief about what was likely to happen. It would always be easier to exploit the enemy's ingrained fears and preconceptions than to root them out and plant something foreign in his mind. If there was one strategic concern which Hitler and Churchill shared, it was the significance of the Balkans – Churchill always wanting to strike a blow there, Hitler obsessively anxious about their security – and here was food for the British Intelligence staffs. At the same time, it was so unlikely that the Allies would risk sending convoys of troops and warships from Tunisia *eastwards*, that is through the narrow straits within reach of German airfields in Sicily, that it was necessary to devise a deception plan which would indicate two Allied targets – Greece by the Eastern Army under General Maitland Wilson and Sardinia by the Western Army under General Alexander. But perhaps Ewen Montagu's most brilliant touch was in suggesting that the document in question should show that the Allied intention was to try and convince the Germans that *they were going to invade Sicily*! This document was no less than a letter from the Vice Chief of the Imperial General Staff, Lieut. General Sir Archibald Nye, to General Alexander. Dated 23 April, 1943, it made two things clear – first that the *Husky* objective was Greece; second that another operation, *Brimstone*, was to be mounted from North Africa with another unspecified objective, but obviously one further west; furthermore the cover plan for this latter operation would be – *Sicily*. The wording of this letter was masterly. Its authoritative tone together with the kind of intimate language that two generals, who were close friends, would use to each other hit exactly the right note. In discussing the cover target the letter reads: 'The C.O.S. Committee went into the whole question exhaustively again and came to the conclusion that in view of the preparations in Algeria, the amphibious training which will be taking place on the Tunisian coast and the heavy air bombardment which will be put down to neutralize the Sicilian airfields, we should stick to our plan of making it cover for *Brimstone* – indeed, we stand a very good chance of making him think we will go for Sicily – it is an obvious objective and one about which he must be nervous'. Indeed it was so obvious an objective that Churchill, when commenting on the proposed operation, gave it as his opinion that the risk of revealing Sicily as a target did not much matter because 'anyone but a damned fool would know it is Sicily'. But perhaps the most striking part of the operation was the method of delivering this vital document into enemy hands.

Having had the idea of using a dead body for a different reason fed into his mind by a colleague, Ewen Montagu asked a question which gave birth to the means of executing Operation *Mincemeat*: 'Why shouldn't we get a body, disguise it as a staff officer, and give him really high-level papers which will show clearly that we are going to attack somewhere else? We won't have to drop him on land, as the aircraft might have come down in the sea on the way round the Med. He would float ashore with the papers either in France or in Spain; it won't matter which. Probably Spain would be best, as the Germans wouldn't have as much chance to examine the body there as if they got it into their own hands, while it's certain that they will get the documents, or at least copies'. Montagu's book describes the immense and sometimes gruesome detail with which the operation was launched. What mattered was that it worked. On 30 April the body of a Major Martin, Royal Marines, the man who never was, was picked up by Spanish fishermen near Huelva. The documents he carried duly received the expected treatment by the Spanish authorities, copies were made available to German agents, and the whole process of evaluation and consequent action because of the information contained in them got under way.

The results were gratifying and did much to reinforce the view that one of the great purposes of deception measures was to comfort the enemy by confirming his preconceived ideas. At the beginning of May Hitler was still regarding the Mediterranean as his most vulnerable area, and was especially fearful of the Peloponnese of Greece and of the Western Mediterranean. When, therefore, the *Mincemeat* documents fell into the Abwehr's hands, his fears seemed to be confirmed. Certainly the Abwehr's head, Canaris, was convinced. Hitler was more circumspect. 'Couldn't this be a corpse they have deliberately played into our hands?' he demanded of a staff officer at his headquarters. Whatever his private doubts, the Intelligence staffs were taken in. *Mincemeat* had worked. It was, as Ronald Lewin recorded, only one part of an extremely complicated deception plan for the invasion of Sicily, but it was at once the most renowned and the most effective. Hitler's directive issued on 12 May made plain that defensive measures concerning Sardinia and the Peloponnese would take precedence over Sicily. This being so, what would the Axis defensive measures on the island be like, and what were the Allied plans for overwhelming them?

Responsibility for the defence of Sicily rested with the Commander-in-Chief of the Italian 6th Army, General Guzzoni, who had taken over from General Roatta at the beginning of June. He had two Italian Corps, the 12th in the West, 16th in the East. Each Corps had two mobile divisions and about three coastal divisions plus some mobile or tactical groups. Italian troops totalled 200,000. In addition there were 32,000 German Army troops and 30,000 ground troops from the Luftwaffe. The German Army divisions were both experienced and powerful. In the West with 12th Corps was the majority of 15th Panzer Grenadier Division, and to the east with 16th Corps was the Hermann Göring Panzer Division with nearly a hundred tanks, including Tigers, and the rest of 15th Panzer Grenadier Division. Although these German formations were nominally under command of the Italian C.-in-C., in practice they took their orders from General von Senger und Etterlin, who was Kesselring's liaison officer with Guzzoni. Both Guzzoni and Kesselring expected that the Allies would assault in the south-eastern part of the island,* and in this they were right. Where they disagreed was in the tactical method of countering an assault, Guzzoni being in favour of light defences on the coast and strong mobile reserves held back so that, as soon as the main enemy landings had been identified, they could be powerfully counter-attacked, while Kesselring stuck to established German doctrine of holding strongly in forward positions in order to defeat the initial enemy landings before they could be reinforced by heavier weapons. The decision finally reached between them was swayed by Kesselring's views – enemy landings would be attacked initially by coastal divisions, then by Italian mobile divisions, with the Germans ready to deliver the coup de grace. Each landing must be eliminated before it could consolidate with its neighbour.

The Allied plan to capture Sicily would have five phases, as laid down by General Alexander: first the preparatory operations by naval and air forces to neutralize enemy sea activity and get air supremacy;

---

* Despite the success of *Mincemeat* and other measures which influenced Hitler, Kesselring and Guzzoni were very much alive to the likelihood of a descent on Sicily by the Allies, whose shipping concentrations alone pointed to Sicily as the most probable target. The *timing* of the invasion did, however, surprise them.

next the assault by sea and air to seize airfields and ports – Syracuse and Licata; then gaining a firm base from which Catania and Augusta ports and the Gerbini airfields would be captured; fourth the actual capture of these objectives; finally the reduction of Sicily as a whole. All very neat and logical; who was to do it and how was it to be done? In answer to the first of these questions, we may recall what the *Official History* had to say: 'The number of ships, craft, and men engaged in the assault on Sicily had never been surpassed in a single amphibious operation'. There were no fewer than 180,000 troops and the naval forces, which totalled nearly 2,600 vessels, included more than 500 warships, 1,700 landing craft and more than 200 merchant ships. Some two weeks before the invasion Admiral Cunningham commented in a letter to Sir Dudley Pound, First Sea Lord, that the idea of having to turn back such a prodigious fleet, should bad weather intervene, was daunting, adding that 'the soldiers seem to think that they will be landed at the exact spot they expect to be, that the weather will necessarily be perfect, and that naval gunfire will silence all opposition'. Given the soldiers' experience of war up to this time, some of them might have thought that, although they might hope for such desirable conditions, they no longer *expected* them. In any event none of the sailors' or soldiers' expectations could be realized unless the Allied air forces had successfully done their stuff.

The air plan had three distinct parts. From the moment that Axis forces had surrendered in Tunis, Allied bombing began to prepare the way for Sicily's conquest, while attempting to conceal that Sicily was in fact their next objective. Right up until a week before the invasion, strategic targets would be airfields in southern Italy, Sicily and Sardinia; ports in the same area – Naples, Cagliari, Messina, Palermo; industrial centres; from the U.K. the Royal Air Force would attack Germany and northern Italy; bombers from the Middle East would concentrate on the Aegean. All this was the first part. During the week up to D-Day [10 July] the theme would be much closer to the real objective. Enemy air forces and bases likely to interfere with the Allied landings would be subject to intense engagement, as would all communications with Sicily – land, sea and air – which the Axis had. Radar installations were to be attacked. This was the second part. Finally, after the landings had been made, Allied air forces would concentrate on maintaining air supremacy and neutralizing enemy air bases in Sicily. As in all such operations of war, the activities of the soldiers and airmen were complementary. The more airfields the soldiers captured, the fewer enemy aircraft there would be. The more enemy aircraft Allied airmen destroyed, the easier would be the soldiers' task. What exactly was the soldiers' task?

Broadly expressed, 8th Army's task was to assault between Syracuse and Pozallo, get itself firmly established on the line between Syracuse, Ragusa and Pozallo, and make contact with Patton's 7th Army on its left. 8th Army would also capture Augusta and Catania, and the Gerbini airfields. For this job Montgomery would have four infantry divisions, an independent brigade and an airborne division. 7th U.S. Army with five divisions was to assault between Cape Scaramia and Licata; capture the latter, plus airfields at Ponte Olivo, Biscari and Comiso; protect 8th Army's left flank. Montgomery was in no doubt as to who should exercise overall control, and as early as 2 May had signalled to Alexander: 'Consider proper answer would be to put U.S. Corps under me and let my Army HQ handle the whole operation of the land battle'.* It was not surprising, in the interests of Allied harmony, that this signal did not go further than Alexander's headquarters. Much more to the point were Montgomery's declarations concerning the importance of getting ashore. If his divisions could be landed successfully, he was confident of the outcome. '8th Army must get ashore; this is the really difficult thing; given success here, the other points are easy.'

Montgomery's concern about getting ashore was certainly borne out by events. To start with the airborne operations were, as General Sir William Jackson put it, 'a fiasco in which the most carefully selected and highly trained soldiers from both armies were literally thrown away by inexperienced and inadequately trained aircrews.' Montgomery had given to his 1st Airborne Division the task of seizing the Ponte Grande bridge on the south side of the road to Syracuse. An entire brigade was to land by glider. Only twelve gliders out of 134 succeeded in getting to the right area. The rest were either released prematurely and came down in the sea, or landed somewhere else in Sicily. The remarkable thing was that the few men who got to the bridge did hold it until reached next day by ground troops. Patton's airborne troops did little better. He had required a parachute regiment of four battalions to seize

---

* 'He is an egotist and a braggart,' said Disraeli of Wolseley. 'So was Nelson.' A similar comment might be made of Montgomery, but, alas, he lacked an Emma. Nevertheless, like Nelson, Montgomery became a national hero.

high ground north of Gela inland from the objective of his 1st Division. Only one of the four battalions dropped anywhere near the correct place. All the others were either on the beaches, in the wrong divisional area or – such was the degree of inaccuracy – in the British zone. If nothing else, however, it was a lesson for the future.

Seaborne landings had their difficulties too – strong winds, errors of navigation, faulty launching of assault boats, lateness of arrival at the rendez-vous – all contributed to the confusion and to troops being landed on the wrong beaches at the wrong time. The recollections of those who took part in the operations bring the whole thing alive. Dudley Davenport was First Lieutenant of HMS *Tetcott*, a destroyer responsible for escorting one of the convoys of transports, and noted in his diary:

9th July The convoys move on towards Sicily, unmolested and apparently unsighted, and tension grows as we wonder whether the enemy is aware of our approach and is storing up a warm welcome for us nearer his own shores. . . . The sea becomes choppy and the wind freshens to force 5, only to drop to flat calm again . . . is the Almighty on our side again?

10th July 0200 Still no sign of the Landing Craft. There must be something wrong. I hope we aren't in the wrong position. . . . The whole thing seems so peaceful, just lying off the coast, stopped and for all the world miles away from the war.

0215 Here they are, coming up astern. Yes, that's them one, two, four, six, eight . . . they are steering straight towards us. . . . 'Steer North 65 West' shouted to the Landing Craft, carrying about 60 men each. They pass round our bows and steam on into the darkness.

0240 Here come the second wave, steering straight for us again. We hail them and give a course for the beach. Still no sign of activity from the first wave. They must be nearly ashore by now. We close in nearer to the shore. Now we have shown the Landing Craft the way, our job changes to bombardment. Putting out of action any batteries or searchlights which make a nuisance of themselves.

0415 At last a sign from shore. Some green Verey lights from our beach. They must have captured it without much opposition. There's a searchlight shining out to sea. . . . That searchlight is becoming a nuisance. . . . The battery behind the searchlight is firing on the beaches almost continually now. we must have a shot at it.

0605 Our men ashore seem to be getting on well. The beaches are all in our hands. . . . The first Tank Landing Craft are discharging on the beach and the whole operation seems to be going very smoothly and according to plan. There are a pair of enemy fighters overhead, circling round, but they don't worry us and we leave them alone. Mutual understanding! After months of seeing only Egypt and Libya, the coast of Sicily looks pleasantly clean and peaceful with its olive groves and vineyards.

0945 We are ordered to leave the beach and go on anti-submarine patrol to seaward of the shipping.

1500 All troops from the personnel ships seem to have been landed . . . more and more Tank Landing Craft seem to be arriving and discharging over the beaches.

2030 At dusk we make a smoke screen to cover the shipping, and there is a fairly heavy raid. Our people seem to have got quite a lot of guns ashore, mainly Bofors, as they put up a decent barrage. There is not much activity throughout the night, and on the whole things are pretty quiet.

It was by means of comparable activities across the entire invasion coast that no less than eight Allied divisions established themselves in Sicily during 10 July, 1943. Montgomery's fears about the difficulties of getting ashore had not been fulfilled. His prediction that the rest would be easy, however, was also wide of the mark. And it was during the operations which followed the initial invasion that his unseemly row with George Patton developed. But before we follow the course of the campaign which conquered Sicily, we must see what effect the invasion itself had had upon Hitler and Mussolini.

In July, 1943, Hitler might have been excused if he had reflected that the game was beginning to go wrong, for during that month the Allies set foot in southern Europe, Mussolini fell and the Russians, despite the German attack at Kursk, mounted a gigantic offensive. Hitler's reaction was like Macbeth's when confronted with the double shock of Birnam wood moving to Dunsinane and Macduff not being born of woman in the normal sense – 'Yet I will try the last'. As Hitler told Mussolini when they met on 19 July, there was only one thing to be done, to go on fighting – in Italy, in Russia, on all fronts. What mattered was the unconquerable will to go on resisting. Mussolini had little to say in response to the 'voice of History'. Indeed before long he had little to say about anything. The Allied landing in Sicily was preceded – it was a matter of only five days – by the launching, after many delays, of *Zitadelle*, the German attack on the Kursk salient. All these delays had guaranteed its failure, had ensured that the Red Army would not simply be ready for it, but would positively welcome it, for after defeating it the Russians took the initiative, never again to lose it. Four days before the German attack began on 5 July, Hitler addressed the senior commanders at his headquarters, *Wolfsschanze*. Much of what he had to say laid blame upon Germany's allies, particularly Italy. The Italians, he declared, had completely let them down. Africa would never have been lost if the Italian fleet had escorted supply ships to North Africa. Even now the Italian warships were skulking in harbour being smashed up by Allied bombing. The Italian Army had failed wherever it had fought – in Russia, in Africa, in Greece. There was, of course, some comfort to be gained from the fact that German soldiers had taken over in Greece and Crete, and that German troops were in Rhodes, Sicily, Sardinia and Corsica. If the Italians alone had been there, they would have surrendered them already. He went on to say that 'where we are, we stay'. In Russia they would yield nothing. The Russians were biding their time. They must not be allowed to create further crises in the coming winter. It was necessary to disrupt them. Hence *Zitadelle*.

But the time the Russians had already been allowed had enabled them to create a huge defensive zone, some 200 miles deep, with belt after belt of positions manned by anti-tank guns, tank-killing teams, massed artillery, tanks mounting 122mm and 152mm guns, and a million soldiers. Against this formidable defence were launched Model's 9th Army and Hoth's 4th Panzer Army, between them mustering no fewer than seventeen panzer divisions. Hitler's hope was that he would succeed in driving the Russians back to the Don, even the Volga, and at last be able to roll up and capture Moscow from the south-east. Events were to show otherwise. Blitzkrieg could work against an ill-prepared, linear defence and armies of low morale and poor weaponry. It had little chance against defences of immense strength and depth, soldiers of high courage, and seemingly inexhaustible reserves. After a week during which Hoth's Panzer Army had simply indulged in a 'death ride' and had encountered such numbers of Russian tanks that they seemed to swarm like rats all over the battlefield, the offensive was called off. It was not only here,

1. Mr Churchill, in the uniform of the 4th Hussars, with General Leese (*left*) and General Alexander, Italy, August, 1944.

2. Marshal Stalin, President Roosevelt and Mr Churchill, Teheran, 1944.

3. Generals Alexander, Montgomery and Brooke, Italy, December, 1943.

4. General Marshall and General Brooke.

5. General Montgomery talking to men of 231 Brigade, Sicily, September, 1943.

6. General Dwight D. Eisenhower and General Mark Clark.

7. Mussolini bids farewell to Hitler. On the right
are Goering and Ribbentrop.

8. Field-Marshals Rommel and Kesselring.

9. (*left*) Field-Marshal Albert Kesselring.

10. (*below left*) General Heinrich von Vietinghc

11. (*below*) General Lucian Truscott.

12. Ribbentrop, Ciano and Hitler.

13. The Sicilian Landings, dawn, 10 July, 1943.

14. Landing at Salerno, 9 September, 1943.

15. Salerno: British troops of 5th Army advance past a burning Mark IV special.

16. Fifth Army Front: British troops in the mountains above Teano, November, 1943.

17. British Sherman tank lands at Anzio, January, 1944.

18. Sappers of 78 Division built this Bailey bridge in two days while under continuous fire, May, 1944.

19. After the crossing of the Rapido, May, 1944.

20. American troops among the ruins of the
town of Cisterna di Latima, south of Rome,
June, 1944.

21. British troops in the town of Cassino, May, 1944.

22. The ruins of the Abbey on Monastery Hill, Cassino, May, 1944.

however, that Hitler had a crisis on his hands. There was Sicily too.

During the first two days of their attack on Sicily, the Allies succeeded in landing about 80,000 men, 300 tanks, 900 guns and 7,000 vehicles. The Gela airfields and the ports of Licata, Syracuse and Augusta were in their hands. The first two phases of Alexander's plan had been completed. On 13 July he gave further instructions:

> Operations for the immediate future will be for Eighth Army to advance on two axes. One to capture the port of Catania and the group of airfields there, and the other to secure the network of road communications within the area Leonforte-Enna. Seventh Army will conform by pivoting on Palma di Montechiaro-Canicatti-Caltanissetta, gaining touch with the Eighth Army.

The Americans did not take kindly to a supporting role, and when, three days later, after the Germans and some of their Italian allies were successfully holding 8th Army's attempts to break through to Catania, Alexander issued further orders which required Patton simply to protect the rear, while Montgomery broke through into the Messina peninsula, Patton exploded, visited Alexander's headquarters and got agreement to drive on Palermo. This he did with dash and rapid success, entering Palermo on 22 July. It was now clear that the Axis forces under General Hube, whom Hitler had despatched to Sicily with two more German divisions on 13 July, were establishing a strong defensive position pivoted on Mount Etna which protected the north-eastern part of the island. It became necessary for Alexander to think again.

Meanwhile Hitler and Mussolini had met at Feltre, near Treviso. On 18 July the Duce had telegraphed to the Führer asking for a meeting 'to examine the situation together attentively, in order to draw from it the consequences conforming to our common interests and to those of each of our countries'. Their discussion was not fruitful. Richthofen, who was present, reported that Hitler spoke for two hours about how to conduct war. None of the Italians understood a word, except Mussolini, who later tried to make Hitler appreciate the danger of Italy being crushed by the combined weight of Britain and the United States. Italy's power of resistance and morale had been badly damaged. In reply Hitler promised air and army reinforcements to defend Italy, which was in Germany's highest interest too. The crisis, Hitler made plain, was one of leadership. Indeed it was, and immediately after his meeting with the Duce, when he was back at the Berghof, he had seen a report from Himmler, which not only predicted a coup d'état to get rid of Mussolini and instal Marshal Badoglio, but also stated that Badoglio would then initiate peace talks as soon as the Allies had completed the conquest of Sicily. Within a few days the first of these predictions had become a fact. On 25 July King Victor Emmanuel III dismissed Mussolini and appointed Badoglio as head of government.

When the news reached Hitler at his Headquarters, he flew into a rage, but did not allow anger to cloud his judgment. Rightly suspecting that Badoglio would opt for surrender of one sort or another sooner or later, he began to make plans to prevent the military situation in Italy getting out of hand. Even though it might be necessary to wait for further information before taking action, the planning could be done here and now – and this on the very evening of Mussolini's fall. As so often in the past Hitler's political intuition was cold and clear: 'Undoubtedly in their treachery they will proclaim that they will remain loyal to us. Of course they won't remain loyal. . . . We'll play the same game while preparing everything to take over the whole area with one stroke, and capture all the riffraff'. Four plans were rapidly made and the forces to carry them out earmarked. These plans were for the rescue of Mussolini [which was subsequently carried out after the armistice and once the fallen Duce's whereabouts were known to the Germans]; the occupation of Rome and restoration of a Fascist government; the occupation of Italy by German forces; and the seizure or destruction of the Italian fleet. Further, on 26 July Hitler signalled to von Mackensen, German Ambassador in Rome: 'For reasons of principle we shall be interested in receiving the names of about thirty important personalities in the army, politics, and the royal family known to be notorious opponents of ours. Reich Foreign Minister requests your reply by secret cipher tonight'. As Lieutenant-Colonel von Plehwe has recorded, Mackensen named Ciano, Volpi, Grandi, Cerutti, Suvich and the Princess Isabella Colonna. He undertook to supply military names after consulting his military attaché, General von Rintelen. It was then that von Rintelen showed outstanding courage and integrity in refusing to supply a list which would have endangered the innocent. The wording of the telegram he drafted for Mackensen's signature was such that it would give maximum irritation and minimum information to its recipients:

> Military Attaché reports to me as follows . . . 'There is no evidence that individual leading personalities in the Italian army can be described as definite enemies of the German Reich. In the Italian officers' corps rigid discipline and alignment with royal family prevails in attitude to allies or enemies. Also Fascism did not tolerate definitely anti-German elements among senior commanders. . . . Nevertheless it is a fact that as a result of military events of the past year, confidence in and admiration for the German army has generally declined . . .'

In the absence of the information requested, Hitler's staff simply listed all the names of senior Italian commanders as being hostile and suspect. Hitler did not yet act in arresting leading Italian personalities, but he made sure that, when the time of Italian collapse came, he would be ready to establish a proper military grip on the whole peninsula. Army Group B under Rommel began to concentrate with its headquarters at Münich and would comprise no less than eight divisions, mainly drawn from France, while later – about a week before the Germans withdrew from Sicily – a newly formed 10th Army under General von Vietinghoff was to take command of all German divisions in the south of Italy. Here we may anticipate events in order to show how greatly contrasted were Hitler's correct interpretation of likely developments and his rapid, ruthless action in order to control them, and, on the other side, the slowness and feebleness of the Allied reaction to an opportunity which their longed-for aim of 'knocking Italy out of the war' was finally to present them with.

Hitler had always been concerned that the Allies would take full advantage of Italy's 'treachery'. He totally overestimated both their inclination and ability to act quickly and their strategic boldness when at last they did act. An entire six weeks were to pass between the time of Mussolini's overthrow and the declaration of an armistice between Badoglio's government and the Allies. During those six weeks Hitler had not only deployed sixteen German divisions in Italy and put himself securely in control of the country; he had disarmed and immobilized the Italian Army. He even welcomed the new situation. It would now be much easier for Germany to continue the struggle 'free of all burdensome encumbrances. . . . Tactical necessity may compel us once and again to give up something on some front in this gigantic struggle, but it will never break the ring of steel that protects the Reich'.

And indeed the ring of steel in Italy was the hardest one of all for the Allies to break. There was not to be much giving up anything on the Italian front, and we may recall Norman Stone's judgment that 'Hitler was able to meet the Allied invasion of Italy almost without serious disruption of the war elsewhere'. On the other hand, these sixteen divisions had to come from somewhere, and by deciding to hold fast in Italy, Hitler was removing divisions from East and West, and so conforming to Allied Mediterranean strategy in making the southern front a distraction from German effort on other fronts.

Why was it that the Allies had found themselves incapable of bolder action at the time of Mussolini's dismissal? Part of the answer to this question is to be found in the war diaries of Harold Macmillan, at that time British Minister Resident in North Africa. His entry for Monday 26 July 1943 contains the following passage:

> While it was inevitable that our military reaction to the fall of Mussolini would take time – Alexander estimated that Sicily would be reduced by the end of August and that landings on the Italian mainland might begin in late September – it was vital that our political reaction should be prompt. We must encourage the new Italian Government to make peace, and be ready for them when they offered to do so.

Quite apart from the general faintheartedness of this approach – letting I dare not wait upon I would, like the poor cat i' th' adage – it simply spoke of unpreparedness. Why should it be inevitable that military reaction should be so slow? One of the joint planners' ideas examined before the Washington conference in May had been how to exploit this very situation – Italy's collapse before either the Allies invaded or the Germans reinforced. Alas, it had not been pursued. And while it was understandable that the Allies would not wish to forfeit the advantages of a wavering Italy by imposing dishonourable terms or conditions on them, history had shown time after time that swift and decisive military action soon led to acceptable political solutions. But to search for the latter first – and Macmillan's diary goes on to talk of draft armistice terms containing *forty* clauses – before taking military action was simply to invite the Germans to impose their own conditions – political, military, strategic, everything. Even the bold and far-sighted Churchill could do little more than send telegrams to President Roosevelt, arrange for directives to the Combined Chiefs of Staff to be drafted and complete the arrangements for the next top-level meeting between the two Allied leaders, which was to take place at Quebec in August.

It was already clear, however, that there was one fatal flaw in the whole concept of a Mediterranean strategy which had been designed to exploit Italy's weakness and Germany's concern to bolster up her weaker partner. When the moment came to strike and strike decisively, there were insufficient reserves and inadequate preparations to do so. The fact was that the Allied armies were still struggling with a relatively honest trifle – the conquest of Sicily. Moreover, the Allies were confronted by a difficulty of their own making in that there was no master-plan for the conduct of operations in the Mediterranean after the conquest of Sicily. Michael Howard has made the point that 'Hitler's continuing uncertainty even after the invasion of Sicily whether the main Allied thrust would really be directed against the Italian mainland was well-founded. The Allied leaders still did not know themselves.' It was not for want of trying on Churchill's part. After the Trident Conference in Washington he had flown to Algiers with Brooke and had attempted to persuade Eisenhower and Marshall to commit themselves to an invasion of the mainland as soon as Sicily was conquered. But the Americans chose to be circumspect, to wait and see how the Sicilian campaign went before deciding on the next step. They argued that the extent of resistance in Sicily would itself determine what should be done next. In this way the deadening effect of the compromise reached in Washington was beginning to make itself felt. Imperfect strategic calculation and decision was beginning to impose such tactical restraints on the conduct of operations that no large dividends could be realized. At the same time tactical uncertainties inhibited the possibility of great strategic prizes. And this was to be the pattern of affairs throughout the Italian campaign.

The result of disagreement at Algiers was that any decision about future operations was postponed until after the Sicilian invasion had got under way. Just before it did, both the British Chiefs of Staff in a telegram to the Combined Chiefs, and Mr Churchill in a letter to Eisenhower, reiterated their views. In the first case it was made clear that the British were convinced that the Allies must exploit *Husky* by taking offensive action on the mainland of Italy and so eliminate Italy from the war. Moreover, such action would contain the greater number of German forces. Churchill urged Eisenhower to 'put your right paw on the mainland as soon as possible. Rome is the bull's-eye.' As things began to go well during the first few days of the Sicilian battle, the Prime Minister minuted the Chiefs of Staff in stirring language:

> The question arises . . . why we should crawl up the leg like a harvest-bug from the ankle upwards? Let us rather strike at the knee. . . .
>
> Once we have established our Air power strongly in the Catanian plain and have occupied Messina, etc, why should we not use sea power and air power to land as high up in Italy as air fighter cover from the Catania area warrants?
>
> Let the planners immediately prepare the best scheme possible for landing on the Italian west coast with the objective the port of Naples and the march on Rome, thus cut off and leave behind all the Axis forces in Western Sicily and all ditto in the toe, ball, heel and ankle. It would seem that two or three good Divisions could take Naples and produce decisive results if not on the political attitude of Italy then upon the capital. Tell the planners to throw their hat over the fence; they need not be afraid there will not be plenty of dead weight to clog it.

It was just such bold and imaginative ideas that the Germans feared. They too need not have worried. Apart from the dead weight, there were the realities of the campaign in Sicily, which we shall look at shortly. But at least Churchill did succeed, while this campaign was still in progress, in getting Allied agreement to the invasion of the Italian mainland. His views were admirably expressed in a letter to Field-Marshal Smuts: 'I will in no circumstances allow the powerful British and British-controlled armies in the Mediterranean to stand idle. . . . Not only must we take Rome and march as far north as possible in Italy, but our right hand must give succour to the Balkan patriots. . . . I shall go to all lengths to procure the agreement of our Allies. If not, we have ample forces to act by ourselves.' His passionate concern both to help the Russians defeat the Germans and ease the way for the cross-Channel operation in the following year by doing what would bring honour to British arms is readily comprehensible to us now. Indeed what else could he have done? The tragedy was that success in Sicily, albeit with difficulty and Allied friction, was not to be matched by comparable success in Italy.

While Hitler and Mussolini had been conferring at Feltre, Eisenhower – spurred on by Marshall to consider the possibilities of a 'direct amphibious operation against Naples . . . if the indications regarding Italian resistance make risks worthwhile' – after consulting his commanders asked for formal approval of his recommendation that the war should be carried into Italy as soon as the reduction of Sicily had been completed, approval that was instantly forthcoming. All this enabled the British Chiefs of Staff to initiate further planning – for two eventualities, the first for an attack in the Naples area, the second an attack in the south of Italy. In his customary way, Churchill turned this into his picturesque language in a signal to Alexander:

> It would seem that after *Husky* is finished or has become certain you can use both the right and the left hand like a boxer and strike or feint as you choose. Only the Germans count. If they mass in the toe, ball and heel, great advantage will be gained by cutting in above near the knee if that is physically possible. . . .
>
> On the other hand if the Germans mass two or three divisions around Rome or Naples and you feel that their strength is beyond your powers, there is quite a good secondary gambit by capturing the toe, ball and heel and reaching out with seaborne supplies, agents, commandos and air power into Albania and Yugoslavia.

This planning gave rise to a further request by the British Chiefs of Staff that Allied resources in the Mediterranean area should in no way be diminished until the situation was clearer. But such a move, which to the Americans was further evidence of the British reluctance to stick to agreed priorities with regard to the Far East and *Overlord*, was most unwelcome to them, and they made it plain in their reply that as far as a possible attack in the Naples area was concerned, General Eisenhower would have to make do with the resources already made available to him. The U.S. Chiefs of Staff were certainly not intending to support any operations which would demand an increase in those forces agreed to for post-*Husky* activities. In any case, at this time, shortly after mid-July, 1943, the battle for Sicily itself was not going all that well.

We last saw Alexander 'thinking again' after giving 8th Army its orders on 13 July to capture Catania and the Leonforte-Enna road communications. Alexander, although renowed for his courage, charm, gentlemanliness and ability to get on with allies, was not in fact a great battlefield commander. Brooke observed that he 'had many very fine qualities, but no very great strategic vision'. Montgomery went further, describing Alex as 'a very dear person, but definitely not a commander in the field on a high level – nor does he understand the higher conduct of war. . . . He has never himself commanded an Army or a Corps in the field. . . . He does not understand the offensive and

mobile battle; he cannot make up his mind and give quick decisions. . . .
He does not think and plan ahead.' Above all Alexander did not 'grip'
the battle in Sicily [nor later in Italy] and, with two such subordinates
as Montgomery and Patton, grip was not merely desirable, it was
indispensable. In the absence of firm direction from above, Montgomery tried to grip the whole thing himself. On 12 July he recorded in his
diary:

> It was now becoming clear that the battle in Sicily required to be gripped
> firmly from above. I was fighting my own battle, and 7th American Army
> was fighting *its* battle; there was no co-ordination by 15 Army Group
> [Alexander]. Without such co-ordination the enemy might well escape;
> given a real grip on the battle I felt convinced we could inflict a disaster on
> the enemy and capture all his troops in Sicily.

Montgomery therefore attempted to get on without co-ordinating with
the Americans. But his efforts to break through into the Catanian plain
and to outflank the enemy to the left by pushing up the Vizzini-Enna
road failed, and 'with their failure,' wrote Nigel Hamilton, 'the Sicilian
campaign became for 8th Army a war of attrition'. In doing so it set the
scene for the entire battle for Italy. The trouble was that in this war of
attrition, the Germans were never worn down to the point where they
could hold on no longer until May, 1945, when, with the Russians
surrounding Berlin and about to link up with Eisenhower's armies on
the Elbe, with the Führer dead in his bunker, and the Wehrmacht in
ruins, the war was over anyway.

After Patton's triumphant capture of Palermo, he turned east to
advance along routes 113 and 120, determined to win the race for
Messina. 8th Army had been making little progress against the San
Stefano Line, and Patton's drive was checked by the combined efforts
of 15th and 29th Panzer Grenadier Divisions. On 25 July, therefore,
Alexander conferred with Montgomery and Patton to co-ordinate, at
last, the final stages of the campaign. The U.S. 7th Army was to aim at
Messina via San Stefano and Nicosia, while 8th Army would capture
Adrano and Paterno, thus forcing the enemy to withdraw from Catania.
Two days later Kesselring gave orders to his commanders that they
were to be prepared either to defend the San Stefano Line at all costs,
or to fight a covering battle to ensure their successful evacuation. The
issue was settled by the success of both the 7th and 8th Armies in their
attacks. By the end of the first week in August the Allies had captured

Catania, Adrano, Troina and San Fratello. General von Senger und Etterlin told Kesselring that if the German divisions were to be saved to fight again, as Hitler wanted, the time to order evacuation had arrived. Kesselring agreed and appropriate orders were sent to General Hube. Meanwhile Hitler had been tightening his grip on Italy itself.

The end of the Sicilian campaign – Patton's forces entered Messina on 16 August, while the remaining Axis troops crossed over to the mainland early next morning – coincided with Hitler's orders to Rommel that he should move his troops across the Italian frontier. We may consider first the significance of what had happened in Sicily, before looking at the strategic problem facing the Allies as they began to contemplate the invasion of Italy. The Sicilian campaign had lasted for 38 days.* Cost to the Allies had been some 20,000 men; the Axis had lost 164,000 in dead, wounded and mostly prisoners. Of these 130,000 were Italians. As General Sir William Jackson has put it, the race to Messina was won, not by the British or the Americans, but by the German commander, General Hube, who succeeded in evacuating 60,000 of his troops, complete with weapons and vehicles, to reinforce the growing strength of the German Army in southern Italy. Neverthe-less the Allies had achieved great successes and acquired invaluable experience. The handling of great armadas of warships and transports, together with their landing craft; the problems of airborne operations, to say nothing of close air support during amphibious assaults; the logistic requirements of landing supplies across open beaches; the sheer business of directing Anglo-American armies, with all the sensitivities created by *prima donna*-like commanders in the mould of Montgomery and Patton – all these were to be exploited in the great enterprise of *Overlord*, which was still almost a year away. Besides, Italy's leader had been toppled, his successor was on the point of breaking the Axis once and for all and the so-called Mediterranean strategy was paying off by giving the Allies two of the great tricks they had been playing for – diversion of German divisions from Russia and France and freedom of the Mediterranean Sea itself. Yet as General Jackson observed: 'The main strategic lesson of Sicily remained unnoticed at the time'. He was referring to the courageous and skilful way in which the Germans had conducted their defence. They had shown themselves to be masters of delay and withdrawal even in the

---

* The Italian campaign lasted 607 days.

face of overwhelming material strength in the air and on the ground. 'The performance of Hube's hard-pressed Panzer Corps,' wrote William Jackson, 'in the ideal defensive country which abounds in southern Europe should have made the strategic planners pause for a moment.' If it did not give them pause there and then, it would not be long before it did. By the time the Allies actually set foot in Italy, the Germans had *nineteen* divisions there. Twelve of them were mobile – panzer, panzer grenadier or parachute; seven were infantry, mountain or Jaeger divisions. Against this force the Allies, as we shall see, were proposing to throw a comparable number, but they would, of course, enjoy the advantage of choice of striking place and concentration. In their choice they amazed and delighted the Germans.

In making his plans for the invasion of Italy, it had of course been necessary for General Eisenhower to bear in mind what Badoglio and the Italian Government might do, and how the Germans would then react. The plans had to be adaptable to circumstances. No sooner had he given his decisions on 16 August, just as the conquest of Sicily was completed – the plan was that 8th Army under Montgomery would cross the Straits of Messina between 1 and 4 September while a week later, about 9 September, 5th Army under General Mark Clark would land at Salerno – than he heard that General Castellano had presented himself to the British Embassy in Madrid asking that arrangements should be made for Italy to change sides. What Hindenburg had warned Hitler about and Hitler himself had foreseen was about to come true.*

At this time the British Ambassador to Spain was Sir Samuel Hoare. General Castellano, who was the principal military assistant to the Italian Chief of General Staff, asked Hoare not only to accept an Italian surrender as soon as Allied troops set foot in Italy itself, but that agreement must be immediate because of the Germans' rapid reinforcing of Italy, which would mean that the Italian Army's freedom to act would soon cease. Hoare's consequent telegram to London contained some dramatic stuff:

> General Castellano informed me that he had come officially and with full authority from Marshal Badoglio to put before His Majesty's Government

---

*Lord Gort, when CIGS before the war, had commented to the German Military Attaché in London when he heard of the Pact of Steel: 'It's your turn this time'. Gort added, when the prospects of war between Germany and Great Britain were touched on, that if it should happen again the result would be the same as before.

the Italian position and to make a specific and very urgent proposal. The Marshal wished His Majesty's Government to know that Italy was in a terrible position. Practically the whole country was in favour of peace, the Italian Army was badly armed, there was no Italian Aviation and German troops were streaming in by the Brenner and the Riviera. Feeling against the Germans was intense. The Italian Government however, felt powerless to act until the Allies landed on the mainland. If and when, however, the Allies landed, Italy was prepared to join the Allies and fight against Germany. If the Allies agreed in principle to this proposal General Castellano would immediately give detailed information as to the disposition of German troops and stores and as to co-operation that the Italians would offer Mihailovic in the Balkans. General Castellano was also empowered to concert operations, eg. connected with the Allied landings from Sicily. Marshal Badoglio regarded it as essential that action should be taken immediately as every hour meant the arrival of more German units in Italy and at present there were thirteen Divisions and the German plan was to hold the line of the Apennines and Ravenna.

Although what Castellano had to say on two counts – Italy's readiness to surrender, even change sides, and Germany's steady reinforcements – seemed to show that the Allies were being successful in their dual aim of knocking Italy out of the war and obliging Germany to divert military forces there, his prediction of German intentions to hold a line so far north, even though at one time Hitler, anticipating bolder Allied action, feared he might have to do so, turned out to be so wide of the mark that it was not until the autumn of 1944 that the so-called Gothic Line became the scene of battle. And it was not until the following spring, the April of 1945, that it was finally broken by the Allies. All this meant that the whole purpose of following up from Sicily onto the mainland of Italy had been blunted almost out of recognition.

Yet to Mr Churchill, when he received a copy of Hoare's telegram in Quebec – where with the Chiefs of Staff he was conferring with the President and his advisers – the chance was not to be missed. The Allied leaders agreed that Castellano's proposal should be acted on at once. Accordingly Eisenhower was to be instructed to liaise with Castellano by sending staff officers to Lisbon with the so-called Short Terms. These stipulated that hostilities would cease at a time to be laid down by Eisenhower, shortly before Allied forces set foot on the mainland; the Allies and the Italian Government would announce the Armistice simultaneously; the Italians would instruct their armed forces and people to resist the Germans and collaborate with the Allies; Allied prisoners of war would be released; Italian shipping, naval and merchant, plus aircraft would move to Allied ports and airfields; those that could not were to be destroyed; until the Armistice was declared the Italians would resist passively. Although Eisenhower acted promptly, it was not until 27 August that General Castellano was back in Rome. As it had been agreed that the Italians must indicate their acceptance of Allied terms by 30 August, there was little time for them to make up their minds.

Meanwhile in Quebec the British and American military chiefs had been having familiar discussions and disagreements relating to the Mediterranean part in overall strategy. The Americans still harboured suspicions that the British were not wholly committed to *Overlord* at the time and with the strength already agreed. They thought, wrongly, that the British were still playing the Mediterranean game with a view to post-war political advantages. It was not so. What was true was that the British still believed that exploiting advantage in the Mediterranean would do more to help the success of *Overlord* than would the mere transfer of military strength from the Mediterranean area to the United Kingdom. Accordingly the British Chiefs of Staff summed up their position by making three recommendations: first, that *Overlord* should be carried out on the basis of the agreed plan as near as possible to the target date; second, that Eisenhower should fully exploit his victories and aim at the Milan-Turin area in order to ensure conditions for *Overlord*'s success; third, that resources for the Mediterranean campaign should be restricted to those necessary to produce those conditions essential to *Overlord*'s success.

The American position differed first in broad strategic concept. Whereas formerly some opportunism had been forced on the Allies by lack of resources, now it was necessary to abrogate opportunistic policies and stick to sound military plans which would result in the conduct of decisive operations at times and places of the Allies', not the enemy's, choosing. *Overlord* would do this, and therefore *Overlord* must not be jeopardized by exploiting local successes in secondary theatres. The second difference was the American reluctance to see what General Brooke described as 'the close relation that exists between cross-Channel and Italian operations'. They insisted that *Overlord* would always have over-riding priority where resources were short. This insistence verged on rigidity of view, giving no rein whatever to the possibility of a change of strategic priorities. It was a total dismissal of Churchill's concept of flexible manoeuvre – left-handed, right-handed or both-handed as opportunity, circumstances and material dictated. In particular the Americans were adamant that the seven battle-experienced divisions from the Mediterranean theatre, promised for *Overlord*, must be sent. In the end the two sides were able to agree that some flexibility was necessary, and that the two operations, in North-West Europe and the Mediterranean, *were* inter-dependent in effectively conducting the war for defeating Germany. While the main object would be to ensure the success of *Overlord*, it was acknowledged that such success would be contributed to by what happened elsewhere. This concession was made clear by a sentence in the paper which referred to 'the maintenance of unremitting pressure on German forces in Northern Italy and the creation, with available Mediterranean forces, of the conditions required for *Overlord* and of a situation favourable for the eventual entry of our forces, including the bulk of the re-equipped French Army and Air Force, into Southern France'. Ironically enough, although both the conditions required for *Overlord* – a sufficient diminution of German air and ground strength in western France – and a situation allowing entry into southern France *were* created, there was no question of unremitting pressure on German forces in northern Italy, at least not for a year. Hitler had made sure of that.

Rommel's record of his discussion with the Führer in East Prussia on 11 August summed up the latter's views. Like Rommel himself, Hitler did not believe in the Italians' honesty. They were playing for time and then would defect. The reason Churchill and Roosevelt were conferring was to persuade the Italians into treason. Hitler wanted to restore fascism as this was the only way of guaranteeing Italy's continued support [Rommel was already certain that the Fascist party, so hopelessly corrupt and so swiftly swept aside, would never be restored]. Hitler was displeased with Mackensen, Rintelen and Kesselring, because of their confidence in Badoglio. Although Rommel and Hitler saw eye-to-eye on the likelihood of Italian defection, Hitler would not agree that Kesselring should be removed, leaving Rommel in sole command of the German forces in Italy. He did, however, accept Rommel's broad concept of operations – delaying action in Sicily until forced to withdraw to the mainland, then fight from four defensive lines across the peninsula, first Cosenza-Taranto, then at Salerno, next Cassino, finally the Apennines. Three out of the four were to become battlefields of great moment.

In order to force the Italians to reveal their hand, Hitler instructed Rommel and Jodl to present them with a proposed joint plan for the defence of Italy. They met the Chief of Italian General Staff, General Roatta, at Bologna on 15 August. His reaction to the idea that Rommel was to command all German forces north of the Apennines and his own ideas as to positioning Italian formations where they could block the Germans further south told Jodl and Rommel all they needed to know. Jodl simply signalled to Hitler that their grounds for suspicion were confirmed. Hitler acted at once. Sicily would be evacuated, Vietinghoff's 10th Army was to move some mechanized divisions to the Salerno-Naples area, Rommel was to tighten his grip in the north. Hitler's directive made it plain that he now expected Italy to surrender to enemy pressure, sooner or later. It turned out to be sooner. Although Canaris's *Abwehr* failed to produce information, Himmler's intelligence agencies discovered on 26 August that Badoglio had asked the British for an armistice. Four days later the orders went out from Hitler's headquarters to prepare for Operation *Axis*. When execution was ordered, Italy would be occupied by the Germans, the Italians disarmed, all their weapons seized, and plans completed for the German forces to conduct a fighting withdrawal from the south towards Rome.

As had already been shown in Sicily, the Germans were very good at conducting withdrawals. Hitler had declared in December, 1942, that it was a thousand times easier to storm forward with an army and gain victories than to bring an army back in an orderly condition after a reverse or a defeat. Yet it was in this latter endeavour that the German Army was to show itself at its most admirable. Of course, it was to have much practice – on the Eastern Front, in the South and later, except for the extraordinary defiance of the Ardennes counter-offensive, in the West. For all that, to continue to contend every inch of the way back with courage, determination and tenacity, to say nothing of expert fieldcraft and economy, in the face of overwhelmingly superior resources on the ground and in the air, to counter Allied strategic ironmongery with tactical excellence – to do this was to write in the chronicles of military achievement something which every soldier of today is bound to award his approbation. In his own special way, Montgomery, even before the battle for Sicily was over, had been given a preview of what was to come and in a letter to Mountbatten he commented:

> I am now operating in very mountainous country – with Mt Etna towering above everything. It is ideal defensive country and the Bosche is fighting well and bravely, and with great determination. There is no doubt he is a very good soldier; he is far too good to be left 'in being' as a menace to the world, and *must* be stamped on. He was thrown right off his balance by the speed and violence of our initial assault; but he recovered well on the Etna line and is now fighting a very skilful delaying battle.

One glance at the nature of the Italian country is enough to show how ideal it is for defence and delay. Metternich once described Italy as a geographical expression. And now it was Italy's geography which would once again be dominant, for it greatly assisted and shaped the Germans' strategy and tactics, which in their turn cabin'd, cribb'd and confin'd Allied aspirations and endeavours. The Germans would not be thrown right off balance again – not at Salerno, nor Cassino, nor Anzio, nor the Gothic Line. The Allies were about to embark on a campaign which turned into a series of slow, slogging, indecisive and bloody battles, crossing river after river, storming mountain after mountain, in mud, rain and cold, with only discomfort, death and disillusion as company, and the disagreeable reflection that there would always be one more battle to fight.

6

OPPORTUNITY AND ADVANTAGE

Monty is tired out and Alex fails to grip the show.
Alanbrooke December, 1943

Disraeli once observed that the most important thing in life, next to knowing when to seize an opportunity, was to know when to forgo an advantage. In contemplating this aphorism we may discern the essential difference between the Germans' and the Allies' conduct of the Italian campaign. The Germans seized every opportunity going and never forewent an advantage. The Allies almost never failed to forgo advantage and let slip opportunity time and again. It was, of course, only when Italy was out of the war that the battle for Italy began in earnest. And it was in its beginnings that this respectively expert and inexpert juggling of advantage and opportunity may be illustrated.

Taking bold action to exploit opportunity and advantage is greatly facilitated when your military and political intelligence is good. In this respect the Allies appeared to have most of the cards in their hands. They *knew* that the Italians were going to get rid of Mussolini; they *knew* that Badoglio's government was prepared to conclude an armistice; they even *knew* when and how. The Germans guessed. Yet whereas the Allies' reactions were slow and cautious, and their commitment of resources niggardly, the Germans had no hesitation in harnessing those two great decisive assets, speed and concentration, and so stabilizing a dangerous situation. Before we look at the Allied action in more detail, we may recall that six weeks passed between the dismissal of Mussolini and the declaration of an armistice with Badoglio's government, six weeks in which Hitler tightened his hold on

Italy to the extent that he would be able to choose where and how to conduct defensive operations, six weeks during which the Allies had talked much and done little. It is true that Montgomery's 8th Army had crossed the Straits of Messina on 3 September to land on the toe of Italy in what Ronald Lewin described as an 'unopposed crossing, supported by a cascade of fire from his own artillery, from naval guns and from the air . . . pure *opéra bouffe* in which it is said that the only casualty was a puma that escaped from the zoo at Reggio'; it is also true that 5th Army landed at Salerno on 9 September, but the battle there became a desperate one, so much so that, when by the end of 1943 the Allies were still only seventy miles north of Salerno, Hitler agreed that Kesselring should establish the Winter Line across the peninsula only just north of Naples. The so-called Gustav Line, with its almost impregnable core, Cassino, was to give the Allies many months of struggle, frustration and bloodshed.

Initial disappointments of the Italian campaign were hardly to be wondered at. On 20 September, 1943, Montgomery noted in his diary:

> One cannot get away from the fact that I was ordered to invade the mainland of Europe without being given adequate resources, and without even being given any object . . . the High Command in this Mediterranean Theatre of War invaded Italy, and thus embarked on a major campaign on the continent of Europe, without having any clear idea – or plan – as to how they would develop the operations and fight the land battle. There was no object laid down. The whole affair was haphazard and untidy.

It was now, more than ever before, that the fundamental difference of view as to what could or could not be achieved in the Mediterranean theatre, held respectively by the Americans and the British, damaged their conduct of war. It explains why there was no proper directive to Eisenhower or Alexander or anyone else. Churchill had always been sympathetic to the idea of pursuing an offensive campaign in Italy; Marshall – for Roosevelt left much of America's strategic thinking to his Army Chief of Staff – still hoped for the best of both worlds, that is not too much commitment to Italy in view of *Overlord*, yet still pining for cheap victory. But, as Nigel Hamilton writes: 'The battle for Italy could not be won on the cheap, however much Eisenhower might fret about missed opportunities.' The fact is that once the Germans had deployed nearly twenty divisions to hang on to the bulk of Italy – arguably in itself more than sufficient justification from the Allied point of view in going to Italy at all – there were but two courses of action open to the Allies, either simply to keep roughly that number of German divisions busy while decision was sought on other fronts, or to concentrate so decisively on the Italian front that they would sweep everything before them. The latter option would never have been accepted by the Americans, so that all Eisenhower's talk blaming the Allies for lack of boldness which resulted in an expensive and unrewarding campaign really goes for nothing. The resources to be bold both in Italy and Normandy did not exist. Even Eisenhower's idea that the proposed airborne drop on Rome, which was quickly abandoned once the likely reaction of the Italians themselves was understood, ought to have been executed has little to support it.

The pity of it is that even those imaginative operations which were proposed and were practicable received little support from Alexander's headquarters. For example, William Stirling, commanding 2nd S.A.S. Regiment, had proposed that in September, 1943, some 300 men in jeep patrols landed by glider or simply dropped by parachute could disrupt communications in northern Italy to such an extent that reinforcements by rail or road from the north would be immensely difficult. Alas, he was not listened to. Nor was the legendary Shan Hackett who suggested a similar task for his own 4th Parachute Brigade. Brigadier Hackett had also made the memorable comment that if his brigade were to be employed at Salerno, using among other equipment United States Army gliders, the first people to be rounded up on landing would be the American glider pilots, who were liable to be much more of a nuisance than the Germans. How in fact, while Montgomery's 8th Army was making its way towards Bari and Foggia – Taranto had already been taken by the British 1st Airborne Division – was the battle of Salerno going?

As far as the first week went, not well is the answer. The landings had been timed to coincide with the Italian surrender – 8/9 September – and it was another instance of hoping for a quick and cheap victory, of gambling with insufficient resources and against all the odds of what the Italians and Germans were likely to do. It was a gamble that very nearly failed altogether. In the end it paid a small dividend. On 8 September Hitler, moved by his astonishing *Vorhersehung*, his intuition as to the occurrence of some great event, had flown from the Ukraine back to his East Prussian headquarters, primarily because he was worried about the situation in Italy, and whether when it came to the point the entire eighty Italian divisions at Badoglio's disposal would not defect to the enemy, and so create a problem there which might be beyond his capacity to solve. Sure enough on arrival at *Wolfsschanze*, he was shown a message indicating that the Italian peace proposals had been accepted by the British and were still under discussion with the Americans. Shortly afterwards the BBC announced Italy's surrender. By 8 pm that evening the codeword *Axis* had been signalled to Rome, where General Student took instant action. The Italian Army was disarmed, the King and Badoglio had fled to the south, German divisions deployed, Rome surrendered and Kesselring found himself master of Italy. Meanwhile the Allied convoys were sailing towards Salerno.

General Clark's 5th Army had the task of seizing the port of Naples and securing the airfields in that area, so establishing a firm base for further offensive operations. Although the landings themselves were successful, the German build-up against the beachhead enabled them to mount such dangerous counter-attacks that at one point General Clark contemplated re-embarking one of his corps to reinforce the other. But naval and air fire power, plus the approach of 8th Army from the south, together with the sheer dogged fighting of the Allied troops, won the day eventually. It had been a close-run thing. General Alexander's telegram to Mr Churchill dated 16 September shows how serious the situation had been:

I have just returned from an extensive tour of the Fifth Army front. . . . I am happier than I was twenty-four hours ago. The Germans have not put in a serious attack since night of 13th. This has given us time to improve our position somewhat, rest for very exhausted troops, and get some reinforcements of men and material in. Eighth Army are also drawing near. I have been able to issue certain directions. . . . Hold what we have gained; at all costs consolidating key positions by digging, wiring and mining. Reorganise scattered and mixed units and formations. Form local reserves and as strong a mobile reserve as possible. Inform troops of rapid approach of Eighth Army and flow of reinforcements now arriving day and night. Germans have been able to concentrate strong forces quicker than we have been able to build up sufficient forces to hold what had been gained in first rush. Germans hold most of the dominating features and overlook us onto the beach. Our troops are tired. There is very little depth anywhere; we have temporarily lost the initiative.

Nothing could more eloquently illustrate the hard realities of Salerno – an initial success in landing; a dangerous seesaw phase in which the German build-up and counter-attacks threatened the very existence of the beachhead; grim hanging on by the Allies with strong naval gunfire support and just enough reinforcement to enable the approach of 8th Army to persuade the Germans to retire. But the nature of the gamble was plain. The Italians had done nothing to support the Allies and the Germans had been free to concentrate against the landings, while holding 8th Army off with relative ease during the first crucial days. Montgomery's view of it all was hardly flattering to the Allied High Command:

> The original idea was that my Army was not to operate beyond the Catanzaro neck. But in actual fact I had to operate some 200 miles beyond that neck, and go very quickly too, and if I had failed to do so the whole of 5 American Army would have been pushed into the sea.
>
> As it turned out I just arrived in time to relieve the pressure, and make the Germans pull out.
>
> Even the enemy admits this. . . .
>
> The more one reflects on past events the more one is forced to the opinion that every operation teed-up by 15 Army Group heads straight for disaster and has to be pulled out of the fire by Eighth Army.
>
> If the High Command in the Mediterranean Theatre had not got such a first class army to do the business for them, they would have had one long series of disasters; in fact we would still be fighting in Africa.

Montgomery had recorded this in his diary on 20 September. Four days earlier General von Vietinghoff, commanding 10th Army, had advised Kesselring that the Allies could not now be turned out of Salerno. The beachhead was too strongly established. Kesselring agreed and the Germans went over to the defensive in order to slow down the subsequent advances of both 5th and 8th Army. In this they were notably successful.

One incident from the Salerno battle shows how tight the beachhead was. 10th British Corps was commanded by that great cavalry soldier, General Dick McCreery, and Alexander has recalled that although the Salerno landings caused him some anxious moments, it was the personal example and dynamic influence of McCreery and his Corps which ensured that a firm footing was obtained. Indeed there are those who suggest that had McCreery not shown his American colleague what to do, the U.S. 6th Corps would have been driven into the sea.

McCreery was constantly seen dashing about in his jeep by himself when the battle was not going well. His calm, almost casual, manner was an inspiration to everyone. Always determined to see things for himself, he very nearly landed himself in enemy hands, and as it was, was subjected to a nasty ambush and a close shave. As he described it:

> The bridgehead position was very restricted at the time, but near the boundary between two divisions, there was an area of no-man's-land where I thought we had established reconnaissance patrols. I wished to have a look for a good Observation Post in this area. We drove forward and I suddenly suspected that we had gone rather far. I got out and ordered the scout cars to turn round while I looked through my glasses. Just as we were doing so, anti-tank guns opened up at very short range on the vehicles, setting them on fire, and small arms fire made it pretty hot for us. We had almost done what had been done so often in the war – motored straight into the enemy.

The officer accompanying McCreery, Hugh Vivian-Smith, remembered that while they were peering through their binoculars a deafening explosion brewed up the leading armoured car, instantly followed by a second one going up in flames, and that, after taking cover for a few minutes, McCreery announced that he was going to run for it. As they started off together, Vivian-Smith saw a bullet strike the sand between them. 'Look out, Sir,' he cried. 'What's the good of looking out, you bloody fool? Come on,' was the uncompromising reply. They succeeded in walking out of the ambush, although disturbed by a low-flying Messerschmitt spraying machine-gun fire all over the place. 'My God, we're a couple of bloody fine soldiers,' observed the Corps Commander as they found their way back to McCreery's headquarters. 'There,' remembered Vivian-Smith

> General Alex was walking about waiting. I myself was covered with sweat and dust and had twisted an ankle, but the Corps Commander was as though he had just washed and shaved, and entered directly into a discussion with General Alex.

It was not every Corps Commander who was keen to be so far forward in the battle area. McCreery was an exception, and two of his subordinate divisional commanders, Keightley and Templer, often found their Corps Commander in front of them. On one occasion Templer was told by him, 'Ah – it's all right for you to go on now.'

Hitler's reaction to Salerno had been characteristic of his attitude to military developments from 1943 onwards. *Festung Europa* was to be inviolate. Defiance was the order of the day. The invaders would be thrown back into the sea. Not a yard, not an inch of territory was to be yielded. Then, when the harsh unrealities of such a notion were demonstrated beyond doubt, comfort was to be drawn from such reflections as: 'No more invasions for them! They are much too cowardly for that. They only managed the one at Salerno because the Italians gave their blessing'. Further comfort was to be forthcoming, as David Irving has pointed out, from the apparent incompetence and lack of daring which the Allies were showing. There had been no attempt to land in the Balkans where a welcome from the local inhabitants awaited them. There had been no question of exploiting the Italian defection by boldly landing north of Rome. And the ponderous progress of the Allied armies already in Italy – all these things reassured him. Moreover, the rescue of Mussolini had been a spectacular success.

It had been a long time – five and a half years in fact – since Hitler had assured Mussolini, because of his neutral attitude at the time of the *Anschluss*, that he would never forget him, that he would stick to the Duce if ever he were in danger or needed help, whatever happened, even though the whole world were against him. He was as good as his word. After Skorzeny had effected his daring airborne rescue of Mussolini on 13 September, the two dictators had met once more at Hitler's headquarters. It could not be said that Mussolini was still 'the greatest son of Italian soil since the collapse of the Roman Empire'. All he desired now was to be done with politics for ever and retire to his home in the Romagna. But such an exit did not fit Hitler's ideas at all. The Duce must still play a part, be restored as the Leader of Fascism, in theory head of the new Italian Socialist Republic, in practice a prisoner of the S.S., hated by his own people, held in contempt by his gaolers, and even obliged to hand over his own son-in-law, Ciano, the former Foreign Minister, to be executed by a Fascist firing squad. Hitler, with that colossal self-delusion that only he was capable of, convinced himself that the world, and in particular the British, would applaud such staunch friendship. 'The British will say: "He's a friend indeed".'

It was, of course, Nelson who had repeated that phrase in referring to Collingwood just as the crescendo of Trafalgar was about to break over the British and Franco-Spanish fleets, Nelson, who possessed the four aces of leadership – imagination, ability to inspire, proper use of subordinates and the offensive spirit – all wrapped up in such an understanding and love of the lower deck that he became the observed of all observers, the hero of all heroes, the model to which so many subsequently aspired. The idea that Hitler could be anyone's 'friend' simply reminds us of Macbeth's pact with the weird sisters and taking a bond of fate. Yet it cannot be denied that if we forget all about the magic that Nelson inspired in his band of brothers, Hitler did possess to an extraordinary degree the leadership aces. His imagination was unbridled; he held an entire nation spellbound by sheer force of personality alone; his use of subordinates was ruthlessly efficient; and the offensive spirit in him never died until he himself did. The essential difference was that whereas Nelson made the whole Fleet, and indeed the whole nation, love him, Hitler was in Churchill's words 'an evil man, a monstrous abortion of hatred and defeat'.

Not that Hitler was prepared to recognize, even late in 1943, the possibility, let alone the likelihood, of defeat. Yet the situation in the East deteriorated relentlessly. After the failure of the Wehrmacht's Kursk offensive, the Russians advanced and simply went on advancing. All those strategic centres which had gone down to the Germans so easily in 1941 now fell to the Russians like a row of dominoes – Orel and Kharkov in August, 1943, Poltava and Smolensk in September, Kiev in November, Zhitomir in December. The Donetz basin and the Crimea, whose capture had been of such great consequence before, now were lost or cut off. The whole game in the East was going wrong, and in doing so, by virtue of Hitler's inflexible defensive methods, resulted in huge losses of men and equipment which could never be made good. The Battle of the Atlantic had been lost. The battle for the skies of Germany was hardly contested by the Luftwaffe. In the West invasion was awaited. Only in the South did there appear to be any sort of stability. Hanging on to Greece and Crete was easy enough. There was no enemy incursion there. And hanging on in Italy, where indeed the enemy were in strength, did not seem too difficult. Certainly neither 5th Army under Clark nor 8th Army under Montgomery posed too great a threat. How in fact were these armies getting on and why were they so slow?

Winston Churchill called it 'Deadlock on the Third Front', which might well be taken as a fitting comment on the entire Italian campaign. Once Hitler had accepted Kesselring's advice that the battle for Italy should be waged as far south as possible and allowed him the military resources to wage it soundly, there was only one way in which the Allies could have reversed the situation – by committing so much strength to Alexander's 15th Army Group that he could have beaten Kesselring by sheer weight of numbers alone. Far from doing this the Allies were about to deplete Alexander of what superiority he had. The winter line chosen by Kesselring was one of immense natural strength. On the Adriatic side it was based on the River Sangro, then ran across the mountainous centre to the River Garigliano in the west. It was a defensive position enhanced by mountains and river lines, which the approaching winter weather was to make even more formidable, and it was to be manned by troops who were not only skilled in defensive fighting, but brilliant and bold improvisers at every level of command.

By mid-September, with the Salerno bridgehead secure and 8th Army heading for Potenza, Alexander wrote to his two Army commanders, Clark and Montgomery, outlining the way in which he saw operations developing during the next month or so. Rarely can there have been a grosser misappreciation of either what the Germans would do or his own Armies be capable of. He foresaw operations in four phases: first consolidation of the general line Salerno to Bari; next the capture of Naples and of the Foggia airfields; third the taking of Rome and its airfields; then getting Leghorn and the communication centres of Florence and Arezzo. There was even a broad timetable to go with this plan – Gaeta to Termoli by the end of the first week of October; the Rome-Terni area a month later; Lucca – Ravenna by the end of November [Ravenna was not to fall to the Allies until *a year later!*]. How quickly disillusion was to set in! Naples was taken by the end of September and Foggia too, but thereafter the Germans rapidly stabilized their positions on the Volturno-Termoli line. By 24 October Alexander was painting a very different picture, summed up in a review of the situation submitted to Churchill and Roosevelt.

He pointed out that at the time of the Salerno landings and the announcement of the Italian armistice, there had been some eighteen German divisions in Italy – two in Calabria, one in the heel, three to the south of Rome able to interfere at Salerno, three more near Rome itself and nine in the north. It had been accepted that there would be risks in landing at Salerno, but that the great adaptability which the Allies enjoyed by virtue of their amphibious capability and air superiority, together with the German need to deal with a dangerous internal problem, would justify these risks. Moreover, Allied landing craft would enable them to deploy some twenty divisions by the end of the year, backed up by appropriate air forces. Now, however, the situation was very different. Not only had the Germans got nine divisions in the line, with fifteen more in the north, possibly nineteen, but the Allies, with a mere eleven now deployed, could not achieve a rate of build-up to match the Germans. At best 15th Army Group would have thirteen divisions by the end of November, perhaps two more a month later, and at most a total of seventeen by January, 1944. The enemy, on the other hand, could if they chose rapidly build up their strength to *sixty* divisions despite Allied air superiority. Moreover, Alexander's report went on:

> A stabilized front south of Rome cannot be accepted, for the capital has a significance far greater than its strategic location, and sufficient depth must be gained before the Foggia airfields and the port of Naples can be regarded as secure. This being so, the seizure of a firm defensive base north of Rome becomes imperative . . . we cannot afford to adopt a purely defensive role, for this would entail the surrender of the initiative to the Germans.

Alexander's report went on to say that the German intention was clearly to hold a line south of Rome in country favourable to the defence, where it would not be possible to take advantage of Allied superiority in tanks and guns. The inevitable bad weather would hinder use of air power. And whereas the enemy would find it easy to relieve tired troops from the north, the Allies would not be able to do so. It appeared therefore that the Allies would be

> committed to a long and costly advance to Rome, a 'slogging match' with our present slight superiority in formations on the battle-front offset by the enemy opportunity for relief: for, without sufficient resources in craft, no outflanking amphibious operation of a size sufficient to speed up our rate of advance is possible.

How right Alexander turned out to be about the slogging match. It may be questioned, however, whether he remembered his words about the outflanking amphibious operation when the Anzio landings turned out to be such a disappointment. His conclusions from this survey were that although things had looked fairly rosy in September, the position now was that the battle of the build-up was not being won by the Allies and that the resources available for amphibious operations confined such ventures to ones of 'local character'. Delay south of Rome might be such that the initiative might pass to the Germans. In this way, we may comment, the opportunity created by the Italian defection and the advantages conferred on the Allies by sea and air power, together with a clear holding of the initiative then, had been more or less chucked away to produce little more than stalemate. To Churchill conclusions of this sort were intolerable. He signalled to Roosevelt on 26 October:

> You will have seen by now Eisenhower's report [Eisenhower had simply forwarded Alexander's paper to the President and Prime Minister] setting forth the condition into which we are sinking in Italy. We must not let this great Italian battle degenerate into a deadlock. At all costs we must win Rome and the airfields to the north of it. The fact that the enemy have diverted such powerful forces to this theatre vindicates our strategy. No one can doubt that by knocking out Italy we have enormously helped the Russian advance in the only way in which it could have been helped at this time. I feel that Eisenhower and Alexander must have what they need to win the battle in Italy, no matter what effect is produced on subsequent operations.

It was on this last point that the American and British leaders would never be able to reach agreement. Marshall's view was clearly that the commanders in Italy had adequate resources to fight the battle there. That they were adequate to fight battles was made plain by subsequent events. It was equally clear that those battles would not be decisive.

Having decided to establish a winter line based on the Garigliano and Rapido rivers in the west, then through Cassino and the central mountain range and on along the Sangro, Kesselring's task was clear – to delay the Allied advance and exact as many casualties as possible until this winter line was ready. So it turned out. In October and November Montgomery's 8th Army made their way slowly and painfully to the Sangro, while 5th Army under Clark crossed the Volturno and edged their way towards the series of mountainous ridges which barred their progress to Cassino. Fred Majdalany, who fought so gallantly in the campaign and whose book about Cassino has never been bettered, described precisely the frustrating and seemingly insoluble problem facing the Allies at this time:

> The pattern of battle seldom varied. The Germans would hold a position for a time until it was seriously contested: then pull back a mile or two to the next defendable place, leaving behind a trail of blown bridges, minefields and road demolitions. There was always a new defendable place at hand. The Allied armies would begin with a night attack – ford the stream or river

after dark, storm the heights on the far side, dig themselves in by dawn, and hope that by the time the Sappers, following on their heels, would have sufficiently repaired the demolitions and removed the obstacles to permit tanks to follow up and help consolidate the new positions. The Germans, watching these proceedings from their next vantage point, would attempt to frustrate them by raining down artillery and mortar fire on their own recently vacated positions.

This pattern persisted throughout the campaign. A year later, while contesting the Gothic Line positions, we were still doing the same thing. While this ponderous advance was taking place, Montgomery was noting in his diary that the Germans were bringing more divisions into Italy – once they had decided that the Allies were not going to invade the Balkans, there were more divisions to spare. This reinforcement, together with the arrival of the Italian winter – in its recipe of cold drenching rain and endless mud it was quite as effective a stop to military operations as the sheer cold of the Russian version – made it impossible for the Allies to achieve spectacular results. Progress, observed Montgomery, was bound to be slow and difficult. He went on to touch the nub of the problem. As the Allies had not got the resources to conduct two major campaigns simultaneously, one or the other must have priority. 'If Western Europe is to be the main theatre, then turn the tap on there; in this case you must not expect spectacular results in Italy.' Quite apart from this there was the continued lack of grip, which Montgomery had been decrying throughout the campaign. Montgomery himself was shortly to leave Italy in order to take a proper grip of *Overlord*. Before he went 8th Army succeeded in crossing the Sangro, but there was no pursuit, no rapid advance to Pescara, no cracking of the German winter line. There was always another river in the way – there was the Sangro, the Moro, beyond that the Foro, and then the Pescara. As it became clear to Montgomery that there would be no question of taking Rome in 1943, he was writing to the Director of Military Operations in the War Office, General Simpson, that if there were to be a front opened up in Western Europe, then Italy should simply be held during the winter months and then in the spring used, by means of an offensive into the Po valley, to draw enemy divisions from France, and at the same time provide an alternative theatre for a main effort in the case that the offensive in France were not wholly successful. In this we hear an echo of Churchill's 'left-handed, right-handed or both-handed' strategy.

Montgomery was also highly critical of the way in which Clark committed 5th Army formations piecemeal, as he saw it, combat teams fighting enemy combat teams all along the front with no proper concentration anywhere. Certainly, in spite of dogged fighting for the Mignano Gap, in particular for Monte Camino and Monte Trocchio, 5th Army had exhausted itself – eight divisions had taken six weeks to advance seven miles and had suffered 16,000 casualties – and all this, not for the German main defensive positions, but merely for delaying positions short of the main defences. The distraction for the Allies, and the cost in men and material [the use of 200,000 shells at Monte Camino had earned it the title of Million Dollar Hill] were becoming formidable indeed. As Fred Majdalany put it: 'It consummated the pattern of fighting in Italy: the monotonous, heart-breaking, exhausting, seemingly pointless battle for one great obstacle only to be faced immediately afterwards by another.' If this was to be the cost of reducing a mere delaying position, Majdalany went on to ask, what was it going to be like 'when the finest German troops, the geography of Italy, and the full fury of midwinter conspired together in defence?' The answer was to be found in one word – Cassino.

Yet even before the Battle of Cassino had been joined, plans were being made to speed up the campaign in order that Rome could be captured earlier. We have seen that after the Cairo Conference Churchill was quick to seize on the possibility of retaining some landing craft in order to loosen up the Italian front. When Montgomery heard of the idea of a landing near Rome, he dismissed it as 'complete nonsense', pointing out the uncertainty of the weather, the ease with which German panzer divisions could concentrate against a landing, and the relatively few suitable places for such a venture, all of which would be watched. His view was shared by the highly competent British Deputy Chief of Staff, HQ 5th Army, Charles Richardson, who even echoed Montgomery's language, calling Anzio 'a complete nonsense from its inception'. It had always been clear, he maintained, that unless the Germans panicked – not much of a likelihood if their customary behaviour was anything to go by – any landing force would quickly be contained. So, as we shall see, it turned out. Yet if there were to be any alternative to climbing up the leg of Italy like a harvest bug, another attempt to strike higher up would have to be made. What surprised the Germans was firstly how unimaginatively far south the blow fell, and secondly the utter lack of drive and initiative shown by the Allies after their landing had been effected. Even Anzio made little difference to the slow and ponderous way in which the Allies were to advance. It looked as if Montgomery's prediction that, if the Allies wanted Rome, they would have to fight their way forward by land would prove accurate. Montgomery would not be there to see it. In his reflections on the Italian campaign, he summed up the post-Salerno operations like this:

> After the Salerno front had been saved, the two armies lined up side by side. We then moved North-West up Italy; there was no co-ordination, no plan, no grip; I did what I liked, Clark did what he liked. Finally we arrived at a situation on 17 November when the Fifth Army was exhausted, and was incapable of further action.
>
> I had to continue the battle alone, and this made it easier for the Germans.
>
> 15 Army Group definitely failed to grip the battle and to co-ordinate the action of the land armies. . . . Ad hoc plans were suddenly produced for various situaitons; there was no planning ahead, and no firm grip on the campaign after it had started. . . . Alexander knows nothing about it; he is not a strong commander and he is incapable of giving firm and clear decisions as to what he wants. In fact no one ever knows what he *does* want, least of all his own staff; in fact he does not know himself.

Without Montgomery there, how would Alexander get on? As it transpired, he was able to supervise two successful battles – one the battle for Rome, the other, the final battle of the campaign. He was also able to raise Churchill's hopes – hopes which were, alas, never fulfilled – that a reversal of the Allied decision to invade southern France in support of the Normandy landings would result in a great coup which, as part of his Mediterranean strategy, would transform the war situation. Alexander's name would also live on in his connection with two military epics which figure so prominently in the annals of British and German wartime endeavour – Anzio and Cassino. But it was quite plain that his name would never be associated with the bold exploitation of opportunity or advantage. This distinction he surrendered to his opposite number, Field-Marshal Albert Kesselring.

7

THE BATTLE FOR ROME

And death is on the air like a smell of ashes!
Ah! can't you smell it?
And in the bruised body, the frightened soul
finds itself shrinking, wincing from the cold . . .

D. H. Lawrence

The Battle of Cassino lasted for more than four months, from 15 January, 1944, when Allied shells first fell on Monastery Hill, until 18 May when the Poles occupied the Abbey itself. It began too soon and went on for too long. It started early in order to help bring about success at Anzio. Success at Anzio would have ended the battle much more quickly, but there was to be no success there. Once again opportunity and advantage were squandered. The Allies might afterwards congratulate themselves on dogged courage in the face of skilled and determined resistance and counter-attack, but the whole idea of Anzio was to break the deadlock. It did nothing of the sort. On Christmas Day, 1943, Churchill had sent a telegram to Roosevelt after conferring with Eisenhower and his principal commanders. He reported:

General Alexander is prepared to execute the landing at Anzio about January 20 if he can get a lift of two divisions. This should decide the Battle for Rome, and possibly achieve the destruction of a substantial part of enemy's army . . . For this purpose eighty-eight L.S.T.s are required. These can only be obtained by delaying the return home of fifty-six L.S.T.s due to leave the Mediterranean from January 15 onward . . . Having kept these fifty-six L.S.T.s in the Mediterranean so long, it would seem irrational to remove them for the very week when they can render decisive service.

Churchill went on to deplore the idea of allowing the Italian battle to stagnate and fester further. They could not afford to leave a huge unfinished job behind them. Therefore the effort to bring off Anzio with two divisions on about 20 January commended itself to all those conferring, and Alexander had been instructed to make preparations. 'If this opportunity is not grasped,' the Prime Minister concluded, 'we must expect the ruin of the Mediterranean campaign in 1944.' Thus he sought the President's agreement to keeping the fifty-six landing craft for three more weeks after 15 January. Three days later Roosevelt signalled his agreement on the understanding that *Overlord* remained the paramount operation and that its agreed timing would not be delayed. Churchill recorded his delight at this decision. Alexander's plan was to use one American and one British division under an American corps commander. The attack was planned for 20 January* and some days before that Alexander would launch an offensive against the Cassino line in order to draw enemy reserves away from areas where they might be well placed to interfere with the Anzio landings. There was, however, one snag to this admirable strategic idea. If the attack on Cassino were to precede the Anzio landings on 22 January by any proper interval, there would be no time for a prepared battle. It would be a continuation of an advance that had been going on for months in bad weather conditions and with exhausted troops. As Fred Majdalany put it: 'The fact remains that the first assault on one of the most powerful defensive systems of the war was an *ad hoc* affair, hastily undertaken without anything like proper pre-paration.' It was hardly surprising, therefore, that the strategy failed.

On 12 January Alexander had given his directions to Clark's 5th Army. The momentum of the advance had to be maintained to the absolute limit of their capabilities. The enemy would then be obliged by the landings in his rear [at Anzio] to react to this threat to his communications, so weakening his main defences and thus allowing a breakthrough there, which in turn would permit the two thrusts by 5th Army to link up. One of 5th Army's intelligence summaries at this time suggested that the enemy's strength in the Cassino line would be insufficient to withstand a co-ordinated Army attack. It went on to argue that as this attack would be launched before the

---

*Later postponed to 22 January.

Anzio landings, the two things together would cause him to withdraw. Never was there a greater mis-appreciation of the Germans' capacity or perseverance. Clark had decided to implement his directive like this. On 17 January McCreery's 10th Corps would assault across the River Garigliano to the extreme west, then turn east towards the Liri valley; three days later the U.S. 2nd Corps would cross the Rapido, some five miles to the south of Cassino, and break through to the Liri valley, while the Free French Corps would make their way through the mountainous country north of Cassino and then turn south-west; finally, two days after that, on 22 January, the ace of Anzio would be played. As things turned out, the British and French Corps made some progress, but not enough to affect the crucial centre where the 36th Texas Division tried to cross the Rapido in a two-day battle which ended in disastrous and costly failure. At Anzio itself, despite gaining surprise, the American corps commander, Lucas, made no attempt to exploit his initial success, push on inland to gain depth and establish a proper defensive zone. He simply sat down by the sea and allowed Kesselring to seal off the beachhead. Churchill's memorable comment was that a wild cat hurled ashore had become a stranded whale. How had it all come about?

General Westphal, Kesselring's able Chief of Staff, subsequently commented that one of the advantages enjoyed by the Germans was that they had made many contingency plans for dealing with possible Allied invasions, so that if and when the Allies landed here or there in Italy, the mere issue of a codeword would initiate the appropriate counter action, with troops to be used, routes, timings all laid down and understood by those required to execute these prearranged plans. At the time of the Anzio landings, apart from a few coastal batteries, there were only two German battalions in the neighbourhood. 'The road to Rome,' wrote Westphal, 'was open. No one could have stopped a bold advance-guard entering the Holy City.' But to the Germans' further surprise, their enemies kept quiet and simply got on with the business of building up their beachhead. Two days later sufficient reinforcements had arrived and, under command of von Mackensen's 14th Army, the sealing-off operation got under way. Nor was this all. Hitler had also made it clear that the Cassino defences of the Gustav Line must be held at all costs. The Führer expected the 'bitterest struggle for every yard'. He was not disappointed. On 28 January Churchill, already seriously concerned about the slow progress being made, signalled to General Alexander his satisfaction on learning that Clark was about to visit the Anzio beachhead – 'It would be unpleasant if your troops were sealed off there and the main army could not advance up from the south'. He could hardly have been more prophetic. On the same day Hitler sent a message to Kesselring, couched in the dramatic language which he used to conceal the gravity of his strategic situation:

> In the next few days the Battle for Rome will break out . . . It must be fought in holy wrath against an enemy who is waging a pitiless war of extermination against the German people, who shuns no means to that end, who is devoid of all higher ethical purpose, and who is intent only on the destruction of Germany and thereby of our European culture.

In fact the battle for Rome had already broken out. The Allies, alas, could not break out. Few battles in Italy caused so much controversy as Anzio. We must remember that when the U.S. 6th Corps landed early on the morning of 22 January they met virtually no opposition. A few hundred sleeping German soldiers, who had been withdrawn from the Cassino line for a rest, were rounded up and that was all. By the end of that day the best part of two divisions, nearly 40,000 men with some 3,000 vehicles, were safely ashore. Alexander, in reporting to Churchill, told him that they had gained almost complete surprise and that he had given instructions for strong mobile patrols to be pushed boldly forward to make contact with the enemy. Churchill replied that he was glad to know that claims were being pegged out, rather than the troops just digging in on the beachhead. There was every reason for doing this since Allied intelligence, which proved to be remarkably accurate as to the likely German reaction, had made it clear that the first two days would be crucial for moving inland, seizing some of the important ground there and giving the invasion forces some proper depth to their defences when the inevitable German counter-attack materialized. Yet General Lucas, commanding 6th Corps, made no attempt to exploit his initial success or push on deep inland. He sat down, occupied the beachhead and built up troops and supplies. A week after the landing four Allied divisions were holding an area some fifteen miles long and about eight miles deep. Facing and containing them were components of eight German divisions, none of which had been withdrawn from the Cassino position. The gamble had failed, and Churchill, principal architect of the venture, was bitterly disappointed that what he had regarded as so splendid an opportunity had been thrown away. When he was informed that two weeks after the landing there were 18,000 vehicles, not counting tanks, in the beachhead to serve a total of some 70,000 troops his comment was that the Allies must be enjoying a great superiority of chauffeurs. But what good was that? It was infantry that mattered.

By 11 February Alexander was signalling to Churchill that the first phase of the operation, which had promised so much, was over because of the speed with which the enemy had been able to concentrate against the beachhead. Now would begin the second phase – that of defeating the enemy's counter-attacks. Then with that done, the offensive would be renewed to push forward and cut enemy communications between Rome and the Cassino position. If we leave aside the success of the initial landings, it might be said that the only other success achieved was that of defeating these counter-attacks by von Mackensen's 14th Army which took place between the middle and end of February. By this time General Truscott had replaced Lucas, and Truscott, who showed himself to be a brave and competent commander, dismissed all ideas in his memoirs written after the war of there being an opportunity to charge forward, cut German communications and move swiftly on to Rome. His view was that the whole concept had two fatal flaws – an over-estimation of the effect such a landing would have on the German High Command and an under-estimation of their ability to counter the landings. He made much of Kesselring's own post-war point that Anzio was a half-way measure and not powerful enough in its initial phase. The basic mis-appreciation, of course, was that the Anzio landings would cause the Germans to withdraw from or weaken their Cassino defences.

All this is very well, but does not alter the fact that in the first two days Lucas had great freedom of manoeuvre, that he could have advanced further inland and seized good tactical ground, and so have been in an even better position to withstand and defeat the counter-attacks, which would come sooner or later, from a properly organized defensive position with some depth to it. Ronald Lewin in his *Ultra* book points out that Mark Clark's subsequent claim that 6th Corps had to dig in because Ultra sources had revealed German reinforcements to be on the way is specious and absurd, since these reinforcements could not possibly arrive until a week had passed. As General McCreery said to the British Liaison officer with Lucas: 'You're a cavalry officer. Why didn't you push on?'

In all this we may sympathize with Churchill's frustration and disappointment. It was he who had pressed so hard for the war to be taken into Italy; it was he who had constantly urged bold strategic moves which would make maximum use of the Allies' undoubted superiority in air and amphibious resources; it was he who had persuaded Roosevelt to keep certain landing craft in the Mediterranean area so that the Anzio operation could take place; he had even telegraphed to Stalin telling him of the launching of a big attack against the German armies defending Rome and gave promise of good news before long. But Churchill was getting used to disappointments and the account he gave to the House of Commons on 22 February as to the course of the Anzio battle did to some extent produce a justification of his strategy:

> It was certainly no light matter to launch this considerable army upon the seas – forty or fifty thousand men . . . with all the uncertainty of winter weather. . . . The landing was virtually unopposed. Subsequent events did not, however, take the course which had been hoped or planned. In the upshot we got a great army ashore. . . .
>
> The German reactions to this descent have been remarkable. Hitler has apparently resolved to defend Rome with the same obstinacy which he showed at Stalingrad, in Tunisia, and recently in the Dnieper bend. No fewer than seven extra German divisions were brought rapidly down from France, Northern Italy, and Yugoslavia, and a determined attempt has been made to destroy the bridgehead and drive us into the sea. Battles of prolonged and intense fierceness have been fought. At the same time the American and British Fifth Army to the southward is pressing forward with all its strength.
>
> On broad grounds of strategy, Hitler's decision to send into the south of Italy as many as eighteen divisions, involving something like half a million Germans, and to make a secondary front in Italy is not unwelcome to the Allies. We must fight the Germans somewhere, unless we are to stand still and watch the Russians. This wearing battle in Italy occupies troops who could not be employed in other greater operations, and it is an effective prelude to them.

In this way Churchill consoled himself that the Italian campaign was paying the right sort of dividend. Yet it was still not really of great concern to Hitler. He had, of course, hoped that the Anzio beachhead could be eliminated. 'If we can wipe them out down there,' he observed, 'then there won't *be* an invasion anywhere else.' But he was not willing to back this wishful thinking to the extent of denuding France of freshly formed panzer divisions, and when it became clear at the beginning of March that von Mackensen's attempts to drive the Allies out of Anzio had failed, he reconciled himself to a mere holding operation in the South. What was happening in the East, and what he suspected was about to take place in the West – these things were of far greater moment. But what was the fighting in Anzio like?

We have no better recorder of events from the infantryman's point of view than Raleigh Trevelyan. His Anzio diary gives us the feel and the smell and the comradeship of battle. At one time his slit trench was so close to the enemy's positions that he and his companions had little to fear from mortars, but there were plenty of other unpleasantnesses:

> Snipers and hand grenades were the main worry, not counting shells falling short and airbursts. All night long the artillery and mortars of both sides kept up a non-stop barrage. The screeching and whirring of the shells over our heads might have been some furious gathering of witches on Walpurgis Night. Sometimes the explosions were close enough for us to see shreds of flame spurting upwards in the dark, and the sharpnel would come hissing at us on all sides. We grew to distinguish the sound of various guns, as if they were voices – some were alto, some bass, some grumbly, some like baying wolves, some as retchy as the cough of a tubercular in his last stages. But all these were more or less noises off; nearer to hand were the staccato *eugh-eugh* of two-inch mortars, the snarly spandau-ripple, the more deliberate bren-crackle, and the swift searing whine past of a single bullet, generally tracer and half-seen like a miniature comet.

One of the men in his platoon seems to be showing signs of what became well known as 'bomb-happiness'. Why were they at Anzio, this soldier would ask? Why didn't they either get on or get out? It was just a waste of men on both sides. He didn't want to kill a German, any more than a German wanted to kill him. Trevelyan noted:

> This boredom *does* get you down, and there's no doubt that one's nerves are worn thin by the mere lack of news and the nagging feeling all the time that something is brewing up. We do nothing but watch and wait. Stag comes at dusk, and again at dawn. Twice a day we expect the attack that never materialises. Our weapons are cocked, our eyes strain into the twilight; the slightest gust of wind causes palpitations. It will be a relief to be in danger again.

He did not have long to wait:

> Yesterday we had to fetch back the Browning ammo from the observation post, so I went up the gully with four men. As we came round the last corner, I could see the arch of the bridge thirty yards off, quite distinctly in the moonlight. I was afraid to go on, and I could sense that the men were faltering too. The frogs were not croaking. Then it happened like this: from the trenches ahead there was a rattle of bolts, a shout – *Feuer* – and a spandau, then two spandaus, opened up at us. I saw red rods darting by me, and the little flames from the barrels of the spandaus.
>
> We doubled back round the corner. I was untouched, but three of the others were wounded, one very badly with a bullet in his neck. The fourth, Jolly – he was nineteen – I think was killed. We haven't yet been able to recover him.

If Raleigh Trevelyan was our best chronicler of Anzio, Fred Majdalany was of Cassino.

We have seen that the battle of Anzio began to be fought in order to render unnecessary a battle for Cassino. Now that Anzio was failing to do this, more and more battles at Cassino became necessary in order to ensure that the battle of Anzio was not irretrievably lost. In early February, therefore, at a time when the German 14th Army was clearly preparing for an all-out assault on the Anzio beachhead and when it was clear that the American 34th and 36th Divisions had done all they could, Alexander decided that a new formation, the 2nd New Zealand Corps, under the legendary General Freyberg, and comprising two excellent, battle-hardened divisions, 2nd New Zealand and 4th Indian, should be given the formidable task of capturing Cassino and so opening the gate to the Liri valley. Freyberg's plan for doing this was to assault Cassino from the north and from the south-east at the same time, 4th Indian Division being responsible for the northern sector in order to seize Monastery Hill and the Monastery itself, and so be able to cut Highway 6, while the New Zealanders would capture the railway station, about 1,200 yards south of the town, which the Germans had made into a strong defensive position. In this way the gate would be opened, and the U.S. 1st Armoured Division would be free to sweep into the Liri valley. As the various regiments and battalions of these two veteran divisions took over their positions prior to the attack, however, it became more and more clear to the commanders at all levels that the dominating feature of the Monastery itself which commanded observation over all routes, and which was of course in

German hands, might – if not in some way neutralized – spell failure all round.

Freyberg made it clear to his Government [to which he reported directly about all operational matters – a unique distinction among Allied armies] that from the Monastery the enemy could watch and thus bring down fire on any troop movement either on the roads and tracks or the open country below. His view was supported by Kippenberger, commanding the N.Z. Division, who was certain that the Germans were using the Monastery as their main observation post. General Alexander himself referred to it as an integral part of the German defensive system because of its superb observation. General Tuker, who commanded 4th Indian Division, went further and demanded that the Monastery be reduced by heavy bombers, thus originating another great controversy of the war. Much of this controversy centred on whether or not German soldiers were actually occupying the Monastery buildings, and here opinion is divided, the Germans not surprisingly denying it, the Allies in some cases claiming to have *seen* enemy soldiers and wireless aerials in the Abbey during a reconnassance flight over it. But Kippenberger made one of the most sensible observations about it to the effect that whether the Abbey was occupied or not was immaterial. If not occupied on one day, it could be on the next; reserves could always be positioned there, or could withdraw into shelter when under attack. He felt it was impossible to ask troops to attack a hill with a building on top of it which could house and protect hundreds of enemy soldiers, ready to emerge at a critical moment. His own troops certainly supported the policy of destroying the Abbey before the hill was stormed. With both his divisional commanders in favour of this policy, Freyberg was reluctantly compelled to support them. The fact is that the Monastery had to some extent itself become an enemy in the eyes of the soldiers. There was, as Fred Majdalany explained, a psychological aspect to the whole issue:

> Because of the extraordinary extent to which the summit of Monte Cassino dominated the valleys: because of the painful constancy with which men were picked off by accurately observed gunfire whenever they were forced to move in daylight within its seemingly inescapable view: because of the obsessive theatrical manner in which it towered over the scene, searching every inch of it, the building set upon that summit had become the embodiment of resistance and its tangible symbol.

General Mark Clark, in whose 5th Army Freyberg's Corps was, claimed after the war that he had no responsibility for the decision to bomb the Abbey, whereas he actually gave the order to do so. Like all Clark's other apologias, his writing is so blinded by his dislike of the British and so distorted by vanity and self-vindication that we need not take his claim seriously. It was in any case Alexander who accepted responsiblity by expressing his total acceptance of Freyberg's judgment. In a somewhat curious aside which appeared years later in his memoirs, Alexander referred to a mistaken translation of an intercepted wireless message transmitted over the German military network. *'Der Abt ist noch im Kloster'* means, of course, 'The Abbot is still in the Monastery', but for some extraordinary reason the interceptors and translators assumed that *Abt* was an abbreviation for *Abteilung* [the gender of which is feminine, ie. *die Abteilung*], a word which, with some stretching of the imagination, could be thought of as referring to a military department or division of some sort. But no one could believe that the decision to bomb or not to bomb was taken upon such flimsy and doubtful evidence as this. What mattered was that Freyberg had, however reluctantly, come to the decision that the Monastery must be reduced by bombing for both tactical and psychological reasons. The real tragedy was that in the end the bombing was not coordinated with the ground attack, and therefore, as Fred Majdalany wrote: 'It achieved nothing, it helped nobody'.

The second main battle for Cassino began with this bombing on the morning of 15 February. 450 tons of bombs were used to reduce the Monastery. The tactical, as opposed to psychological, value of the appalling destruction caused, was questionable. To some exent the ruined rubble made better defensive localities than a building intact would have done. But there were two sides to this question too. General von Senger und Etterlin, commanding 14th Panzer Corps, maintained after the war that the bombing had actually helped with their defences. All experience in street fighting, he argued, led to the conclusion that for the defence, houses and buildings had to be demolished in order to convert them from being mouse-traps into defensive bastions. But the Allied commanders had taken this well into account. Kippenberger took the view that on balance the Monastery provided better protection for the Germans if it were undamaged. Once knocked down the uneven heaps of debris, although providing certain defensive advantages, were far more vulnerable to artillery, mortar and ground-attack fire than would have been the building intact. In the event the Allied attacks failed irrespective of what had happened to the Monastery itself. The 4th Indian Division had to seize a knoll between their own positions on Snakeshead Ridge and Monastery Hill – it was called Point 593. Three nights of desperate fighting followed. What happened to a company of the 1st Royal Sussex on the first night, 15 February, does much to explain why all subsequent attempts failed:

> They moved in normal formation of two platoons abreast, the third following behind in reserve. They moved very slowly. On this ground there was a danger at every step of a stone being dislodged and rattling against another: and in these high places sounds of this kind were audible a long way off. On this ground, too, it was fatally easy to turn an ankle or stumble. It was especially easy for a man laden with something heavy, such as a Bren gun. With every single step there was a danger of breaking the silence that was essential to their approach, with an alert enemy a bare seventy yards away.
>
> The leading troops had advanced no more than fifty yards when they came under a withering fire of machine-gun and grenade. They went to ground. They wriggled across the sharp, stony ground from one position to another, trying to work round to the flanks. Time after time individuals and groups made a new effort to find a way round, a way closer to an objective that was so near and yet so inaccessible. But the steep ground defeated them. And their grenades began to run short, though the Germans, sending them over in showers from their positions up the slope, had unlimited quantities. To help them out grenades were collected from the other companies of the battalion, and passed forward, but long before dawn these too had been used up.
>
> If they had remained in the open after daybreak they would have been wiped out to a man. Before first light therefore they were ordered to withdraw. February 15th, a calamitous day for Monte Cassino, had not spared at the Royal Sussex either. Of the three officers and sixty-three men who had undertaken this exploratory trial of strength against a preliminary objective, two officers and thirty-two men had been killed or wounded no more than fifty yards from their start-point. It was a foretaste of things to come.

If the 4th Indian Division, despite the utmost valour and perseverance, fared ill in their attempt to take Monastery Hill from the north, the New Zealand Division with comparable courage and determination had had some initial success, which was later wrested from them by German counter-attacks. The 28th Maori Battalion actually captured Cassino railway station on the night of 17 February, suffering 128 casualties, killed or wounded, and by dawn next morning they were dug in. *But* they had no tanks or anti-tank guns with them. All the superb efforts of the New Zealand sappers in bridging a canal and the River Rapido, clearing mines, making usable tracks – always under shell and mortar fire – had not quite brought the thing off. One blown gap remained unbridged by daylight. It was impossible for the work to be done during the day, such was the power that observation everywhere gave to the Germans. Indeed to have attempted it would have been suicidal. This meant that the Maori battalion would have to hold on to the railway station, pivot of the whole position south of Cassino, until night fell, when the sappers' work could be completed, and tanks and anti-tank guns could reach the dug in infantry. The Germans were well aware of the key importance of the station and about three o'clock on the afternoon of 18 February they put in a co-ordinated attack with tanks, artillery and infantry, which not all the gallantry of the New Zealanders could withstand. After losing a number of men, killed, wounded and taken prisoner, they were obliged to withdraw. The second battle for Cassino was over, and the Allies had little to show for it except a crossing over the Rapido. It was clear from the relief shown by Kesselring and Vietinghoff at having recaptured the railway station how close-run a thing it had been. Thus with Cassino still untaken and the German attempts to pinch out the beachhead at Anzio, stalemate presided over the Italian campaign.

A word must be said here about the defenders of Cassino. All of us who actually argued the toss with the German Army in Italy or anywhere else know what brave, skilful and dedicated soldiers they were. Often their tactical improvisation in defence and counter-attack, their superb fieldcraft and concealment, their brilliant use of mortars, above all their perfected practice of fighting with the all-arms team – tanks, guns, infantry – taught the Allies, who in the later stages of the war were too apt to rely on sheer ironmongery and weight of fire power, lesson after lesson. None were better at it than the 1st German Parachute Division, whose fanatical bravery and unshakeable morale, together with exceptional fighting ability, held together the whole foundation of the astonishing defence of Cassino.

By the beginning of March, then, there was once more deadlock in Italy. As Churchill wrote: 'We could not break the main front of Cassino and the Germans had equally failed to drive us into the sea at

Anzio.' What is more, the relative strengths were such that no decision either way seemed probable. The Allies had some twenty divisions in Italy, the Germans about twenty-four, of which five were in the north, nineteen south of Rome. Rome was still an objective, but the timing for *Overlord* was getting nearer and nearer, with all the controversial questions concerning Operation *Anvil*, the projected landing in southern France, which was designed to assist the forthcoming battle for Normandy. In this it signally failed. Since most of the resources for it were to come from Alexander's armies, however, *Anvil* did succeed in robbing Alexander of the one remaining opportunity he was to have of capping slogging tactical victory with decisive strategic gains. Before we look at the final battles for Rome, which were on that city's fall instantly eclipsed by the descent on France, we must see what was to happen on Hitler's Eastern and Western fronts and what effect this was to have on the south.

Not only that, but in view of the extravagant claims made about the major contribution which the Italian campaign made to the success of operations elsewhere, it is important to understand just how great or how insignificant this contribution was. On the Eastern front, quite apart from having to stomach the loss of the Ukraine, Hitler was obliged to witness *débâcle* in the Crimea where, in a five-week battle, the Wehrmacht lost over 75,000 soldiers. After that the Russians remained relatively quiet until the latter part of June. There was, therefore, between April and June no denuding of the eastern front because of what was happening in Italy. Indeed, there – as Hitler put it – Kesselring was holding the Allies at bay 'with his little finger'. Even in late May, when Alexander's final offensive to capture Rome was well under way, and von Richthofen, commanding the Luftwaffe in the South, had come to see the Führer in the Berghof, what was going on in Italy was simply regarded as a ruse to persuade the German High Command to divert Army and Air Force reserves away from France, and von Richthofen noted in his diary on 23 May:

> 3 pm with the Führer. He's grown older, good-looking, very calm, very definite views on the military and political situation, no worries about anything. Again and again one can't help feeling this is a man blindly following his summons, walking unhesitatingly along the path prescribed to him without the slightest doubt as to its rightness and the final outcome. . . . The unpleasant military occurrences at Cassino and since this

morning at the Anzio beachhead are contemplated by him quite calmly: as he puts it, we can be thankful that we are still fighting so far down. After all, last September [1943] we all thought, and he did too, that this summer [1944] would see us fighting in the Apennines or even in the Alps.

It can hardly be disputed that those who labour the argument of how great a distraction the Italian campaign was to the Germans need to bear in mind its actual effect on the mind of the man who called the tune for so much of the Second World War. He even called the tune as to the fate of Rome itself when its inevitable capture by the Allies became plain. Kesselring wanted to destroy the Tiber bridges and so slow down the Allied advance. Hitler would not hear of it. His enemies might destroy the Monte Cassino monastery, but he would not go down in history as the destroyer of Rome. But what was happening in Rome during the first week of June, 1944, had little effect on the far more momentous activities in Normandy. So concerned was Hitler by what his generals had to say on 11 and 12 June, by which time it had become clear that the Normandy invasion had succeeded and that the Allies were in France to stay, that he ordered the 9th and 10th S.S. Panzer Divisions to entrain from the Eastern front for Normandy. Yet this step was taken at the very time when Hitler was expecting a major offensive by the Red Army, whose *Schwerpunkt* he intuitively and correctly suspected would fall on Army Group Centre. And while Montgomery was tightening his grip on Normandy and Brittany, the Red Army was about to overcome Army Group Centre like a summer's cloud – something that demanded even Hitler's special wonder. At his conference on 6 July he was told by General Heusinger that losses during the last two weeks amounted to *twenty-eight divisions*, some 350,000 soldiers. It is when we contemplate figures of this magnitude that we are perhaps able to get the side-show of Italy into perspective. Yet three days earlier Hitler had been telling Kesselring how vital it was to delay the enemy's advance well south of the Apennines – for after Alexander's final success in breaking the Cassino position, combined with the Allied advance from Anzio, which we must return to shortly, there was only the German Army's courage and skill to stop them, and Kesselring was complaining of shortages of troops and air cover, a familiar pattern for the Wehrmacht by this time. General Koller, Luftwaffe Chief of Staff, recalled the meeting between Kesselring and Hitler:

The Führer explains just why we have to fight for every square metre of ground – because for us gaining time is everything now.* The longer we can hold the enemy off at the periphery the better. Perhaps the individual soldier or NCO may not grasp why he is asked to fight in the Abruzzi mountains instead of the Apennines, but his Supreme Commander must understand why and comply, because the interests of Germany's fight transcend those of the individual soldier.

Kesselring fears that he will be breached in his present position if he holds it too long, and he wants to fall back on the Apennine line early on. But the Führer wants that postponed as long as possible, as there is nothing else behind the Apennines, and if the enemy gets through there, the entire lowlands of Upper Italy will be lost.

Hitler need not have worried. The Allied armies in Italy were kept at the periphery all right, and did not break through the Apennines into the lowlands of Upper Italy until the war had been totally lost to the Germans on other fronts. But now we must see how they closed up to the Apennines in the first place.

The third battle of Cassino began on 15 March, and although bombing had failed before, it was tried again, this time with the aim of obliterating the German defences in the town of Cassino itself. Despite the use of one thousand tons of bombs and a rather greater weight of artillery shells, soldiers of the 1st German Parachute Division survived and went on with the fight. Alexander had expressed the opinion that it was inconceivable that troops should be left alive after eight hours' concentrated hammering. He was wrong. Indeed Hitler, in discussing the Atlantic Wall fortifications which had twenty feet of concrete, had expressed his confidence in their rendering Allied air attacks impotent by pointing out that in Italy enemy air superiority and bombing had no effect on German troops, where they had only slit trenches for protection. The battle lasted for about a week, and although the New Zealanders and 4th Indian Division succeeded in capturing part of the town, Monastery Hill was still not taken, despite its partial occupation by the Gurkhas. The German line held. Churchill, always eager to discover the truth of the matter and never reluctant to offer his senior commanders tactical advice, demanded to know why the strong defences of Monastery Hill could not be outflanked. His signal to General Alexander, dated 20 March, received on the same day a reply

* Hitler placed great faith in the coming jet aircraft and secret V weapons.

which admirably summed up the difficulties and explains why the battle for Rome was so prolonged:

> Along whole main battle-front from Adriatic to south coast there is only Liri Valley leading direct to Rome which is suitable terrain for development of our superiority in artillery and armour. The main highway, known as Route Six, is the only road, except cart-tracks, which leads from the mountains where we are into Liri Valley over Rapido River. The exit into the plain is blocked and dominated by Monte Cassino, on which stands the monastery. Repeated attempts have been made to outflank Monastery Hill from the north, but all these attacks have been unsuccessful, owing to deep ravines, rocky escarpments, and knife-edges, which limit movements to anything except small parties of infantry, who can only be maintained by porters and to a limited extent by mules.

Alexander went on to explain that ravines and mountains prevented a turning movement to the north, and that, to the south, not only flood-water, but the enfiladed artillery fire from German gun positions, made movement very difficult. It was for these reasons that a direct assault on the bastion of Monastery Hill, via Cassino town, following an immense concentration of fire power, had been attempted. It had been but partially successful, and the bombing had itself contributed to failure in that it had so cut up the roads and created obstacles of smashed buildings that tanks and other fighting vehicles could not advance. In paying tribute to the German paratroops defending Cassino, Alexander questioned whether any other troops in the world could have stood up to such a battering and then gone on to fight with such fierceness and tenacity. He concluded by saying that if it were necessary to call off the attack, at least they would be able to hang on to the two bridgeheads over the Rapido and to some other key points. Thereafter 8th Army's plan for finally entering the Liri Valley would be put into effect after the necessary regrouping had been done. Churchill's acknowledgement expressed the hope that it would not be called off. But it was, and almost two months were to pass before the final battle of Cassino was fought and the road to Rome at last opened. Before we see how this came about, we may perhaps recall the experience of some of those taking part in the third battle.

To the ordinary German soldier the bombardment seemed like hell on earth. When a thousand aircraft bombed their positions and artillery concentrations simply went on all day the ground would shake like an earthquake, nothing but dust and smoke was to be seen, there was not a moment's peace, just the dreadful thunder of guns and mortars, enemy aeroplanes always overhead discharging their deadly and terrifying cargo; nothing like it had ever happened before, not even in Russia. Their strong points may have been reinforced with stones, but a direct hit would soon do for them. As if this were not enough, there was snow too. 'You would think you were in Russia. Just when you think you are going to have a few hours' rest to get a sleep, the fleas and bugs torment you. Rats and mice are our companions too.' Yet they held on to Cassino.

Fred Majdalany remembered Cassino: 'It was ours – Monastery, the mountain, the smells. A cemetery for the living.' His battalion was so close to the enemy that neither side had far to move to get to grips with the other. As the hills and mountains were themselves key positions, it was common to find them occupied by both German and British soldiers, one dug in on the near side, the other on the far side. Movement during the daylight hours was not recommended. The enemy's artillery observation posts would quickly smarten you up with a 'stonk'. Movement by night was easier, but more difficult to identify:

> Being attacked at night is particularly unnerving because you cannot tell if there are twenty of the enemy or a whole battalion. If two machine-guns can infiltrate through your positions and open fire from behind, the most dogged temperament finds it hard to resist the impression that it is surrounded. . . . At any moment we expected to hear our machine-guns get to work – if it was a big attack they would be bound to go for the ridge overlooking us. Messages were flashed to the mortars and guns to stand by ready to bring down fire on all the SOS targets. The tension of total alertness temporarily eclipsed one's tiredness. Nobody spoke, unless it was to pass a message on the telephone or wireless. You just stood or leaned or sat motionless – and fancied you could hear your heartbeats. Then the firing seemed to die down slightly – or was it that you wanted it to die down? No, it was definitely easing off. People began to talk again. They made the rather forced little jokes which always follow a period of fear. We still had no idea whether the attack had been made by twenty or two hundred. Twenty minutes later we heard that it had in fact been made by twelve men. One of them had been wounded and taken prisoner. He said it was a fighting patrol of twelve. Its object had been to get a prisoner. One suddenly felt very, very tired.

Tired or not the fighting had to go on, and we shall see shortly how General Alexander orchestrated and conducted his *chef d'oeuvre*.

Meanwhile Churchill consoled himself with the reflection that twenty German divisions were pinned down in central Italy, divisions which might otherwise have been in France. But now there was to be another great controversy as to the allocation of resources, this time concerning the projected landing in southern France, Operation *Anvil* [later *Dragoon*]. Although there were those who affected to believe that the argument about *Anvil* was one of the respective priorities of north-western and southern France, in fact the only argument which counted for anything was whether the resources involved should be used for furthering the campaign in Italy or France. France won, but the resources were dissipated just the same.

The controversy was of long standing. As early as 21 February, 1944, Montgomery, under persuasion from Churchill, had written to Eisenhower strongly recommending the cancellation of *Anvil*. He was, of course, very much against any diversion of landing craft from *Overlord* itself, but his reasons for abandoning the landing in southern France went further:

> As a result of what he [Churchill] told me about the situation in Italy it is my definite opinion that all resources in the Mediterranean should be put into the campaign in Italy. I further consider that we should now make a definite decision to cancel *Anvil*; this will enable the commanders in the Mediterranean theatre to devote their whole attention to fighting the Germans in Italy ... If agreed, then all the craft now being kept for *Anvil* can be released at once for *Overlord*. The effect of this on *Overlord* will be tremendous. ... Let us have two really good major campaigns – one in Italy and one in *Overlord*.

Eisenhower, as was customary with him, procrastinated. He agreed to delay, but not cancel, *Anvil*. His reasons, as Carlo D'Este has so eloquently pointed out in his brilliant *Decision in Normandy*, was not only so that he could mount *Anvil* later and so draw German reserves away from Normandy and protect his southern flank there. It was also to help ensure what he and Marshall had always wanted to ensure, that *Overlord* would preserve its priority and so prevent the British doing what Churchill and Brooke had so frequently favoured – widening the Italian campaign into a major thrust. Ironically, when *Anvil* was finally launched in August, 1944, it did nothing to help what was happening in Normandy. 'Postponement,' wrote A. J. P. Taylor, 'destroyed its purpose, and the Americans insisted on it only from obstinacy. They were determined not to be tricked by Churchill into any further

Mediterranean adventures.' And the further irony of it was that by robbing Alexander of the extra strength to exploit his final success in the battle for Rome, they robbed him too of his last opportunity to cap the British Mediterranean strategy with a dividend, which could have been triumphantly significant, and which those who had for so long struggled in the mud, rain and cold so surely deserved. Meanwhile, the next role clearly cast for Alexander was to time his next great offensive south of Rome so that it could, so to speak, take the place of *Anvil* and ensure that maximum pressure was exerted on the Germans in Italy while Montgomery was about to descend on the beaches of Normandy. Operation *Diadem* was the result.

The object of *Diadem* as laid down by the British Chiefs of Staff was to give the greatest possible assistance to *Overlord* by destroying or containing in the Mediterranean area as many German military formations as possible. Its object was not, it will be noted, to capture Rome or drive on Vienna. The capture of Rome was incidental to the idea. The operation certainly succeeded in containing some twenty-one operational German divisions. That it did not do more damage to von Vietinghoff's 10th Army was the result of the Germans' skill in recovery and withdrawal, together with the vanity of General Mark Clark, who wanted his Army to be the first to enter Rome, and so misinterpreted, or disobeyed, Alexander's orders. The success which *Diadem* did enjoy depended greatly on Alexander's ability to deceive and surprise Kesselring. He did both. While it was impossible to conceal from the enemy that some sort of regrouping was under way in preparation for a further offensive, deception measures as to timing and place were not only possible but highly effective. Thus Kesselring was persuaded to believe that the Allied attacks were likely to start in June, but futhermore that yet another amphibious landing to the north-west of Rome at Civitavecchia was on the cards. Thus when *Diadem* began on 11 May many key German commanders, von Vietinghoff, von Senger und Etterlin and Baade, who commanded 90th Panzer Grenadier Division, were away.

Alexander's plan was simple. 8th Army was to attack on the right, break into the Liri valley, take Cassino and advance along Route 6 towards Rome; 5th Army to the south would drive through the Aurunci Mountains, and advance both along route 7 towards Rome and on the left of the Liri valley. At the right moment the six Allied divisions in the Anzio beachhead would storm forward and cut off the Germans retreating before the main bodies of 5th and 8th Armies. Alexander was very precise in his directive. It was to *destroy* the right wing of von Vietinghoff's 10th Army, then to drive what was left of it and von Mackensen's 14th Army north of Rome, pursuing the whole lot to what was at that time known as the Rimini-Pisa position [the Gothic Line] inflicting maximum losses on the enemy throughout the operation. In his Order of the Day, Alexander made some revealing points:

> Perhaps you are disappointed that we have been unable to advance faster and farther, but I realize full well how magnificently you fought among these almost insurmountable obstacles of rocky, trackless mountains, deep snow and in valleys blocked by rivers and mud against a stubborn foe. The results of these past months may not appear spectacular, but you have drawn into Italy and mauled many of the enemy's best divisions which he badly needed to stem the advance of the Russian armies in the east. *Hitler has admitted that his defeats in the east were largely due to the bitterness of the fighting and his losses in Italy* ... blows are about to fall which will result in the final destruction of the Nazis. ... To us in Italy has been given the honour to strike the first blow. We are going to destroy the German armies in Italy.

Good stirring stuff, no doubt, although as Fred Majdalany has pointed out, the honour of striking the first blow was one that many of those responsible for doing so were happy to relinquish to others. Apart from that we may recall that the disasters in Russia were caused primarily by Hitler's conduct of the war there, together with the seemingly inexhaustible resources of the Red Army. It was the strategic circumstances taken as a whole – what was happening in the East, West and South – which added up to so bankrupt a prospect for the Wehrmacht, rather than the special influence of one battle in the South on another in the East. We may again recall Norman Stone's contention that Hitler dealt with Allied operations in Italy 'without serious disruption of the war elsewhere'.

One of the most striking features of Alexander's offensive was the sheer international character of the Armies which took part in it. The initial attacks were made by American, French, British and Polish divisions. The Commonwealth participants included New Zealanders, Indians, Canadians and South Africans. It was the Poles who eventually

---

* My italics.

took Cassino; it was the French – the Goumiers under General Juin – who outflanked the Gustav and Hitler Lines; it was the Americans who advanced so effectively from Anzio; and by 25 May, two weeks after the offensive began, it was virtually all over. The 5th and 8th Armies from the south had broken through the Gustav and Hitler lines and caused von Vietinghoff's 10th Army to withdraw. General Truscott's force from Anzio had broken out and was driving forward in order to trap the retiring German 10th Army. It was then that General Mark Clark gave his astonishing order to Truscott to change direction and head for Rome, a decision which Churchill with unusual restraint called 'unfortunate' . . . As Ronald Lewin observes in *Ultra*, Clark abandoned his mission 'not for fear of the unknown' for 10th Army's plight was well understood, 'but for personal reasons which have scarcely been disguised'. Much of 10th Army got away to fight more battles, and indeed for all Alexander's Order of the Day calling for the destruction of the German armies in Italy, almost another year was to pass before he finally achieved it and received their surrender.

Before we leave Cassino we may recall what it all seemed like to *The Times*' special corespondent, Philip Ure, who wrote this despatch from inside Cassino on 18 May, 1944:

Here is a scene of utter desolation such as only this war can produce. It is nearing noon, and the last Germans left this relic of a tortured town some few hours ago; they were prisoners. Their last stronghold – Hotel Continental – had gone up with a bang a little while before that; it was the final retreating blow that the Germans in Cassino struck. There were fewer than 30 prisoners taken in Cassino itself. Our men felt bitter about that. "This is the first time I have ever been able to stand outside in the open air", said one of them, "and now I have only seen ten Germans".

He had come into the open air to stand bolt upright for the first time this morning; he had come from a dug-out that was in the rubble of a battered house where the day was dark as night, and where only in the hours of darkness you dared to crawl out so that the next section to hold the post might crawl in.

A little behind us is "the Crypt". Its rightful ecclesiastical name – for it is below the chapel of a convent – remained relevant in the cruel circumstances of war. It had 99 direct hits on it up to the arrival of British troops who took over about ten days ago; since then it has received 15 direct hits.

They say that nothing less than a direct hit from a 1,000 lb bomb would penetrate the crypt. That is some measure of the protection which the Germans enjoyed last March when the allied air forces bombed this town in the greatest strength ever put on a target of comparable size. The crypt inside and out might pass for any front-line soldier's picture of a dug-out. Its dangers were supremely the dangers of the front line itself: one British sergeant whose head was visible in daylight above its entrance for less than a second was killed. Enemy snipers never left the spot uncovered.

Today, in its remnants of shattered walls, Cassino looks just as if it were mainly a series of caves in the hillside. Castle Hill, rising sheer within the town on its north side, stands like a steep crag, its pinnacle a jagged rock now unrecognizable as buildings. The castle itself had remained in our hands since the last part of March; below it the ruins of the houses were in the hands of the Germans. Thus, our own troops on the top of Castle Hill were just above the Germans, who in turn were only about 50 yards from another line of our troops in the opposite direction towards the centre of the town and River Rapido.

One writes about "the centre of the town". Today it is but a guess which or what was the centre of the town. Across there, there is a stinking quagmire with disabled tanks half buried in its mud, craters, dirty yellowish-green with the slime of stagnant water, blasted trees, gaunt remains of stone walls, a medley of twisted metal – all the mess and disarray of horror that comes in the chaos of ceaseless bombardment. That, we were told, was the centre of the town.

Just outside the crypt was another crater; its muddy water had served as washing water – when purified by the medical officer – for a first-aid post within the crypt. The convent beside the crypt stood like a crazy house of cards about to collapse.

In one of its walls was embedded a tank, a reminder of the days when the New Zealanders had fought along this way. Soldiers who had known this scene only though the meagre slits of defensive sentry posts, were looking round freely this morning. They still moved warily, cautious of mines and traps. Ahead of us was a small sangar or pile of stones. Two men had been sitting there a few days ago when a German mortar shell burst exactly between them.

High above the town the abbey stood like jagged spikes of rock on a hilltop; it was no more like any building than is a natural rugged peak of mountain, and yesterday it had been like a sullen smoking crater of some volcano. Today, no longer in German hands, it seemed to have regained almost something of peacefulness; at least it was quiet.

British troops looked down on us from the lesser height of Castle Hill and waved cheerfully. They are irrepressibly cheerful, these men who have endured so much with stolid, simple courage. (One of them is exploring a tank in the quagmire that may be the centre of the town, and shouts across that he has found an old wireless set. "See if you can get us any news" call out his comrades like one man.)

Rome fell on 4 June and Harold Macmillan, who had been at Eton, sent a telegram to General Alexander, a Harrovian, congratulating him on this achievement, adding how thoughtful it was of Alexander to have done it on the Fourth of June. To which Alexander replied: 'Thank you. What is the Fourth of June?' Two days later Churchill announced the liberation of Rome by Alexander's armies in a House of Commons statement. However welcome this news was, it was totally overshadowed by a further piece of news – the Normandy landings. 'Instantly, and irrevocably,' wrote Lewin, 'the Italian campaign had been reduced to a sideshow.' That this sideshow continued to drag on for so long was aggravated by the removal of many of Alexander's divisions for the irrelevance of *Anvil*, and it is this, together with the closing up to the next great German defensive barrier of the Gothic Line, which we must now examine.

8

AN ALMOST BLUNTED PURPOSE

Many of us who followed the Italian campaign still think it was wasteful, and the insensate battering of the Gothic Line in the north appears to have been especially futile.

Alan Moorehead

When the 1st Armoured Division was launched to break through the Gothic Line and blast a path to the Po valley, Venice and the Alps, I had the honour to be in command of the leading troop of the leading regiment, 4th Hussars, and since my map reading was somewhat superior to that of my NCOs, I was actually in the leading tank. It was 3 September, 1944, five years to the day from the war's beginning, and it was perhaps fortunate for my crew and myself that when we were about a mile short of the village of Coriano – it was night-time but with a bright moon – an order was received from the Divisional Commander, Major-General Richard Hull, to halt. Had he instead sent up a company of the 60th Rifles we might have taken Coriano that night and established the whole regiment on that vital ridge with unforeseeable consequences for the 1st Armoured Division's subsequent operations. As it was, we were told to halt. The good fortune from my point of view sprang from the fact that next morning we discovered that, had I advanced a few hundred yards further and turned a corner, my tank would have been directly in the sights of a dug-in and concealed 50mm anti-tank gun. As it was, we were able to deploy at first light on to a ridge overlooking Coriano, where we were subjected to the most disagreeable artillery, mortar and anti-tank fire for most of the day, while the Germans steadily reinforced the Coriano position. During the first few days of the Coriano action – for which the Regiment was later awarded a battle honour – we lost five officers, thirty-five men and nine tanks.

So, all along the line, the initial battles for the German defensive positions astride the Apennines got under way – Coriano, Rimini, the Romagna, and further west the Il Giogo Pass, to the accompaniment of rain, blood, mud and cold. By the end of October, some eight weeks later, it had become clear that the Allied armies would be required to spend one more winter in the mountains. There was to be no break-through to the Po valley in 1944. Despite desperate fighting and the crossing of numerous rivers, the occupation of countless ridges, the Germans established a winter line on the Senio River. It would not be until April, 1945, that a break-through would finally be made. By then the purpose of it was to be all but blunted. Decision as to the war's outcome was being determined at rivers far distanced from the Senio – the Oder just east of Berlin, the Elbe to its west. Yet hopes in Italy had been so high in the summer. What had gone wrong and how was it that the Germans, despite Allied air supremacy, had been able to hold the line?

Kesselring had, of course, promised Hitler that he would do so, but he had also made it clear that stopping the Allied advance would depend on using the right ground, in other words the Gothic Line in the Apennines. As early as June, just after the fall of Rome and the invasion of Normandy, it had become plain to Hitler's staff officers that the strength of the Apennine position had to be exploited, not only to stabilize the Italian theatre, but also to allow greater freedom of operations elsewhere. Such advice was hardly welcome to the Führer, who, sensing as he did that the war was being lost on all fronts, became even more obsessive about contesting every foot of territory until the V weapons could bring England to its senses. Thus when General Warlimont, Jodl's deputy at Hitler's headquarters, reported that it was essential to turn the Apennine position into the main defensive zone for Italy, so that withdrawal from the temporary defences north of Rome to such prepared strength would be possible, Hitler waved his arguments aside. He went further and issued orders to Kesselring that withdrawal must stop and that the line must be stabilized and held astride Lake Trasimene, that is south of Florence. But Kesselring, however he might admire Hitler's political skill and strategic judgement, was not to be bullied as to the way in which he handled his two armies. At a meeting early in July in Bavaria he spoke to the Führer in uncompromising terms, explaining that his troops would fight and die if necessary, but that this was not the point. The point was whether Germany could afford to chuck away two more armies, whether the failures of Stalingrad and Tunisia could bear repetition, whether Hitler was willing to see a way into Germany opened up for the Allies in the south. On the other hand, he argued:

> I guarantee, unless my hands are tied, to delay the Allied advance appreciably, to halt it at the latest in the Apennines, and thereby to create conditions for the prosecution of the war in 1945 which can be dovetailed into your general strategic scheme.

'*I guarantee*' – they are not words which every general would use. But Kesselring was as good as his word. Not only did he hold up the Allied advance as he had promised, but by the end of August when the Allies did close up to the Gothic Line, although it was not completely ready, Kesselring was satisfied with its general strength, particularly on the eastern, Adriatic, side. He felt able to anticipate an Allied assault there with some confidence. Ironically enough, although it had not been Alexander's original intention, it was in the end precisely there that he lauched his first attack.

If things were looking up a bit for Hitler in the south during July and August, 1944, the same could hardly be said of events elsewhere. Even before that the game had been going badly wrong in the West and East. The truth was that even the great German Army was over-extended. The Red Army's summer offensive had caused the German defensive line to disintegrate. Minsk, Vilna, Pinsk, Grodno – all fell to the Russians, who even threatened East Prussia. In Normandy the Allies were winning the battle of the build-up. When Hitler demanded of his two Field-Marshals there, Rommel and von Rundstedt, that the invasion forces be annihilated so that he could turn back to deal with the Red Army, they advised him to end the war. Neither Field-Marshal remained there for long. Rommel was injured when his staff car was strafed by British fighters and von Rundstedt, when he told Keitel that the battle for Normandy was lost and that they should make peace, was dismissed and replaced by von Kluge. But changes of command made no difference, East or West. Rigid defence could do nothing against the superiority in material and mobility enjoyed by the

Anglo-Americans and the Russians. By July the Red Army had broken through into Poland, cutting off the German armies in the Baltic States. The Russians were also advancing without check into Rumania. Only in the centre did Model and Guderian succeed in restoring some sort of defensive line. In Normandy crass interference by Hitler and his staff in the conduct of the battle guaranteed with even more speed and certainty that the battle for Normandy was lost. Suicide by von Kluge and the arrival of the brilliant, bustling Model could not prevent the withdrawal of the Germans across the Seine. The best part of twenty infantry divisions and well over 2,200 tanks and assault guns had been lost. Indeed the war was about to become a battle for Germany itself. The Russians were nearing East Prussia, the Anglo-American armies were approaching the Rhineland. But still the Supreme Commander of the Wehrmacht did not despair. He had already dismissed Jodl's recommendation that Finland, northern Norway, upper Italy and the Balkans should all be evacuated, so that the Army could establish defensible positions along the Tisa and Sava Rivers and on the southern side of the Alps. Hitler would not hear of it:

> Under all circumstances we will continue this battle, until, as Frederick the Great said, one of our damned enemies gets too tired to fight any more. We'll fight until we get a peace which secures the life of the German nation for the next fifty or hundred years and which, above all, does not besmirch our honour a second time, as happened in 1918.

The failed attempt on his life at Rastenburg had in no way weakened Hitler's resolve. Rather it tightened his grip on the Army. Guderian became Chief of the Army General Staff, not only pledging to the Führer 'the unity of the Generals, of the Officer Corps and of the men of the Army', but also conforming to the demand that the Nazi salute was compulsory and that every General Staff officer should declare himself to be a 'National Socialist officer-leader'. And for the time being the Wehrmacht succeeded in holding its enemies at bay. Model and a re-instated von Rundstedt imposed a kind of stalemate west of the Rhine; Kesselring, as we have seen, was firmly established in the Gothic Line; on the Eastern front, East Prussia held. Indeed Hitler insisted on remaining at his headquarters there, Rastenburg, saying that as long as he remained in East Prussia, all would be well. While at Rastenburg, however, he did more than contemplate defence. In mid-September, just before the Allies' ill-fated descent on Arnhem, he told Jodl that he had come to a 'momentous decision', to go over to the counter-attack in the Ardennes with objective – Antwerp!* No such dramatic and spectacular events were to be expected in the South. There slogging frustration for Alexander's armies was to continue to be the order of the day.

In December, 1943, seven Allied divisions had been withdrawn from Alexander's command for *Overlord*. In August, 1944, he lost six more divisions, including the skilled French mountain troops, to take part in the controversial Operation *Anvil [Dragoon]*. This latter juggling of resources was preceded by much inter-Allied wrangling and was followed by futile recrimination. As usual with any matter concerning operations in Italy, Churchill was at the heart of it. In discussing all this, we must bear in mind what had been agreed at Teheran in late November, 1943:

> *Overlord* and *Anvil* are the supreme operations for 1944. They must be carried out during May, 1944. Nothing must be undertaken in any other part of the world which hazards the success of these two operations.

Although the Normandy invasion had in fact been put back to June, 1944, partly in order to allow the disappointingly inconclusive Anzio landings to take place, and although *Anvil* itself had necessarily been delayed because of the shortage of landing craft, there was in the American minds no question of abandoning *Anvil* altogether. But after the capture of Rome Alexander put forward some proposals which awoke a great response in the Prime Minister. There were, Alexander suggested, three things he could do. First, simply advance to the Pisa-Rimini line and stand there, so allowing some economies in the Italian theatre and thus creating possibilities for other more offensive operations elsewhere. Alexander himself did not greatly favour this somewhat negative idea. Yet the C.I.G.S., General Sir Alan Brooke, saw certain virtues in it. At first he felt that by the time Alexander had reached the Gothic Line the Italian theatre would have done its stuff in

---

* For the Ardennes counter-offensive Hitler mustered nearly a quarter of a million German soldiers organized in some twenty-six divisions with 700 tanks and 2,000 guns. Two of the three armies were 5th and 6th Panzer Armies with seven panzer divisions between them. At the time of the Ardennes battles Kesselring had two armies of some twenty divisions. Thus with all three fronts being held, Hitler was still able to administer a shock to the Allies. In this way we are able to see the Italian campaign in perspective.

keeping German divisions away from Normandy and that landings in southern France would therefore be fitting in order to complement what was happening in Normandy. Later, as we shall see, he changed his mind.

Alexander's other suggestions were more exciting. His second idea was that his armies should go beyond the Pisa line and on into north-west Italy and thence southern France. But it was not so much this notion, which was not all that different from *Anvil*, but his third alternative which fired Churchill's imagination. It was no less than an advance on Vienna. Given his present force of twenty-seven divisions – that is no deductions for *Anvil* – he would drive through the Apennines, into the Po valley, go on to cross the Piave, and so to the Ljubljana Gap. Through that Gap ran the main communications from Italy into northern Yugoslavia, and, once in Allied hands, the road to Vienna, with all the political advantages involved, would be open. Never mind all the difficult and mountainous country which barred the way, so Alexander's argument went, what his armies had done in Italy, they could do elsewhere. Not even the Alps would be an obstacle to his skilled and enthusiastic soldiers. At first Brooke was sceptical – they would be embarking on a campaign which would involve crossing the Alps in winter – and there would be three enemies, the Germans, the weather and the mountains. His mind was changed not by Churchill, nor by his American colleagues, but by the Germans. As soon as it became clear from *Ultra* that Kesselring – although ultimately intending to withdraw to the Gothic Line – was planning to delay that withdrawal as long as possible by fighting south of that line astride Lake Trasimene, he insisted that Alexander's strength must be maintained in order to harass and destroy as much of the German Army in Italy *before* it sought refuge in the Gothic Line. A telegram from the British Chiefs of Staff to the Americans tried to make this clear:

> We are convinced that the Allied forces in the Mediterranean can best assist *Overlord* by completing the destruction of the German forces with which they are now in contact, and by continuing to engage, in maximum strength, all German reinforcements deployed to oppose their advance.

General Eisenhower, as we have seen, was firmly of the opinion that *Anvil* should be undertaken at the expense of Allied armies in Italy. He saw the landing in southern France as part of his Normandy battle and was convinced that Allied resources would not permit two major campaigns to strive after two decisive objectives. The American Chiefs of Staff of course supported Eisenhower, and not even Churchill's eloquence with Roosevelt could move the Americans from this position. However much the Prime Minister might press the President that, while *Overlord* should be reinforced to the utmost, yet at the same time opportunities in the Mediterranean should not be missed, Roosevelt insisted that five divisions must be withdrawn from Italy for *Anvil*. [In the event six went.] The remaining twenty-one divisions, plus extra brigades, he maintained, would provide Alexander with sufficient forces 'to chase Kesselring north of Pisa-Rimini'. Even Churchill's attempt later to switch the *Anvil/Dragoon* forces from the south to the west of France failed. *Dragoon* went ahead, having forfeited its purpose.

Although Churchill later wrote that *Dragoon* did not divert German forces opposing Eisenhower's advance from the west – in fact rather the reverse occurred in that advance from the west caused the Germans to speed up their withdrawal north up the Rhone valley – he went further and claimed that 'the army of Italy was deprived of its opportunity to strike a most formidable blow at the Germans, and very possibly to reach Vienna before the Russians'. But, as Michael Howard has pointed out, it is important to be clear that at the time of the controversy what the British Chiefs of Staff, backed by Churchill, were urging was that the *Dragoon* forces should remain in Italy to continue to engage Kesselring's armies in a battle of attrition. In view of the relative ease with which Kesselring held the Gothic Line, it may be doubted whether the extra divisions diverted for *Dragoon* would have caused the total collapse of the German armies in Italy, for there were still reinforcements to hand from the Balkans, and the further north the armies advanced towards Austria, the narrower and more easily defendable the country became. As it was, even with his depleted forces, Alexander had confidence that he would succeed in breaking the Gothic Line. How was he planning to do it?

It has sometimes been said that the art of command in war consists not only in giving good orders, but in ensuring that these orders are carried out. This ability, combined with absolute clarity and confidence as to what it is you are intending to do, clarity and confidence moreover which pervade the whole army from top to bottom – such a coalition of military talent as this usually leads to success. It cannot, however, be said that by such criteria Alexander gets very high marks. Montgomery was under no illusion as to his friend's inability to understand the conduct of war – 'he knows nothing about it; he is not a strong commander and he is incapable of giving firm and clear decisions as to what he wants . . . he does not understand the offensive and mobile battle; he cannot snap out clear and concise orders. He does not think and plan ahead. . . . He has never himself commanded an Army or a Corps in the field. . . . The higher art of making war is beyond him.' Brooke had a similar view and talked of Alexander's lack of strategic vision and said that throughout the African campaign he had been carried by Montgomery as regards the strategic and tactical handling of the campaign. Even Alexander's most sympathetic biographer, Nigel Nicolson, pulled no punches in his final assessment:

> I started off with great admiration for his performance as a soldier. And then as I went into it, particularly after the period when he became C-in-C Middle East, from Alamein onwards, I found that he, well, that he lacked genius. . . . I don't think the end of Tunisia was a very high performance – I mean a performance to go down in history as a great feat of generalship. And then Sicily was mucked up and I think that the early part of the Italian campaign was badly handled. . . . I don't think he had great imagination. He had great courage but not much daring. You can never see in any of Alex's battles or campaigns something that makes you gasp with admiration. . . . You see how much he was dependent on advice and upon very, very brilliant subordinate generals who often disobeyed his orders.

Sometimes it was even worse and subordinate generals, who were *not* brilliant, disobeyed his orders. We have only to think of Anzio, where despite Alexander urging Lucas to push out boldly with strong-hitting mobile patrols in order to discover the situation and gain contact with the enemy, this was not done, and later earned Alexander a relatively gentle rebuke from the Prime Minister: 'I have a feeling that you may have hesitated to assert your authority because you were dealing so largely with Americans and therefore *urged* an advance instead of *ordering* it. You are, however, quite entitled to give them orders. . . . it is their wish to receive direct orders. . . . Do not hesitate therefore to give direct orders just as you would to our own men.' Later, when Alexander did give direct orders to General Mark Clark to advance to close the Valmontone trap on the German 10th Army after the success of the last assault on Cassino and the break-out from Anzio, Clark disobeyed them in order to guarantee being the first in Rome, an action which after the war prompted the comment from General Truscott: 'I was dumbfounded . . . such was the order that turned the main effort of the beachhead forces from the Valmontone Gap and prevented the destruction of the German Tenth Army.' Now that it came to tackling the formidable Gothic Line, would the pattern of Alexander's orders being changed or ignored by his subordinates persist?

Alexander's original intention had been to attack with both his armies, 5th and 8th, in the centre of the Gothic Line, and, having thrust through the Apennines to attempt the destruction of Kesselring's forces *south* of the Po, then to cross the Po north of Ferrara. In the event, however, he was dissuaded from this plan by the 8th Army Commander, General Leese, who liked neither the idea of mountain operations – having lost his French divisions and wanting to exploit his great strength in armour – nor that of operating closely with the US 5th Army. There was irony in this change, for Alexander's deception measures related to the central attack had been designed to persuade the Germans that their main thrust was to be on the Adriatic side, and it was precisely here that Leese did in the end attack. Fortunately Kesselring had temporarily taken his eye off the Adriatic, because he had interpreted the *Dragoon* landings in the south of France as a threat to his western flank. But as was so frequently the case with Kesselring, once he grasped where the real dangers were, his reinforcement of the key battleground was swift and effective. Thus it was decided that Leese's 8th Army would advance to and break into the Gothic Line to the east, through the Rimini Gap and so on to the Romagna – the Rimini-Bologna-Lake Comacchio triangle – and the Lombardy plains. All this area was thought by some of the 8th Army planning staff to be good going for tanks! How swiftly they were to be disillusioned. 8th Army's offensive lasted from 25 August until 20 September – a day we will examine in more detail shortly to help illustrate the futility and frustration which the operations of 1st Armoured Division brought about. Further west the 5th Army would break through the Futa and Il Giogo passes in order to seize Bologna. Both armies' operations came close to success and were characterized by gallant, dogged fighting by the Allied soldiers against the odds of rivers and ridges and rain, and equally by the skilful defensive tactics and imaginative improvisation which the Germans so often displayed and excelled at. But close to success though they may have been, it was not close enough. On 31 August, with the attacks well under way, Churchill had declared that his object in Italy was 'to turn and break the Gothic Line, break into the Po valley, and ultimately advance by Trieste and the Ljubljana Gap to Vienna. Even if the war came to an end at an early date I have told Alexander to be ready for a dash with armoured cars'. There was to be no dash anywhere with armoured cars until May, 1945, and as early as October when the momentum of Alexander's attacks had slowed down, General Sir Alan Brooke, after visiting Alexander's headquarters, noted that 'Alex is getting stuck in the Apennines', talking of his divisions as 'pretty well whacked'. Certainly there were no decisive results, and Brooke, formerly so ardent a supporter of Churchill in the whole strategic notion of exploiting the Mediterranean, now observed: 'I do not consider that there is much future left in this theatre'.

For some of the D-Day Dodgers there was no future at all. A memorable article published in the *Cronaca di Rimini* on 20 September, 1975 thirty-one years after the battle, recalled the terrible fate which overtook one of the regiments of 1st Armoured Division, The Queen's Bays, in their attack at Monte Cieco, comparing it with the Charge of the Light Brigade at Balaklava in 1854: [I have abridged and translated freely.]

The 20th September, 1944, signalled the end of the British 1st Armoured Division, the famous formation which had helped defeat Rommel and his German-Italian army in North Africa and which Alexander had for months been keeping in reserve to launch at the opportune moment against Kesselring's line, break it and advance through the Po plains towards Vienna in order to arrive there before the Russians. 'It is in Italy,' Churchill had forecast, 'where the future of the Balkans and Europe will be decided.' On that day at 1050 am the Division, after the battles at Coriano ridge, was reduced to two-thirds of its strength. However, here on the Via Roveta, which led to the summit of the Coriano-San Fortunato ridge, its huge Sherman tanks filled the Ausa valley and with the roar of their engines gave an impression of irresistible force.

But Lieutenant-Colonel Asquith, commanding The Queen's Bays, which together with the 9th Lancers and 10th Hussars made up Brigadier Richard Goodbody's 2nd Armoured Brigade, was extremely worried. He had been ordered by the divisional commander, Major-General Richard Hull – at 37 one of the youngest British generals – to break out to Montecieco on the axis of Via Roveta. To do this would mean leaving intact the summit of a hill called Point 153, on the right of the San Martino-S. Ermete crossroads. Asquith, and Lieutenant-Colonel Price, commanding 9th Lancers, who were to support the attack, were worried because in front of them was the

90th Light Panzer Grenadier Division, commanded by the legendary Major-General Ernst Baade, one of the toughest German divisions among the twenty-six in Italy at that time. 90th Light [as they were known by the British], pride of Rommel's Afrika Korps, had been mauled by 1st Armoured Division in Tunisia, had been reconstituted in Sicily, had fought on the Sangro, the Moro, the Garigliano and the Liri, where their commander, Baade, had acquired the title 'Hero of Cassino'. Then they had been put into reserve near the Italian-French border, but Kesselring had recalled them to the Adriatic front to block the 8th Army's offensive. 90th had now been on the Marecchia for three days, since 17 September.

For his part, Baade was the most unconventional of German soldiers. He called himself a soldier with the worst characteristics . . . [yet] he was always in the front line, even further forward into no-man's-land, attracting the reproaches of his superior officers because he exposed himself to too much danger. And when he retired from no-man's-land he would mock the British artillery on the radio: 'Stop firing. I'm Baade and I'll be back.' Kesselring called him one of the bravest officers in the whole German Army. His soldiers loved him.*

At Montecieco Baade had studied the position and had no difficulty in understanding the intention of the Sherman tanks. He positioned his infernal 88mm guns accordingly.

At the same time, neither Hull, nor 8th Army Commander, Leese, nor Alexander, were likely to employ reconnoitring tactics and invite their subordinates to commit suicide. Goodbody had received orders which he passed on to Asquith – to try and take the houses Balducci and Conti on the left of Via Roveta in order to protect the left flank of the attack. . . .

Where were the terrible enemy anti-tank guns, the infernal 88mms? Securely positioned at Point 153, at S. Paolo, at Villa Gabriella, at Balducci and Conti. To the eyes of Goodbody there was presented a vision like that of the Charge of the Light Brigade, in which, it was remembered, his division's reconnaissance regiment, 4th Hussars, had taken part. . . .

The Queen's Bays had 27 Sherman tanks left from the 52 of three weeks' earlier . . . [when they advanced] the Germans saw them appear from the summit of their crest. The German gunners were incredulous at this spectacle. Each Sherman presented itself to be shot at, like a pigeon at a clay pigeon shoot. It was a massacre . . . 24 Shermans out of the 27 were destroyed. 64 men were killed or wounded.

No one got any marks for this action. It cannot be said that Hull had handled his division properly. Where was the infantry brigade with

---

* The gallant Baade was killed on the last day of the war.

which it would have been easy to take Point 153 before the advance started? 1st Armoured Division was broken up soon afterwards. Goodbody was sacked. Hull was given another division to command. If this was the best the British could do after five years of war, it was no surprise that they did not break through quickly and reach the plains of Lombardy. What remains astonishing to those of us who fought in and survived the Gothic Line battles was: first, the amazing optimism displayed by the higher British commanders, who seemed not to have grasped after all the experience they had had that the German soldiers were masters of defence, would never give up lightly, were commanded by skilled, determined generals and that the higher direction of the war by Hitler was such that he would never willingly give an inch of ground, as Kesselring had so ably and for so long demonstrated in his brilliant conduct of the Italian campaign: and secondly, given the great superiority of material, particularly of artillery and air power, and given also that indispensable commodity in war – time – why it was that we did not deploy our soldiers in the way the Germans did, in teams of tanks, infantry, anti-tank guns, artillery and sappers, making use of every skill and every ounce of fire-power in coordinated and carefully prepared attacks, rather than driving forward with tanks, virtually unsupported by anything else, and simply writing them off as a result? My own regiment, 4th Hussars, had been invited to advance to Coriano, unsupported by any infantry, and had neither made progress nor dented the German defences. All that had been achieved was loss of men and machines. The Queen's Bays had had an even more bitter and futile experience.

By October, 1944, it was clear that Alexander's hopes of seriously damaging the German armies and pushing on across the Po to the north and Vienna had faded away. There was even some doubt about his continuing to contain as many German divisions as before. Bologna had still not been taken. 8th Army, now commanded by McCreery, had halted on the line of the River Savio at Cesena, with Bologna nearly fifty miles away. Clark's 5th Army got much nearer, but was stopped, as he put it, not because of any particular obstacle or at any special time. 'It merely ground to a halt because men could not fight any longer against the steadily increasing enemy reinforcements on our front. . . . At the time I felt that with a month of rest we might yet be able to break into the Po valley before winter clamped down on the Apennines. After all the effort that had been expended, after all the casualties we had suffered, it seemed almost impossible to give up the idea of completing the breakthrough that autumn . . . at the end of October, a definite date was set for renewal of both the Fifth and Eighth Army attacks on Bologna, but we never kept the date'.

Kesselring was in no doubt about the importance of Bologna, observing later that if the positions south of that key town could not be held, then all the positions to the east would have to be evacuated. But he did hold on. He had guaranteed to Hitler that the Apennine position would be successfully defended, so giving the Führer both the time and opportunity to conduct the war elsewhere free from any danger that Allied troops would break into Germany from the south. If the Italian campaign is remarkable for anything, it is for this.

Thus all Alexander's optimism came to nothing. Even as early as mid-September when the Gothic Line battles were at their height, he had expressed his disappointment at the lack of support he was receiving. When Harold Macmillan visited him near Siena on 15 September, Alexander seemed tired and strained. While he understood the need to concentrate on operations in France, which caused him the loss of seven divisions and nearly three-quarters of his air forces, he had hoped that something might be raked up from the Middle East or elsewhere. What perhaps may strike us as extraordinary is that in talking things over with Macmillan and accepting that the Germans had twenty-six divisions, and he himself only twenty – albeit larger ones – Alexander still felt he had some chance of a breakthrough even though he admitted that the Gothic Line was a natural defensive position stronger than Cassino. At the morning conference next day, Macmillan listened to the briefing to discover that the 5th Army was advancing on the Futa Pass and that 8th Army was pushing forward on the Rimini front. Macmillan noted that it would be a race against time; with the weather about to break and then with rivers in spate, it would be impossible to get through the mountain range until spring. He then motored with Alexander to a village north of Florence and climbed a hill with a tower on top:

> From this tower one could see the whole great Apennine range stretched before one's eyes, and for two hours with glasses and maps we watched the fierce battle which was taking place. The main effort of the Fifth Army troops was concentrated round the Futa Pass and an attack was in progress upon a certain Monte Catria to the south-east. This proved partially successful, but *the miracle to my mind is that any progress can be made at all in ground so wonderfully adapted to the defence.**

* My italics.

On the way back they stopped in Florence, and Macmillan noted that the wonders there – the Duomo, Baptistery, Giotto's tower, the Palazzo Vecchio, Loggia di Lanzi, S. Maria Novella – were undamaged. But there was destruction elsewhere – the bridges, except Ponte Vecchio, and many houses by the Arno, all wrecked by the Germans. Alexander clearly took great pride in the fact that his campaign had spared the great cities of Rome, Florence, Pisa, Siena, Assisi and Perugia. Just as he husbanded the lives of his soldiers, so he took care of Italy's artistic treasures. But, Macmillan added, 'Alex is not confident about the issue of the battle'.

This lack of confidence as to great results there was reflected in the second Quebec Conference at which Churchill and his advisers met Roosevelt and his. In spite of Churchill's initial telegram to Wilson, the Supreme Allied Commander, Mediterranean and Middle East, and Alexander, in which he made it plain that there was to be no weakening of Alexander's army 'till Kesselring has bolted beyond the Alps or been destroyed', the actual military recommendations made by the Combined Chiefs of Staff struck a soberer and more realistic note:

> We have examined a report by General Wilson on operations within his theatre. In so far as the battle in Italy is concerned, he considers that operations will develop in one of two ways:
> (a) Either Kesselring's forces will be routed, in which case it should be possible to undertake a rapid regrouping and a pursuit towards the Ljubljana Gap (and across the Alps through the Brenner Pass), leaving a small force to clear up north-west Italy; or
> (b) Kesselring's army will succeed in effecting an orderly withdrawal, in which event it does not seem possible that we can do more than clear the Lombardy plains this year. Difficult terrain and severe weather in the Alps during winter would prevent another major offensive until the spring of 1945.

More realistic, but not realistic enough. Kesselring did more than effect an orderly withdrawal. He effected a staunch defence on a further winter line, and moreover actually mounted a counter-attack on the Serchio, which fluttered some doves in the 92nd U.S. Division. The attack was mounted on Boxing Day, 1944, by German and Italian divisions [troops still loyal to Mussolini] and although it was stopped by 8th Indian Division, coming as it did so soon after the Ardennes counter-offensive, which was still having limited success despite

Patton's relief of Bastogne, it gave Alexander pause. He decided that the time had come to go on the defensive. The winter line ran along the Senio River in the 8th Army sector, with a slight northern bulge towards Bologna, thence south-west to a position some twenty miles north of Pisa and so to the west coast south of La Spezia. Now would follow a period of re-training and preparation for the last great offensive.

In his excellent book about the Gothic Line battles, Douglas Orgill, who fought there, reminds us of the beautiful military cemetery which lies on the slopes of the Coriano Ridge. He points out that although there are many other cemeteries in northern Italy, this one is specially significant 'for it was here that the autumn campaign was decided'. In trying to answer the question – why all these hundreds of soldiers who lie there died – Orgill takes some comfort in the reflection that, seen as a great distraction of German forces from fronts where their presence might have been more decisive, the Italian campaign may be justified. Yet he adds that even though Alexander and other Allied leaders agree with this view – indeed Alexander's final conclusion was that the campaign in Italy did fulfil its strategic mission of drawing German troops away from the more vital battlefields directed at the heart of Germany – we must also bear in mind that Kesselring too felt he had achieved his strategic aim of pinning down Allied resources and giving to the Führer those ever-to-be-desired military commodities, time and space.

Not all the results of the Gothic Line battle, however, were disagreeable. On returning from some minor action with my troop, in which I thought we had acquitted ourselves with credit, one of my fellow troop leaders looked at me with distaste and told me I was turning yellow. It took me a moment or two to realize that he was talking, not figuratively, but literally. A glance in the looking glass confirmed it. I *was* yellow. I was soon to learn, however, that to get jaundice was a not wholly unwelcome fortune of war. It is true that you are forbidden alcohol, but this is a small price to pay for three weeks of clean sheets, regular food and respite from the uneasy feeling that the shell with your name on it, although overdue, has not decided to cut the rendezvous altogether. As by this time operations seemed to have settled down to a matter of holding the line until the spring, I determined to make the best of my bout of jaundice. What I had not expected was that the highlight of it would be ten days' convalescence in, of all places,

Beniamino Gigli's sumptuous villa at Porto Reconati, some 20 miles from Ancona. Said to have cost an unthinkable number of lire, it was perhaps a little bizarre when eyed with the critical gaze of the classicist, but as a convalescent home it was ideal. Warm, big, bright and comfortable, it was run by the British Red Cross who, in the absence of its master, had sensibly retained his staff in the kitchen, the laundry and the gardens.

The superb *tagliatelli*, the delicate *lasagna*, the simple but satisfying *risotto con funghi* are treasured recollections even today. These delights coupled with strolls in the handsome, palely sunlit gardens were restoring my physical condition to its peak form. Nor was another of the senses unadministered to. Most of us during our year in Italy had either discovered or further indulged a liking for the opera. Its enjoyment varied from provincial companies in places like Bari or Taranto to an occasional treat on leave in Rome and Naples. Being stationed nearby for a time, my regiment developed a great affection for the Bari repertory company. All the classic roles were performed by the same three singers, baritone, tenor and soprano, and so attached to them did we become that the sight of an Amazon-like Butterfly clutching a diminutive Pinkerton to her bosom touched us without exciting our ridicule. Somehow we enjoyed all this more than the grand but less intimate performances in Rome.

But, of course, at Porto Reconati, I had the best of all worlds – one of the greatest tenors, the most renowned recordings, a music room which was everything it should be, comfortable, spacious, beautifully furnished and equipped – and above all there was a master of ceremonies who by his devotion to Gigli's voice and person, and by his introductions to and explanations of each opera and song, enhanced the appreciation of each in a way at once unique and endearing. It was he, the major-domo, christened Malvolio by us convalescents, who was in undisputed command of the heterogeneous collection of cooks, gardeners, kitchen maids and footmen, and who quickly earned our affection and respect. He had two great loves – *la caccia* [he meant shooting, of course] and His Master's Voice.

Every recording that Gigli had made was in the music room, and each Tuesday and Thursday evening after dinner Malvolio would treat us to a concert. He announced each piece before playing it, told us when and with whom his beloved master had first sung it, and although he must have heard them all a thousand times, sat as spellbound as any of us. His selection was unerring. He would follow the cynical and reckless Duke of Mantua with a few simple songs, and then move on to the impassioned and noble dying fall of Edgardo. These gramophone concerts cemented my affection for Verdi, Donizetti, Puccini and the others in a way that has made them figure largely in my own modest collection of records.

For his second love, *la caccia*, Malvolio literally dressed to kill. Equipped with baggy pantaloons, a voluminous jacket hung about with game bags and cartridge belts, a feathered alpine sort of hat and a shotgun, he was a transformed man. I was always rather disappointed to see him return not with pheasant, partridge and hare, but with what looked like larks, sparrows and starling. I consoled myself with the reflection that 'there's a special providence in the fall of a sparrow', but it is as the devoted disseminator of His Master's Voice that I shall remember him best. He ensured that my convalescence was complete.

Meanwhile both Alexander's and Kesselring's armies were convalescing from the grim and costly battles of the Gothic Line. But if Hitler could draw comfort from the way in which things had been stabilized in the south, elsewhere it was a different story. Alexander's purpose might have been blunted; that of Eisenhower's and Stalin's armies was not. In January, 1945, one of Hitler's S.S. staff colonels had suggested that Berlin would now be the best place to establish headquarters: 'We'll soon be able to take the streetcar from the eastern to the western front'. And indeed by January, 1945, with the Ardennes counter-offensive in ruins, Hitler had disposed his military strength in such a way that the front which was most vulnerable – that in East Prussia and Poland – was also in relative terms the most weakly defended, and thus the one least likely to be capable of withstanding the appalling knock it was shortly to receive. At this time there were seventy-six divisions in the West, twenty-four in Italy, ten in Yugoslavia, seventeen in Scandinavia – that is a total of 127 divisions deployed on fronts other than the East. Only a very few more, 133 divisions, were on the Eastern front, and lining up against them was the staggering total of 300 Red Army divisions and twenty-five Tank Armies. The attacks now being planned by the Russians were designed to end the war – in the North two army groups commanded by Chernyakhovsky and Rokossovsky would converge on East Prussia; in the centre Zhukov and Koniev would drive on Berlin and Upper Silesia; further South two more army groups were to take Budapest and Vienna, clearing Slovakia as well; Petrov would re-occupy the Northern Carpathians. It is when we contemplate the sheer scale of the Red Army's operations – some seven Army Groups operating over vastly broad fronts – that the relatively minor numbers and narrow fronts of Italy may be seen in their true perspective. In Italy the toss was being argued by some twenty divisions on either side. On 12 January, 1945, Stalin launched 180 divisions with four tank armies, *each* of which contained 1,200 tanks, on the 600-mile front of Poland and East Prussia. The Eastern front collapsed like a house of cards and two weeks after starting their offensive the Russians were on German soil. On 16 January Hitler moved to the Chancellery bunker in Berlin. He was to stay there directing the operations of imaginary armies until his suicide in April. By then Model's Army Group in the Ruhr had been surrounded, the American armies reached the Elbe, Königsberg and Vienna had been taken by the Russians, the way to Berlin had been opened by the Red Army's breach of the Oder defences, and Alexander's armies had at last broken into the Po valley. In short the German Army had been totally defeated in the field, and it is to how this came about in Italy that we must now turn our attention.

9

A FLUID SITUATION

Gleaming successes marked the end of our campaigns in the
Mediterranean.

Churchill

Alexander claimed that the last battle in Italy had been as hard as the
first, but we may question the significance of this claim, for the first
battle was not hard and the final battle was certainly not as hard as those
at Anzio, Cassino and the Gothic Line. By the time the last Allied
offensive was mounted in Italy in April, 1945, there had been changes
of high command on both sides and also changes in the number of
divisions which each side deployed. Alexander had taken over from
Wilson as Supreme Allied Commander, Mediterranean, Clark now
commanded 15th Army Group, McCreery 8th Army, and Truscott
5th Army. On the German side Kesselring had been appointed
Commander-in-Chief, West, in March, while von Vietinghoff, formerly
in charge of 10th Army, had succeeded Kesselring. The Germans had
some nineteen divisions in the operational zone, the Allies seventeen,
but of course their divisions were larger and supported by powerful air
forces. The Allied plan was that 8th Army should begin the offensive,
attacking across the Senio on the night of 9 April, force their way from
Bastia to Argenta, which was a strongly defended gap, flooded on
either side, and then on to the more open ground further north; 5th
Army would attack later, on 14 April, bypassing Bologna to the west,
press on to the Po and join hands with 8th Army there, in order to
destroy as many German forces as possible south of the Po, then
pursue to the Adige.

General McCreery, the greatest cavalry soldier of his generation and at the same time that rare coalition of a brilliant staff officer and higher commander, had long been puzzling how to solve the problem of extensive flooding with which the Germans had aggravated the terrain difficulties. The only ground firm enough for large-scale tank movement was the Ravenna to Ferrara road, and the village of Argenta was a crucial part of this route. 'Several times,' wrote McCreery later, 'I went up in an Auster to look at the other side of the hill to try and solve the problem of the Argenta Gap. It was here, we hoped, that the amphibious tanks would help turn the Germans' eastern flank.' McCreery's plan was broadly a two-corps attack directed on Argenta and Bologna with a further Corps available to keep up momentum and an armoured division ready to be launched when the break-through was certain. Having made his plan McCreery was concerned that he could pass on his own confidence and conviction to his subordinates. In this he succeeded totally. The Commanding Officer of the 17th/21st Lancers, Colonel ffrench-Blake, recalled that as a boost to morale McCreery arranged for a race meeting to be held at Cesena, only thirty miles from the front line – McCreery had, of course, been an outstanding amateur rider himself and he used a racing metaphor in his address to all senior commanders four days before the battle started. ffrench-Blake remembered the occasion:

> In his quiet, almost apologetic voice, he said that the theatre had been stripped of troops for France; that the Army was like an old steeplechaser, full of running, but rather careful; that it was his intention to destroy the Germans south of the Po, rather than allow them to withdraw to further defence lines in the north. The plan was then outlined.

ffrench-Black particularly noted how well McCreery's message got through to his troops, for when he passed it on to his regiment, the thrill of excitement which ran through the soldiers remains one of his greatest memories. They were not to be disappointed. Two days after crossing the Senio, 8th Army had reached the Santerno – even at this stage of the campaign there was still river after river, but happily the mountains were behind us – and the attack by amphibious troop-carrying armoured vehicles, Buffaloes, with both Commandos and part of 56th Division had successfully landed at Menate, some three miles behind the German positions. By 14 April there were more successes. Imola had fallen to the Polish Corps; 78th Division had captured the Bastia bridge and joined 56th Division in their advance on Argenta; the New Zealanders, supported by a squadron of 4th Hussars [more on this in a moment] had crossed the River Sillaro. The whole hinge of the German position was in jeopardy, and von Vietinghoff proposed a withdrawal to the Po before his position became untenable. It must have come as no surprise to him when Hitler dismissed any such notions in a sharp reprimand from Jodl to the effect that any proposals for altering strategy from theatre commanders were to cease. There was to be no question of wavering or adopting the kind of defeatist attitude that seemed to prevail at von Vietinghoff's headquarters. 'The Führer expects now as before the utmost steadfastness in the fulfilment of your present mission, to defend every inch of the north Italian areas entrusted to your command.' Before we see the disastrous results from the Germans' point of view of this refusal to countenance tactical withdrawal, I may perhaps be permitted a personal recollection of what it was like to be supporting the New Zealand Division in their crossing of the Senio and subsequent operations which led to what we had all been hoping for for so long – a tour of northern Italy without being shot at by the Germans.

Having been instructed to lead the squadron across the Senio – by this time, I should add, the squadron consisted of some fifty armoured personnel carriers in which we carried infantry into action, a role which, though less traditionally pugnacious than having tanks, turned out to be rather more dangerous and exciting as we got so much closer to the enemy – I had, like General McCreery, but in a much less important sense, viewed the ground over which we were going to advance from an Auster light aircraft, mainly used by the artillery for observation. It was fascinating to observe that, whereas south of the Senio all was activity, preparation, movement and bustle, north of the river there was nothing to be seen. The Germans were masters of camouflage and concealment. Having picked out my route and noted some landmarks which I hoped would be easily recognizable from the ground too, I returned to the squadron. By this time we had joined the New Zealand battalion which we were to carry into action next morning. That evening there was an artillery barrage of unprecedented violence and duration, combined with huge air attacks on enemy targets [it reminded me of one Italian farmer's melancholy question, put to me some weeks earlier: 'When are you going to stop destroying our farms and livelihood?'], and at first light we crossed the river. We were further supported by a squadron of New Zealand tanks and artillery observers, and succeeded in pushing on with a few skirmishes over another river, without much interference from the Germans. So confident did the New Zealand battalion commander become – he was travelling with me in my vehicle – that he turned and said: 'This must be the breakthrough.' No sooner were the words out of his mouth than we were subjected to the most vicious shelling and mortaring imaginable, and all my fellow officers who were carrying the marvellous New Zealand infantrymen reported stiff opposition at a relatively small river ahead. A prolonged artillery duel was followed by a night attack which succeeded in dislodging the German opposition. At dawn we resumed the advance and I found myself proceeding down a country road with the troops I was responsible for deployed on either side. Suddenly that fearsome tearing noise, like an express train going past, occurred and it was clear that someone was firing armoured-piercing shot at us. I moved off the road to a large, strong-looking farmhouse where I found the New Zealand battalion commander. I asked him what the situation was, and have always admired his answer, which was a splendid euphemism for admitting that he had no idea. He looked at me steadily and replied: 'Fluid!' Shortly afterwards I was informed by my Commanding Officer that a number of German self-propelled guns were heading towards me. Being in a vehicle without any armament other than a machine-gun, I demanded by radio that these unwelcome intruders should be engaged by maximum artillery fire. I received no reply, but happily the German S.P. guns did not appear. After a few more scrappy actions and struggles to get over rivers whose bridges had been blown up and whose banks were mined, we found ourselves advancing faster and faster towards the Po. It was maps we needed now rather than ammunition. It was the break-through and a wonderful feeling of freedom swept over us. The situation was fluid indeed.

This collapse of German resistance had been brought about by the concerted actions of 8th and 5th Armies. On 14 April, five days after the Senio crossing, 5th Army had begun their attack west of the Pistoia-Bologna axis. By 20 April they had broken through the mountain country, crossed the main route leading west from Bologna and headed north. Whatever orders he might have had from Hitler it was clear to von Vietinghoff that the only hope of saving anything of his armies was to conduct a withdrawal to the Po and he signalled Hitler accordingly:

> Resolved by my unshakeable will to hold the Italian front under all circumstance and to carry out your orders to the last, I report to you, my Führer, that as a result of heavy battle losses our forces in the Italian theatre are strained to such an extent that, if we persist in our policy of static defence, an enemy break-through at Lake Comacchio, Bologna and La Spezia can in all probability not be prevented despite the heroic resistance and determination of our officers and men. All available forces have been concentrated in the focal points of the battle, and other sectors of the front, not under direct heavy attack, have consequently been denuded to provide reinforcements. Mobile reserves are no longer available. Thus, the enemy threatens to achieve his object, ie. to split and subsquently crush the German front. In a mobile strategy, however, I still see a possibility of preventing this threat from being carried out and of continuing our resistance with a chance of success. Difficult as it is for me, I consider it my duty, my Führer, to send you this report at this hour and to await your orders.

Hitler, however, was not going to give many more orders. He would shortly be in a way to study a long silence. Yet we may still marvel, with all power slipping from him, at the way he exercised so persistent a fascination over his subordinates. We cannot forget his uncanny gift of making others think that he could make fortune change sides. Field-Marshal Ritter von Greim visited Hitler in the Bunker on 27 April, 1945. The end was but three days away, but somehow or other the customary spell was cast. There was no need for despair, von Greim told the incredulous General Koller on the telephone. Victory was inevitable. 'Everything will be well. The presence of the Führer and his confidence have completely inspired me.' There was to be no such inspiration for von Vietinghoff, and in any case he had left his decision for fighting a mobile battle and withdrawing to the Po too late. 8th Army rushed forward with 6th Armoured Division to Ferrara, Bologna was captured by the Poles, 5th Army reached the Po, the Allied air forces wreaked destruction on retiring German columns, thousands of Germans were cut off by the juncture of the 5th and 8th Armies, the Po was crossed, the fleeing remnants of von Vietinghoff's forces were pursued to the Adige, then that river was crossed and Allied troops, unhindered by opposition, made for Padua, Treviso,

Venice, Vicenza, Trento, Brescia and Alessandria. On 29 April Churchill was able to signal Stalin:

> I have just received a telegram from Field-Marshal Alexander that after a meeting at which your officers were present the Germans accepted the terms of unconditional surrender presented to them and are sending the material clauses of the instrument of surrender to General von Vietinghoff, with the request to name the date and hour at which conclusion of hostilities can be made effective. It looks therefore as if the entire German forces south of the Alps will almost immediately surrender.

They did. On 2 May almost a million German soldiers became prisoners of war. The Italian campaign was at an end. In a special message sent tо his officers and men next day General McCreery summed up what had happened:

> On 9 April the Eighth Army started the last great battle in Italy. Twenty-three days later, on 2 May, the enemy surrendered unconditionally. We achieved our object of destroying the enemy south of the River Po. North of the Po a relentless pursuit prevented the remnants of the enemy from making a further stand. This final and decisive victory in the history of the Eighth Army was achieved only after hard and bitter fighting. In the first seventeen days the enemy's best troops were smashed and reduced to remnants. The enemy had great advantages of ground, strong defences on a succession of river obstacles, extensive flooding and deep minefields, but all difficulties were overcome by the splendid fighting spirit, skill, determination and endurance shown by *all* Ranks, and the excellent co-operation of all Arms. In this battle, as always, the decisive factors have been the magnificent fighting qualities of our soldiers and good junior leadership.... The unconditional surrender of the enemy brings the Eighth Army many new and urgent tasks. We have a big job to do in helping to win the peace.

Although Alexander's armies had triumphed, they had still, of course not threatened the heart of the Third Reich. On 21 April when the Supreme Commander of the Wehrmacht was conducting one more battle from the depths of the Bunker, Marshal Zhukov had reached Berlin's eastern suburbs and his fellow Marshal, Koniev, was about to reach Dresden. On that same day General Eisenhower gave orders that his victorious armies should halt on the line of the River Elbe in order to avoid accidental clashes with the Red Army and link up with his Russian allies there. Eight days later, on 29 April, on the same day that Churchill had telegraphed to Stalin the news of the impending

German surrender in Italy, Hitler held his final military conference. The Berlin Commandant, General Weidling, had described the military position and stated that, as the Russians would probably reach the Chancellory and the Bunker within three days, the time had come for the defensive troops to break out. Hitler predictably pronounced against this course of action and there the matter ended. Next day he ended his life, and thus made it possible for others to bring the war itself to an end. If it is true to say that the Allied armies in Italy had but an indirect influence on this end, the same might be said of their influence on the peace which followed. For what happened next had been largely decided at Yalta.

It is ironical to reflect that, whereas late in 1943 Churchill's close advisers had been sanguine enough to anticipate that the war might be ended during 1944, more than a year later, on 12 January, 1945, with the German Ardennes counter-offensive already clearly a failure, the British war cabinet estimated that the war might not be over until the last day of 1945! They were to revise their view when the startling successes of the Red Army's January offensive became plain, but, in spite of this, when Churchill proceeded to Yalta to confer with Roosevelt and Stalin, victory in the West seemed far less likely than the unattractive prospect that the war would be won by the Russians. It was at this point that the respective attitudes of the British and the Americans to such a prospect had a profound influence on the outcome of this conference. No one has expressed the difference of these attitudes better than Sir Isaiah Berlin: 'Mr Roosevelt was intrigued by the Russian Sphinx; Mr Churchill instinctively recoiled from its alien and to him unattractive attributes. Mr Roosevelt, on the whole, thought that he could cajole Russia and even induce her to be assimilated into the great society which would embrace mankind; Mr Churchill, on the whole, remained sceptical.'

Under such circumstances it was hardly surprising that when the three leaders met in Yalta from 4 to 11 February, 1945, Churchill found himself in a weak position to press his views. Roosevelt wanted above all a quick end to the war, not only in Europe, but in the Far East too. Stalin's promises of further offensives against Germany, and moreover an undertaking that Russia would enter the war against Japan three months after Hitler's defeat, proved irresistible. It was therefore in vain that Churchill objected to some of the conditions which his two fellow leaders were in agreement about – how much German territory should be given to Poland, who was to govern Poland, and the amount of German reparations. He was obliged to accept that Stalin's word would match his apparent good will. There was, however, one area in which agreement was unanimous – the exaction of unconditional surrender from Germany and maximum effort to finish the war off quickly. As we have seen, the end was not slow in coming. The Red Army's attacks at Küstrin and across the Oder, their sweeps further south in Hungary and Austria, Eisenhower's successful crossing of the Rhine and pursuit to the Elbe – by mid-April no further effective German resistance was possible. And in the South Alexander's armies were pushing forward to the Po and beyond. Deliberations at Yalta had not taken much account of what was happening in Italy, yet later, curiously enough, rumours of separate surrender discussions there had given both Hitler and Stalin great cause for concern.

In February General Wolff, who was the Wehrmacht's principal liaison officer with Mussolini's Republican Government in northern Italy, had, through agents in Switzerland, made contact with Alexander's headquarters with a view to negotiating the surrender of Kesselring's Army Group in Italy. Kesselring's removal to become Commander-in-Chief, West, and his replacement by von Vietinghoff had delayed developments, and in the end it was only Alexander's successful offensive which brought things to a head. But the fuss made by Stalin – in which he accused Roosevelt of authorizing negotiations allowing Anglo-American troops to advance unopposed into the heart of Germany, while Germany continued to fight against Russia – apart from provoking a spirited reply from the President, caused Churchill to address Stalin thus:

> The President has sent me his correspondence with you about the contacts made in Switzerland between a British and American officer on Field-Marshal Alexander's Staff and a German general named Wolff relating to possible surrender of Kesselring's army in Northern Italy. . . . There were no negotiations in Switzerland even for a military surrender of Kesselring's army. Still less did any political-military plot enter into our thoughts . . . . We consider that Field-Marshal Alexander has full right to accept the surrender of the German army of twenty-five divisions on his front in Italy, and to discuss such matters with German envoys who have the power to settle the terms of capitulation. . . . There is, however, a possibility that the whole of this request to parley was one of those attempts which are made by the enemy with the object of sowing distrust between Allies.

There was in fact no need for the enemy to sow distrust between the Allies. It was already firmly there. It was because of this and because of the absurd belief which Hitler had that sooner or later there would be a positive breach between the Western Allies and the Russians that he had given tacit agreement to the negotiations taking place. At a meeting in the Bunker on 18 April at which Hitler had predicted an armed struggle between his Eastern and Western enemies, going on to say, fantastically, that he would then be offered a high price for participating in a final war, he had listened to what Wolff had to say and finally dismissed him, telling Wolff to return to Italy and continue his negotiations, but to get better terms. Two days later, however, as the Allied leaders wished to avoid a further row with Stalin, Alexander received a signal from the Combined Chiefs of Staff saying that it was now clear that the German Commander-in-Chief, Italy [von Vietinghoff], had no intention of surrendering his forces on terms acceptable to the Allies and that therefore the British and U.S. Governments had decided that the Office of Strategic Services should break off contact with the German emissaries. Alexander could regard the matter as closed. A few days later Wolff received a telgram from Himmler forbidding any negotiations, as 'it is more than ever essential that the Italian front hold and remain intact.' It was much too late. The Italian front had already collapsed and von Vietinghoff authorized Wolff to make his way to Alexander's headquarters. It was on 28 April that agreement was reached for surrender to be effective at six o'clock on the evening of 2 May. By that time the two principals of the Brutal Friendship had paid in full the price of their political ambitions and military follies. Mussolini had been shot by partisans on 25 April. Hitler had chosen self-slaughter five days later.

Churchill deployed all his renowned eloquence in praising those who had successfully carried out his own strategic plans and signalled to Alexander:

> I rejoice in the magnificently planned and executed operations of the Fifteenth Group of Armies, which are resulting in the complete destruction or capture of all the enemy forces south of the Alps. That you and General Mark Clark should have been able to accomplish these tremendous and decisive results against a superior number of enemy divisions, after you have made great sacrifices of whole armies for the Western Front, is indeed another proof of your genius for war and of the intimate brotherhood in arms between the British Commonwealth and Imperial forces and those of

the United States. Never, I suppose, have so many nations advanced and manoeuvred in one line victoriously. The British, Americans, New Zealanders, South Africans, British-Indians, Poles, Jews, Brazilians, and strong forces of liberated Italians have marched together in that high comradeship and unity of men fighting for freedom and for the deliverance of mankind. This great final battle in Italy will long stand out in history as one of the most famous episodes in this Second World War.

Will it? It may be doubted. However successful this last battle might have been, it surely cannot compete in sheer scale, or strategic consequences, or dramatic appeal, or brilliant generalship, or incalculable awfulness with many other battles in Europe alone, to say nothing of the Far East. The battle for France in 1940, Hitler's grip of a faltering Wehrmacht in December, 1941, Stalingrad, El Alamein, *Zitadelle* in July, 1943, Normandy, the Ardennes counter-stroke, the final Russian and Anglo-American advances which cut the Third Reich in two – these battles are likely to be remembered and studied and argued about as long as people go on taking an interest in military history. But side-shows tend to remain side-shows. It was necessary and proper for Churchill to praise the commanders and troops who had brought the Italian campaign, which had lasted a year and ten months, including Sicily, to a successful conclusion. But we may take his words with a pinch of salt, as we may too his contention that 'the principal task of our armies had been to draw off and contain the greatest possible number of Germans'. This was what the campaign was later said to have *achieved*. We should not, however, overlook Churchill's original and constantly reiterated theme that great strategic and political prizes were open to the Allies by exploiting opportunity in the Mediterranean. And indeed there were times when such prizes might have been within the Allies' grasp. But each time, divisions were withdrawn from Alexander to be used elsewhere – either in France or in the battle for Germany on the Western Front. Seven divisions were taken before the battle for Rome was joined, and that battle then bogged down for a complete winter; six more were removed before assaulting the Gothic Line, and then that bogged down for another complete winter; finally the Canadian Corps was taken away before the final offensive, but by then it hardly mattered for decision was being sought and gained elsewhere. Indeed decision was always being sought elsewhere – either on the Eastern or Western fronts, and it is in the contribution which the Italian campaign made to the struggle on these fronts that judgement as to its effectiveness must be made. First we should clear our minds of what Churchill had originally described as 'flexible manoeuvres' pushing left-handed in Normandy, right-handed in Italy, or both-handed, as resources and circumstances dictated. The manoeuvres in Italy were never flexible. There the battle was always one of attrition, and battles of attrition tend to be expensive for both sides. It is with this in mind that we may look again at Alexander's summing up of the Italian campaign.

He pointed out that its value was not to be gauged in relation to ground, for he claimed that the ground was not 'vital' either to the Allies or the Germans. Certainly its lack of importance to the Allies was one of the key arguments endlessly deployed by the Americans, who always insisted on the quickest route through France to the heart of Germany. Its importance to the Germans, however, can be looked at very differently. Here was a piece of ground, the country of an unreliable and probably treacherous ally, which would be easy to defend at relatively little cost and which above all would allow Hitler both time and space with which to conduct the war in the more 'vital' theatres. Seen in this light, holding on to Italy for as long as possible, keeping the Allied armies there at arm's length, containing them, as Hitler put it, with Kesselring's little finger, and at the same time *absorbing Allied military resources* which might have been far more dangerously employed elsewhere – seen thus, to continue successfully to conduct an Italian defensive campaign must have appeared highly attractive to Hitler and the Wehrmacht. Alexander further concluded that the role of his armies was 'subordinate and preparatory' and he went on to argue that his campaign drew away from France a sufficient number of German divisions, whose presence there might have turned the scales against success of the Normany invasion. Moreover, there were in all some fifty-five German divisions committed to the general Mediterranean area in the summer of 1944, a time of great crisis on the Western front.

Here is the nub of the controversy. It can be argued, of course, that Hitler could have moved divisions in the Mediterranean area, which were not committed to fighting, or could have withdrawn to the Gothic Line or even the Alps, much earlier, *had he wanted to*, and so have been able to reinforce the Western, or Eastern fronts. Alexander maintained that his strategic mission had been fulfilled simply because he *did* tie down some eighteen to twenty-six divisions between September, 1943, and May, 1945. Given that this was the correct strategic mission and given that he could not have tied down any more – both questionable assumptions – we may perhaps accept that Alexander did his duty *as he saw it*. But doubts persist both as to the impact of the Italian campaign on the conduct of the war as a whole and on the skill or otherwise with which the campaign was handled, strategically and tactically, by the Allied and German leaders. It is a judgement on these issues which must now be put forward.

10

JUDGEMENT

And so, with the war slowly ravishing the peninsula, and Italy at the bottom of the list for food priorities, the country began to suffer the cruellest sort of revenge for its fatal weakness in allowing Mussolini to have ruled for so long. It was not the war, it was the aftermath of war that destroyed Italy.... It was a campaign which never had a definite and reasonable military object in view. It could end only in the Alps, the worst possible place.

Alan Moorehead

This is a harsh judgement. Alan Moorehead went on to say that the only major loss suffered as a result of the Italian campaign, apart from human lives and Italian cities, was – time. His view is to some extent shared by John Grigg, whose *1943: The Victory That Never Was* tries to show that the cross-Channel invasion, which was at length mounted in 1944, should have taken place a year earlier. Grigg suggests that the four prerequisites for landing successfully in France – air superiority, enough troops, shipping to carry them, and some means of preventing the Germans concentrating against and eliminating an Allied beach-head – either existed or could have been created in 1943. In making this claim, a highly questionable one, he overlooks the very commodity which he is trying to save – time.

The decision to invade Sicily was taken in January, 1943, at the Casablanca Conference. Once this decision was taken there could be no possibility of a mid-1943 cross-Channel invasion, so that in order to allow the latter operation even to be taken seriously, it would have been necessary at the beginning of that year to decide *not* to invade Sicily, indeed not in any way to exploit in the Mediterranean area the clearing of North Africa, which was expected to be completed during the early months of 1943. Even with all the troops available to Alexander and Eisenhower, victory in Tunis was not eventually won until May. To have moved, trained and had ready sufficient troops for a mid-1943 cross-Channel attempt might have jeopardized the North African victory itself, which, because it was so long in coming, was a means of vindicating the decision to go for Sicily and so ensure that time would not be flung away.

From Tunis to Sicily was a relatively easy leap. Tunis to France, via the United Kingdom, would have been hazardous indeed. We have seen that the purpose of invading Sicily was to knock Italy out of the war and to keep Germans busy in the Mediterranean area. We must concede that, in both respects, it was successful. What was not foreseen was that knocking Italy out of the war would put so great a burden on the Allies, as well as on the Germans. Nor was it appreciated that there would be no easy or decisive exploitation of the Italian surrender. On the contrary it presented the Germans with the means of tying down substantial Allied resources at a reasonable cost and giving themselves time to develop operations elsewhere. But whether the Allies had any sensible alternative to invading Sicily and Italy must be doubted.

Quite apart from the Allies' difficulties with time, the other great weakness of Grigg's argument turns on the power of the Wehrmacht to concentrate against a 1943 landing in France. If there had been no Sicily invasion and, we may assume, no fall of Mussolini or at any rate no Italian defection from the Axis, there would have been no serious distraction of German divisions to the south. What is more a June, 1943, invasion of France would have preceded Hitler's great Kursk offensive in Russia of July, during which Hoth's 4th Panzer Army indulged in a death-ride. Such would have been the noise of preparations in the United Kingdom that the Western front would not have been milked for offensives in the East. We must bear in mind too that, even in June, *1944*, when the battle for Normandy was still touch and go, Hitler was squandering *twenty-eight divisions*, 350,000 soldiers in a futile attempt to hold ground in the East. The whole point of getting involved in Sicily and Italy was to help ensure that the Normandy landings when they were made, after proper training, preparation and deception measures, would succeed, while at the same time lending some assistance to the Red Army. Looked at like this, although in one sense time was lost, it was also gained for it kept the Germans occupied albeit in a secondary theatre, while the arrangements for a decisive blow elsewhere were being perfected. It was only when Allied leaders began to look for decisive results in Italy itself that they reaped such disappointment and frustration. And as soon as we acknowledge this point, we are reminded too of Moorehead's objection, which was repeatedly made by Montgomery *at the time*, that the Italian campaign had no master plan, no clear, realizable objective:

> What we want in Italy is a proper and firm plan for waging the campaign. At present it is haphazard and go-as-you-please.
>
> I fight my way forward as I like; I stop and pause when I like; I choose my own objectives.
>
> Clark (Fifth Army) does the same; I have very close touch with him and we see that our actions are so coordinated that all is well.
>
> But we each do *what* we like, *when* we like; the total military power in the two armies is not applied on one big plan. In other words there is no grip or control by 15 Army Group.
>
> As far as I know no high authority has ever said what is wanted. Do we want Rome and its airfields? Do we want the Po valley?
>
> What *do* we want and when?
>
> Until some very clear directive is issued we shall continue to muddle on.

This lack of clarity and lack of grip was intolerable to Montgomery, and the theme outlined above in his diary note of 27 October, 1943, was one he was to return to time and time again. Before long, of course, Montgomery was to go and apply his own very special clarity and grip to the problem of invading Normandy, and after Montgomery's departure Alexander was obliged to take some sort of grip himself, for the German winter line was impeding his advance to Rome. There was still no master plan. Rome itself was thought of as an adequate objective. But Alexander did also intend to knock the 10th Germany Army about. Alexander was constantly seeking some great victory which would enable his armies to sweep forward and capture a significantly political objective like Vienna. It was a victory which as constantly went on eluding him. His idea of a landing at Anzio to break the stalemate of Cassino, an idea which was so enthusiastically taken up by Churchill, was a good one, but it was executed with insufficient strength and a lack of boldness, which simply permitted Kesselring to bring containing and later counter-attack forces against the beachhead, without weakening his defences at Cassino – indeed he had the tactical foresight and audacity to strengthen them. So that, far from Anzio's relieving the pressure at Cassino by getting astride the German communications and obliging Kesselring to withdraw, it was Alexander's offensive of May, 1944 [much of the credit for this plan must go to his Chief of Staff, General John Harding] which allowed the Anzio forces to break out by capturing Cassino and advancing north. Even then, as we have seen, Mark Clark's obsession with his own image by diverting his forces to capture Rome instead of assisting with the destruction of the German 10th Army robbed Alexander of a more conclusive victory.

Undaunted by this disappointment, Alexander again held out hopes of bringing off a decisive coup in the autumn of 1944, and maintained that, provided he could keep the Allied divisons already earmarked for the landings in southern France, he would conquer the rest of Italy and push on through Yugoslavia to Vienna. There was never any chance that the Americans would agree to the abandonment of the *Anvil/ Dragoon* operation in southern France in order to pursue what they saw as a further battle of attrition in Italy. Even Alexander was to admit that it was more the dazzling prospect of a rapid advance to Vienna that was to exercise the minds of his staff, rather than any detailed planning which might make it seem militarily feasible. Any such planning, he conceded, would have been premature until there was some certainty that his armies could get to and advance through the Po valley before the end of 1944. Whether they would have done so with the extra *Dragoon* divisions must still be doubtful, and if they had the Germans would simply have withdrawn to shorter and more easily defensible positions the further north they went. For the rest of 1944 therefore Alexander had to be content with tying down as many German divisions as he could. With the Allied armies firmly established in France and about to win great victories there and the Red Army continuing its inexorable progress to the west, the Italian campaign had done its stuff. Not that it quietened down greatly. The Gothic Line battles were fierce and costly. Alexander's spring offensive of 1945 was a triumph. But the war could not be won in Italy, and in his final despatches about the battles there Alexander admitted as much. 'The Allied armies in Italy,' he wrote, 'were not engaged with the enemy's main armies and their attacks were not directed, as were those of the Allies in the West or the Russians in the East, against the heart of the German Fatherland

and the nerve-centres of Germany's national existence. Our role was subordinate and preparatory.' This, of course, was written after the war. During it there were occasions when Alexander hoped that his role would be primary and a theme all its own. His post-war observations were much nearer to the mark. And in keeping busy, or if not busy deployed away from the nerve-centres of Germany, a number of divisions which might have delayed Germany's defeat still longer, he fulfilled the mission, however subsidiary, that he had been given.

Churchill, as might have been expected, for they shared to some extent a view of the war as a great romantic adventure, gave Alexander his full backing. Alanbrooke was less sure. We find an entry in Brooke's diary for November, 1943, in which he deplores Alexander's inability to think 'big', his lack of vision; 'charming as he is,' Brooke noted, 'Alexander fills me with gloom'. Brooke's own attitude to the Mediterranean theatre generally and Italy more particularly veered from supreme optimism to bitter disappointment. Yet, except perhaps for Churchill himself, he was the most persistent and eloquent advocate of pursuing a Mediterranean strategy. At the *Trident* conference in Washington in May, 1943, he was pleased to obtain American agreement to continuing pressure on Italy, although the exact form which this would take was not then decided, indeed could not be decided until Sicily had been successfully invaded and taken. And even though it was conceded – this was the key point which satisfied the Americans – that Mediterranean operations would be subordinate to the invasion of North-West Europe a year later, Brooke still saw these operations as a proper means of weakening and distracting Germany, while at the same time offering a variety of options, none of them involving too great a commitment of forces, to be taken up in Italy or the Balkans as circumstances and opportunities might allow. In adopting this cautious, yet realistic, attitude, Brooke was surely right. It was only later, when the invasion of Italy was actually under way, that he began to believe that great chances to exploit the situation more boldly were being frustrated by the Americans' refusal to commit more forces there. This change of view was hardly consistent with the agreed Allied strategy that the supreme effort was to be made in North-West Europe while continuing to maintain pressure in the South, specifically to aid the supreme effort. Nor were any ideas about grand exploitations of Italy's collapse consistent with Brooke's previous intention to proceed prudently, step by step, to ensure that the Germans were kept busy in the Mediterranean area. We may understand and sympathize with his disappointment that the advances from Salerno and Calabria did not result in the rapid fall of Rome. It is less easy to comprehend why it was, when the Germans deployed substantial forces to defend the Winter Line south of Rome, that he did not welcome this as a vindication of the very strategy which he had so long been recommending. In the end, of course, the whole matter was one of degree. How *many* German divisions could be kept away from France or the Eastern front? What should be done in Italy and elsewhere in order to ensure that the maximum number of enemy divisions were committed and engaged? Yet in November, 1943, Brooke appeared to be swinging away from the fundamental strategy that he himself had not only agreed, but been a passionate advocate of. Any idea of making the Mediterranean the *main* thrust, despite Churchill's concept of flexible, right-handed as well as left-handed, manoeuvres had long since been dropped. *Overlord* was the thing. Nonetheless, we find Brooke noting in his diary:

> When I look at the Mediterranean I realize only too well how far I have failed in my task during the last two years. If only I had had sufficient force of character to swing those American Chiefs of Staff, and make them see daylight, how different war might be. We should have been in a position to force the Dardenelles by the capture of Crete and Rhodes. We should have had the whole Balkans ablaze by now, and the war might have been finished in 1943! Instead, to satisfy American short-sightedness, we have been led into agreeing to the withdrawal of forces from the Mediterranean for a nebulous Second Front and we have emasculated our offensive strategy. It's heartbreaking!

In another diary entry that month we find Brooke complaining that the Americans have seriously affected Allied Mediterranean strategy and the conduct of the war as a whole. He reiterates that, had they whole-heartedly supported Britain in that theatre, Rome would be securely in their hands. Yet, as Michael Howard has so eloquently observed, the Americans had in fact stood by the agreements reached earlier that year. Far from having abandoned the Mediterranean strategy, the Americans had supported it with the result, entirely satisfactory from their point of view, that the Axis was no more, Italy out of the war, and Germany obliged both to fight a battle for the mainland of Italy and divert forces elsewhere, particularly in the Balkans, to replace Italian divisions which had previously been there. In spite of all this, a feeling of disappointment prevailed among the British. The Prime Minister himself was foremost in trying to swing some emphasis back to Italy. In this he was encouraged by General Alexander, who, conscious of the danger of stalemate on the Winter Line south of Rome and concerned too that it would be all too easy for the Germans to defend that line with minimum forces unless he did something to break the deadlock, was proposing an amphibious attack on the rear and flanks of the German position. It was this proposal, as we have seen, that led to Churchill's getting the Americans to agree to some delay in returning landing craft to the United Kingdom for *Overlord* in order to indulge in the luxury of Anzio.

One consideration in all this veering away from the real purpose and potential of the Italian campaign, this reluctance to settle down to a battle of attrition, and seek instead more decisive results by constantly renewing and reinforcing the offensive, which both Brooke and Churchill seemed intent on, was that it heightened the Americans' distrust of the British being absolutely committed to *Overlord*. Churchill's will-o'-the-wisp hankerings after Rhodes did not help, but in fact, although it may have seemed to the Americans that Brooke was aiming to commit them to greater efforts in the Mediterranean at the expense of the decisive blow in North-West Europe, this was not so. Brooke's loyalty to the agreed strategy did not waver. He did, however, want to make sure that his decisive blow should be given the highest chance of success by weakening the Germans' ability to counter it. Hence his enthusiastic support for the Anzio landings. Alas, they did not achieve what he had hoped for. The beachhead was easily sealed off by Kesselring's forces without any permanent reinforcement of the Italian front, and the logistic strain on Allied resources to keep the beachhead supplied and secure was considerable. Churchill's comment to the effect that, instead of hurling a wild cat ashore that would tear out the bowels of the Boche, they had simply stranded a whale with its tail flopping about, summed it up admirably. The concept no doubt had been sound. Its execution both in power and daring had been inadequate.

But one thing, of course, led to another. If Anzio had shown itself to be incapable of helping break the Germans at Cassino, then Alexander's great offensive, *Diadem*, planned for May, 1944, would help the Allies to break out from Anzio. Besides Brooke was convinced that at this time, with *Overlord* so near and so crucial, it was more important then ever to ensure that the Germans remained firmly committed to an Italian campaign in which, as Hitler so often reiterated, 'every inch of ground' would be stubbornly fought for. Brooke was, with the benefit of *Ultra* intercepts, aware that Kesselring would continue to defend Italy as far south as possible, but his insistence that Alexander should pursue the offensive with all possible strength and so oblige the Germans to remain heavily committed there was sound. It gave rise, however, to yet one more Anglo-American controversy as to the employment of forces in the Mediterranean – the question of landing in southern France, Operation *Anvil*, later called *Dragoon*. Brooke's stand here was not only that he did not believe *Dragoon* would really affect the Normandy battle favourably; he was convinced that this diversion of effort would affect the Italian battle most unfavourably. Brooke tried, as early as March, 1944, two months before Alexander's offensive to take Rome and three months before *Overlord*, to get *Anvil* cancelled. He failed, but it was postponed. By the time it was launched in August, Alexander's armies, having captured Rome, were closing up to the Gothic Line, while the battle for Normandy had been won. A. J. P. Taylor's comment on the landings in southern France was: 'The landing had been planned in order to distract German strength from the north. Postponement destroyed its purpose. . . . It was now the landing in the north which distracted the Germans from the south.' No wonder Brooke returned to the charge in June, 1944, well *before* these landings, in one more attempt to pursue a strategy which he saw as the one most likely to do maximum harm to the Germans. Having previously accepted that, once Alexander's armies had reached the Pisa-Rimini line, they would have played their part in keeping enemy divisions away from the Normandy battlefields, and therefore the landings in southern France could proceed, he suddenly did an absolute *volte-face* when it became clear from *Ultra* that Kesselring intended to fight a defensive battle well south of the Pisa-Rimini line on Hitler's orders. As Brooke saw it, the opportunities to smash Kesselring's armies south of the Pisa-Rimini line far outweighed anything that might be gained in southern France.

As might have been expected Churchill enthusiastically supported Brooke and telegraphed to Roosevelt recommending that divisions should not be diverted from Alexander at a time when there was an opportunity, not only to destroy Kesselring's forces, but to push on to Trieste and beyond. Roosevelt predictably turned him down and insisted on sticking to the strategy agreed at Teheran – exploitation of *Overlord*, advances in Italy and an assault on southern France. His reply contained this passage:

> My interest and hopes centre on defeating the Germans in front of Eisenhower and driving on into Germany, rather than on limiting this action for the purpose of staging a full major effort in Italy. I am convinced that we will have sufficient forces in Italy, with *Anvil* forces withdrawn, to chase Kesselring north of Pisa-Rimini and maintain heavy pressure against his army at the very least to the extent necessary to contain his present force.

There can be little doubt that Roosevelt was right to give the priority to what Eisenhower was doing and, although Kesselring was not exactly chased *north* of Pisa-Rimini, he was chased there and kept there with roughly the same number of divisions until shortly before the end of the whole game. And, as this was after all the strategic mission which Alexander had been given, there was little that Brooke could complain about. As things turned out the Italian campaign continued to play its part in Allied grand strategy, and for this, despite his occasional outbursts of frustration and fury with the Americans, Brooke must take much of the credit. David Fraser pays him a proper tribute when he writes:

> Brooke had, from the beginning, been the strongest proponent of a Mediterranean strategy. Without his skilful advocacy, there might have been no Italian campaign at all. From first to last that campaign fulfilled its purpose. Throughout the years since the landings at Salerno (apart from a short period in 1944) the Germans had always maintained more fighting formations in Italy than the Allies, and this continued until the end. In a country well-suited to defence, against an enemy whose flanks rested on the sea, the Allies had nevertheless attacked continuously. They pinned the Germans to the peninsula by fighting. That was their task. They were, additionally and finally, completely victorious in the field.

Throughout his pursuit of the Mediterranean strategy, Brooke had had a champion who believed in it even more ardently than he did – the Prime Minister. As we have seen in these pages his passionate desire that the British and British-controlled armies should do great things, win decisive victories, meant that his eye was constantly on the theatre where these armies were deployed – the Middle East and Mediterranean. It was he who was the architect of victory in North Africa. In the earlier dark days of the war, when Britain was fighting alone, he had not hesitated to reinforce the British armies in Egypt, even though an invasion threat still hung over Britain. From early 1941 onwards the Western Desert was the one area where the British were fighting Germans on land, so that we may understand the stream of minutes and telegrams with which Churchill plagued commanders on the spot, when he could hardly contain his exasperation that they seemed unable to cap strategic opportunity with tactical success. Even at the nadir of his fortunes, the fall of Tobruk in June, 1942, although he felt deeply the disgrace of it, he did not despair, but managed to pluck from Roosevelt, whose generosity at this time rivalled all other examples of 'a friend in need', the 300 Sherman tanks and 100 self-propelled guns which a few months later assisted Montgomery in turning the tables on Rommel once and for all. It was Churchill too who persuaded Roosevelt that the Anglo-American invasion of French North Africa would be the proper joint strategy for late 1942, a move which not only meant the end of the Axis position in Africa, but yielded a great prize of captured enemy soldiers and equipment comparable with the haul at Stalingrad. 'Africa Redeemed' was how Churchill described the achievement of this great victory, and went on quickly to ask what the Allies should do with it.

He was not slow to answer his own question. As Michael Howard put it: 'As for Mr Churchill himself, and, perhaps, for the commanders of the victorious British armies in Africa, the impulse to carry the battle into Italy was emotional as well as strategic.' That there were sound strategic reasons for doing so has been clearly demonstrated by the results achieved. But it must be admitted that from time to time emotion was in danger of getting the better of strategy. As Axis resistance in North Africa crumbled, British enthusiasm for exploiting success grew. It was fortunate that the Americans, keeping their eye firmly on the main ball, the invasion of Western Europe, were able to resist the more extravagant ideas of the British. Yet throughout the Italian campaign Churchill was always returning, like Brooke, to the idea of some great coup in Italy which would show that a right-handed push could yield spoils of opportunity as spectacular as those which a left-handed push was expected to grasp. Right up until the summer of 1944 Churchill was still pressing for Alexander to retain those forces earmarked for southern France so that he could crush Kesselring's armies south of the Pisa-Rimini line and ride in triumph through the Ljubljana gap to Vienna. The Americans insisted on adhering to the previously agreed strategic decisions, and no responsible commentator would now say that they were wrong. As a distraction from other fronts, as an obligation which Germany could not ignore, the campaign in Italy played its part. We can all agree now that the strategy was opportunistic. Victorious armies were on the threshold of Italy and to Italy they went. And it must also be recognized that, even though *Overlord* itself remained the supreme Allied operation for 1944, Churchill got his way by persuading the Americans to delay D-Day in Normandy and permit Alexander to indulge in one more push in Italy early in 1944 so that something conclusive might emerge. It did not. The Mediterranean theatre remained a subsidiary one, but this was precisely the role allotted to it in Allied grand strategy. It was an essential stepping stone to Allied victory in the West, and all Churchill's dedication to it was wholly vindicated.

If Churchill was intent on exploiting success in North Africa and Italy's defection from the Axis, Hitler was equally determined to minimize the damage which could thereby be done to Germany's strategic position. For him the Mediterranean had always been a side-show. Not all Raeder's eloquence and sound reasoning about crushing the British position in the Middle East, and *then* turning to deal with Russia, moved him. If we look back on it now, we may see that had Hitler chosen to follow Raeder's advice and employed even a small part of the huge forces used for *Barbarossa*, the invasion of Russia; if he had sent to Libya an Afrika Korps three or four times the size of Rommel's tiny force, supported it with a Fliegerkorps or two, and captured Malta – all within the Wehrmacht's capability *before* attacking Russia; if he had done these things, remembering how close-run a thing it was in the desert anyway, it is difficult to see how the British would have maintained their position in Egypt, Palestine, Iraq and East Africa. And then, as the *Official History* has pointed out, with the Eastern Mediterranean lost, with no bases to dispute control of the sea communications there, the Allied task in getting a foothold in Europe might have been something beyond their capability. But it might equally well be said that had Hitler not attacked Russia at all, the power of the Wehrmacht would have remained such that landings by the Allies anywhere in Europe would have had little chance of success. The interesting thing here is that the British Mediterranean strategy itself had an effect, greatly to our benefit, on Hitler's invasion of Russia. British intervention in Greece, although to end in the capture of substantial numbers and the evacuation of more, did distract German forces from *Barbarossa*. Indeed Jodl, head of operations at Hitler's headquarters, went so far as to state at Nuremberg that Germany had lost the war because she had been obliged to divert divisions to meet the British landing in Greece. It is almost always absurd to declare that one single military action, or lack of action, can have so profound an effect on a war fought all over the world, but it is enough to justify the British action to say that, had *Barbarossa* started, say, a month earlier than it did, that is in May, 1941, instead of June, and had been more strongly supported, richer in shock troops, with another month of good weather to campaign in, the German spearheads might have taken Moscow with incalculable consequences. Hitler had always intended to attack in May in order to give himself, as he put it, 'five months to finish the job'.

So we may say that as early as the spring of 1941 the Mediterranean strategy pursued by the British was having an important impact on German operations elsewhere, particularly those about to be undertaken on the Eastern front. It was to go on doing so throughout its course. That the Mediterranean theatre was essentially a secondary one in Hitler's estimate is illustrated by the reflection that the fighting there between the Germans and the British went on for four years without a wholly decisive outcome for either side. In other words Hitler was prepared neither to commit sufficient strength there to obtain decision, nor to allow his strength to drop so much that decision could be taken away from him. He did not even think of Italy as an area of vital interest to Germany. He was to go to extraordinary lengths to rescue Mussolini. For the people and the country he cared nothing, except as a useful defensive barrier by which some of his enemies could be kept at arm's length. After Mussolini's rescue by Skorzeny on 13 September, 1943, the two men met at Hitler's headquarters in Rastenburg. Speer remembered how Hitler embraced the Duce, clearly moved. Speer added:

> On the anniversary of the Three-Power Pact, Hitler sent to the Duce, with whom he declared himself 'linked in friendship' his 'warmest wishes for the future of an Italy once more led to honourable freedom by Fascism'. Two weeks before, Hitler had mutilated Italy.

We have already seen with what lightning speed and total success the Germans took over Italy as soon as Badoglio announced an armistice.

From then on, as far as Hitler was concerned, the war in Italy was simply a holding operation while more important things were seen to elsewhere. In Kesselring he had the perfect instrument for carrying out this policy. And it is significant that at no time during the endless transmission of signals from and to *Oberkommando der Wehrmacht*, the German High Command, which *Ultra* picked up and passed on, was there a cry that the situation in Italy was seriously jeopardizing operations on either the Eastern or the Western fronts. Such was Kesselring's success. But it was success which not only veiled failure on other fronts, but actually contributed to that failure, even though *Ultra* intercepts did not acknowledge the fact. *Ultra*'s relevance to the Italian campaign was a different one, as Ronald Lewin has so effectively shown. 'Once the Allied armies made their lodgement on the mainland of Italy and Hitler accepted Kesselring's policy of holding a line south of Rome rather than pulling back to the Alps,' he wrote, 'it might seem that during a campaign which often looked like a prolonged siege *Ultra* would have been at a disadvantage.'

But Lewin went on to show that in fact the intelligence gained from radio interception was continuous and very accurate. It was certainly not for want of information that the Allied advance was so slow. It was more that Alexander never possessed a sufficient superiority of numbers, particularly infantry, to overcome the naturally good defensive country and the fanatical skill of the German defenders. Lewin also made it clear that Alexander's reliance on *Ultra* never wavered[*]. The information he received as to the whereabouts of enemy formations enabled him to decide on major strategic operations, such as the landings at Salerno and later at Anzio. But once these landings had been made, the outcome depended not so much on the intelligence which had helped determine the strategy, but on the tactical skill and boldness of the commanders on the spot. And, as we have seen, in neither case was the soundness of the strategy rewarded with decisive tactical results.

Another example of this failure to crown the success of good strategy with an outstanding victory in the field, a victory which was made all the more possible by *Ultra*, was to be found in Mark Clark's changing the direction of his breakout from Anzio. Instead of persisting with a drive to entrap and destroy the German 10th Army, he turned away north for the incidental, but publicity-rich, target of Rome. Lewin stresses that,

[*] Like Churchill, whose strategy was profoundly influenced by the information gained for *Ultra*.

when Clark did this, he knew from a variety of intelligence sources – air reconnaissance, *Ultra* and the lower level battlefield radio intercept – what was happening in front of his 5th Army. 'It must therefore be assumed,' he concluded, 'that it was not for fear of the unknown that Clark turned aside from a broken enemy, but for personal reasons which have scarcely been disguised.' Lewin always insisted that the battle was the 'pay-off' for intelligence. The pay-off did not always come up to expectation.

What then was the pay-off for the Allies when we consider the Italian campaign in the round? Over a period of two years, all but two months, if we include Sicily, the Allies fought their way north over the most difficult terrain with an average of some twenty operational divisions opposed by a similar number of German divisions. There were heavy casualties on both sides – over half a million Germans, more than 300,000 Allies. There had been two prolonged and bitter battles – for the Gustav Line from late 1943 until the summer of 1944, and for the Gothic Line from August, 1944, until early 1945. At no time until right at the end did the Allies succeed in mounting decisive mobile operations, while two of their amphibious landings were dangerously threatened by the speed and violence of the German reaction. While all this was going on, decision was being sought and gained on the Eastern and later the Western fronts. How much did Italy's battles contribute to this decision? Historians' views vary. We cannot but wonder at their differences. Chester Wilmot, while deploring the lack of boldness and preparedness to exploit Mussolini's fall, nevertheless maintains that 'the campaign in Italy did bring substantial advantages which could not have been gained elsewhere and which were vital to the success of *Overlord*'. If this last statement were true, then the purpose and achievement of invading Italy would be vindicated absolutely, although it must bring into question whether by August, 1944, with *Overlord* itself successful, it was necessary to indulge in so desperate and costly a series of battles as were fought in the Gothic Line. We remember A. J. P. Taylor's judgements that the British were in the Mediterranean because they were there, and that, after the Normandy landings had been secured, 'British strategy in the Mediterranean lost all significance'. At the same time we have Norman Stone insisting that the Allied invasion of Italy did not seriously disrupt Hitler's conduct of the war elsewhere and that the ponderous caution of the Allies gave fresh hope to some of Germany's generals. Alan Moorehead, as is shown by the quotation at the beginning of this chapter, thought the campaign wasteful and ill-directed. To Churchill, of course, who wrote so much history as well as making it, the Italian campaign was a logical and necessary step in the whole of his Mediterranean strategy, by which he put such store and which was after all the only offensive strategy open to the British in the years from 1941 to 1943. For Churchill an attack upon Italy was not only right, but inevitable, given that Italy was the weak partner of the Axis and that Germany would be bound to come to her aid. And once the campaign had started in Italy, Churchill was determined to wrest every advantage from it.

In this view and policy Churchill was surely right. Indeed to his support comes the Führer himself, who admitted that his unshakeable friendship for Italy and the Duce might well be held to have been an error. Certainly they had done little for him in the military field, losing every battle they fought, and delaying Germany's all-important attack on Russia by their crass intervention in the Balkans. 'It is in fact quite obvious,' Hitler observed after the Allied invasion of Italy, 'that our Italian alliance has been of more service to our enemies than to ourselves. . . . If, in spite of all our efforts, we fail to win this war, the Italian alliance will have contributed to our defeat! The greatest service which Italy could have rendered to us would have been to remain aloof from this conflict.' Just so! Lord Gort's comment to the German Military Attaché, concerning Italy as an ally in war, 'It's your turn this time', had been fulfilled. Yet we must concede, when we examine the contradictory, and at the same time complementary, claims of the opposing supreme commanders, Alexander and Kesselring, to have succeeded in carrying out their tasks of engaging substantial enemy forces, that there is something to be said for both points of view.

At the end of the first paragraph of Chapter 1, I asked four questions about the Italian campaign and the time has now come to answer them. In the first place was the campaign necessary? Who can doubt it? Given the strategic circumstances of early 1943, with the Russians still desperately struggling to wrest advantage from the Wehrmacht, with the invasion of North-West Europe more than a year away, and with powerful Allied forces about to finish off the conquest of North Africa, what else could the Allies have done if they wished to go on keeping German forces committed to the South? Besides, the elimination of Italy was a legitimate and realizable goal. The Allies may have expected too much from it. This was no reason not to go for it. The invasion of

Italy was certainly necessary. Was it significant? My second question must surely receive an emphatic affirmative too. It prompted Hitler to take instant and powerful action to seal off the peninsula, commit himself to a long-drawn-out defensive operation executed by divisions long regarded as the cream of the German Army, and inspired acts of heroism and endurance on battlefields like Cassino, which will live undimmed in the chronicles of war. The Allied effort in men, machines and shipping was enormous, and although the dividends may not have been instant or startling, the slow, bloody slogging match in which the Allied soldiers indulged, year in, year out, made their sure and persistent contribution to what their comrades in arms were endeavouring to achieve elsewhere. The attention which the Italian campaign demanded from the highest Allied counsels right up until the spring of 1945 speaks loudly for its significance. Was it inevitable? Again the answer is Yes! Once Italy's entry into the war in 1940 had turned the Middle East into the only area of operations where the British could harass and damage Germany's weaker partner, Britain's strategy was clear. First make sure of North Africa and the Mediterranean, then take the war into southern Europe by attacking Italy itself. Since Germany would not wish to see Italy defeated, here would be the surest means of continuing to engage German forces on land. Roosevelt's agreement in response to Churchill's persuasion to open a kind of Second Front by invading French North Africa simply confirmed the inevitability of taking the war on to the Italian mainland as soon as North Africa had been cleared. There the Allies were in the spring of 1943 – on Italy's doorstep. Where else were they to go but to Italy itself? Three truths are thus told. The campaign *was* necessary, it *was* significant, indeed it was inevitable. Whether these three truths are happy prologues to the more controversial fourth question as to history's verdict on the campaign is less certain.

It cannot be said to have been decisive; indeed how could it be when its precise purpose had never been defined? All Churchill's talk about striking at the soft underbelly of the Axis turned somewhat sour in the mud and mountains of Cassino fanatically defended by the 1st German Parachute Division. As a distraction to German effort elsewhere, it was all very well, provided we recognize that it was essentially a *defensive* strategy waged by offensive means. It was an operation to hold the Germans on the southern flank in order that advances could be made on the main fronts, and as such turned out to be a major distraction for the Allies too. Yet for the Americans, as indeed for Hitler, it was first and always a side-show, a secondary affair, which must be kept in being, while the main attraction would be featured in another theatre. If we ask, however, whether it was worth doing, the answer, as for the other three questions, must be an unequivocal Yes. In making this answer it is necessary to bear in mind that as an inevitable finale to the whole Mediterranean strategy, which had been designed to draw German forces away from the Eastern and later the Western fronts, the invasion of Italy was simply part of this process. It was not, in Michael Howard's words, 'an end in itself'. We may sympathize with Churchill's passionate desire to pull off some great historical coup which would feature largely in the story of his nation's part in the war, but if we put the campaign into perspective, we may conclude that what sometimes appeared to be great strategic opportunities were in fact illusions, for neither the resources to seize them, not the tactical dexterity to exploit them, were to hand. It is also important to remember once more that the decision to invade Italy was taken at a time when, short of some totally unforeseeable development, the war could not be lost by the Allies. It may not have been clear exactly where and when it would be won, but it *was* clear that it could not be won in Italy. It could only be waged there, something that the Prime Minister had promised his people that he would do as far back as May, 1940. Michael Howard's judgement of twenty years ago that the Mediterranean campaign, as it was carried out, was a proper part of the overall Allied grand strategy and that it still has to be shown that there was a better way of winning the war – this judgement still stands.

It remains only to say a final word about the players. Both sides played well, even though some of the captains were not without their illusions. Churchill in striving always for some great coup was steadfastly backed by Alexander. The ordinary Allied soldier, sceptical though he may have been when listening to the high-sounding promises of his commanders, simply did his duty and slogged on. For the Germans, Italy might have been unpleasant enough. It was nothing to the Eastern front, which so obsessed Hitler that he required Kesselring to ensure that what was happening in Italy did not interfere with it. Those of us who fought the Germans in Italy had nothing but respect for their skill and courage. In his book about the Gothic Line Douglas Orgill recalls revisiting the Coriano Ridge and standing in the military cemetery there among the graves of American, British,

Canadian, New Zealand, Polish, Greek and German soldiers. 'These are the men,' he wrote, 'who tried their best, and did not live to know whether they had won or lost.' Some of them were my friends; others might have been the Germans whom I shot at. When we talk of winning or losing, it is difficult not to remember those lines of Grantland Rice, which have often caused such mockery and mirth:

> For when the One Great Scorer comes
> To write against your name,
> He marks – not that you won or lost –
> But how you played the game.

The lines are fitting here, for nearly all the soldiers who did the fighting in Italy, no matter what army they belonged to, get high marks. No one wrote more truly, movingly or knowledgeably of the Italian campaign than Fred Majdalany who finished his *Portrait of a Battle* like this: 'Cassino, so costly in human life and suffering . . . was in the end little more than a victory of the human spirit: an elegy for the common soldier: a memorial to the definitive horror of war and the curiously perverse paradoxical nobility of battle.' There could be no better epilogue to the Italian campaign as a whole.

BIBLIOGRAPHY

Berlin, Sir Isaiah, *Mr Churchill in 1940*, John Murray
Bryant, Sir Arthur, *The Lion and the Unicorn*, Collins
Churchill, Winston S., *The Second World War*, Vols 4, 5, 6, Cassell
Count, Ciano, *Ciano's Diary*
Fraser, David, *Alanbrooke*, Collins
Hamilton, Nigel, *Monty*, Vol 2, Hamish Hamilton
Howard, Michael, *The Mediterranean Strategy in the Second World War*,
     Weidenfeld & Nicolson
Howard, Michael, *Official History, Grand Strategy*, Vol IV, HMSO
Irving, David, *Hitler's War*, Hodder & Stoughton
Jackson, W. G. F., *The Battle for Italy*, Batsford
Lewin, Ronald, *Ultra Goes To War*, Hutchinson
Macmillan, Harold, *War Diaries: The Mediterranean 1943–45*
Majdalany, Fred, *Cassino: Portrait of a Battle*, Longmans
— *The Monastery*, John Lane The Bodley Head
Montagu, Ewen, *The Man Who Never Was*, Lippincott
Moorehead, Alan, *Eclipse*, Hamish Hamilton
Newby, Eric, *Love and War in the Apennines*, Hodder & Stoughton
Orgill, Douglas, *The Gothic Line*, Heinemann
Plehwe, Friedrich-Karl von, *The End of an Alliance*, OUP
Speer, Albert, *Inside the Third Reich*, Weidenfeld & Nicolson
Stone, Norman, *Hitler*, Hodder & Stoughton
Trevor-Roper, H., Ed., *Hitler's War Directives*, Sidgwick & Jackson
Wilmot, Chester, *The Struggle for Europe*, Collins

INDEX